Caldarola/Schrey

Big Data and Law

Big Data and Law

A Practitioner's Guide

by

Maria Cristina Caldarola
Joachim Schrey

2020

BECK • HART • NOMOS

Published by
Verlag C.H.Beck oHG, Wilhelmstraße 9, 80801 München, Germany,
email: bestellung@beck.de

Co-published by
Hart Publishing, Kemp House, Chawley Park, Cumnor Hill, Oxford, OX2 9PH, United Kingdom,
online at: www.hartpub.co.uk

and

Nomos Verlagsgesellschaft mbH & Co. KG, Waldseestraße 3–5, 76530 Baden-Baden, Germany,
email: nomos@nomos.de

Published in North America by Hart Publishing
An Imprint of Bloomsbury Publishing 1385 Broadway, New York, NY 10018, USA
email: mail@hartpub.co.uk

Suggested citation:
Caldarola/Schrey, Big Data and Law, p. [#]

www.beck.de

ISBN 978 3 406 74393 1 (C.H.BECK)
ISBN 978 1 5099 3193 4 (HART)
ISBN 978 3 8487 6212 5 (NOMOS)

Wilhelmstr. 9, 80801 München
Printed in Germany by
Friedrich Pustet GmbH & Co. KG
Gutenbergstraße 8, 93051 Regensburg
Typeset by
Reemers Publishing Services GmbH, Krefeld
Cover: Druckerei C.H.Beck Nördlingen

CO_2 neutral
chbeck.de/nachhaltig

Preface

Data are often referred to as the “oil of the 21st century” and Big Data applications are seen as a new “oil platform” to extract this lucrative resource. However, like oil platforms, Big Data applications only yield their treasure to those who have not only the right infrastructure and technical expertise but also an understanding of the legal ramifications.

This book has been written to expose and close a gap in German and European legal commentaries when it comes to Big Data. It examines not only data protection and its legal ramifications but also the Big Data environment as affected by laws including the German Civil Code (BGB), intellectual property law and data protection law. Its German language version was published in December 2018 by the Munich-based publishing house C.H.Beck Verlag.

The book deals with personal and non-personal data (factual data or anonymous data), two types of data which are often combined for Big Data analyses. They often come from the different right holders, are subject to different national laws, trigger different legal requirements and/or are used for different analytical purposes.

In this guide, we offer practical and descriptive solutions for setting up a Big Data project by addressing interdependencies – among data types, right holders, applicable law, lawful ground/legal requirements, purposes – and relevant areas of legal practice. It combines these variable aspects for companies in various Big Data scenarios and offers legally reliable and controllable solutions.

With numerous guidelines and graphics, this book is a practical legal guide to gathering, storing and analyzing personal and other types of data in Big Data applications. It provides comprehensive, practice-oriented assistance and reliability for planning in everyday business in a Big Data environment. It is aimed in particular at lawyers, computer scientists, business economists, managing directors, managers, analysts, consultants, auditors, and internal and external data protection officers.

Stuttgart/Frankfurt am Main
November 2019

Dr. iur. Maria Cristina Caldarola, LL.M., MBA
Prof. Dr. iur. Joachim Schrey

Contents

Abbreviations

a. F.	*alte Fassung*; old version
AO	*Abgabeordnung*; Tax Code https://www.gesetze-im-internet.de/englisch_ao/index.html
Art.	Article
BDSG	*Bundesdatenschutzgesetz*; Federal Data Protection Act https://www.gesetze-im-internet.de/englisch_bdsg/index.html
BGB	*Bürgerliches Gesetzbuch*; Civil Code https://www.gesetze-im-internet.de/englisch_bgb/index.html
BGH	*Bundesgerichtshof*; Federal Court of Justice
BVerfG	*Bundesverfassungsgericht*; Federal Constitutional Court
C2P	Controller-to-processor
Data Protection Directive	Directive 95/46/EC of the European Parliament and of the Council of 24 October 1995 on the protection of individuals with regard to the processing of personal data and on the free movement of such data https://eur-lex.europa.eu/legal-content/en/TXT/?uri=CELEX%3A31995L0046
ed(s).	editor(s)
Fn.	Footnote
GDPR	General Data Protection Regulation https://gdpr-info.eu/
GeschGehG	*Geschäftsgeheimnisgesetz;* Trade Secrets Act
GG	*Grundgesetz*; Basic Law https://www.gesetze-im-internet.de/englisch_gg/index.html
GWB	*Gesetz gegen Wettbewerbsbeschränkungen*; Act against restraints of competition https://www.gesetze-im-internet.de/englisch_gwb/index.html
HGB	*Handelsgesetzbuch*; Commercial Code https://www.gesetze-im-internet.de/englisch_hgb/index.html
IoT	Internet of Things
i. V. m.	*in Verbingung mit*; in conjunction with
LG	*Landgericht*; Regional Court
M2M	Machine to Machine
mn.	Margin number
No.	Number
OLG	*Oberlandesgericht*; Higher Regional Court
OWiG	*Ordnungswidrigkeitengesetz*; Regulatory Offences Act https://www.gesetze-im-internet.de/englisch_owig/index.html
p.	Page
PatG	*Patentgesetz*; Patent Act https://www.gesetze-im-internet.de/englisch_patg/index.html
Rs.	*Rechtsprechung*; Case
StVG	*Straßenverkehrsgesetz*; Road Traffic Act https://www.gesetze-im-internet.de/englisch_stvg/index.html
TFEU	Treaty on the Functioning of the European Union https://eur-lex.europa.eu/legal-content/EN/TXT/?uri=celex%3A12012E%2FTXT
TKG	*Telekommunikationsgesetz*; Telecommunications Act https://germanlawarchive.iuscomp.org/?p=692
TMG	*Telemediengesetz*; Telemedia Act
u. a.	*inter alia*; amongst others

UKlaG	*Gesetz über Unterlassungsklagen bei Verbraucherrechts- und anderen Verstößen;* Act on Actions for Injunctive Relief for Breaches of Consumer law and Other Laws
UrhG	*Urheberrechtsgesetz*; Copyright Act https://www.gesetze-im-internet.de/englisch_urhg/index.html
UWG	*Gesetz gegen den unlauteren Wettbewerb*; Act against Unfair Competition https://www.gesetze-im-internet.de/englisch_uwg/index.html
WP	Working Paper

Legend

Glossary

- Purpose
- Lawful ground
- Data economy / data minimization
  (only necessary data as long as essential)
- Client separation
- Applicability of law
- Technical & organizational measurments
- Documentation
- Transparent information, disclosure etc.
- Data erasure concept

- Datum / Information
- Data collection
- Data processing
- Data use
- Lawful ground
- Data controller
- Data subject / personal data
- Employee
- Factual data
- Anonymous data

- Database (empty / with data)
- Cloud
- Fingerprint
- Company

Bibliography

Ahlberg, Hartwig/Götting, Horst-Peter (eds.) *Beck'scher Online-Kommentar Urheberrecht*, 17th edition, 1.4.2017

Artikel-29-Working Party *Working Paper 4/2007*, WP 136, "Personal Data"

Artikel-29-Working Party *Working Paper 5/2014 re Anonymization Techniques*, WP 216, from 10.4.2014

Artikel-29- Working Party *Working Paper 5/2012 re Cloud Computing*, WP 196, from 1.7.2012

Auer-Reinsdorff, Astrid/Conrad, Isabell (eds.) *Beck'sches Mandatshandbuch IT-Recht*, 2011

Auer-Reinsdorff, Astrid/Conrad, Isabell (eds.) *Handbuch IT- und Datenschutzrecht*, 2nd edition 2016

Bitkom Potenziale und Einsatz von Big Data, Ergebnisse einer repräsentativen Befragung von Unternehmen in Deutschland, 5.5.2014, https://www.bitkom.org/Publikationen/2014/Studien/Studie-Big-Data-in-deutschen-Unternehmen/Studienbericht-Big-Data-in-deutschen-Unternehmen.pdf (cited: https://www.bitkom.org/Publikationen/2014/Studien/Studie-Big-Data-in-deutschen-Unternehmen/Studienbericht-Big-Data-in-deutschen-Unternehmen.pdf)

Conrad, Isabell/Grützmacher, Malte (eds.) *Recht der Daten und Datenbanken in Unternehmen*, 2014

Conraths, Timo/Krüger, Stefan Das virtuelle Hausrecht des Online-Spiel-Betreibers, Wirksame Rechtsschutzmöglichkeiten für Online-Spiel-Anbieter abseits des Vertragsrechts, *MMR* 2016, 310 et seq.

Däubler, Wolfgang Gläserne Belegschaften, *Das Handbuch zum Beschäftigtendatenschutz*, 7th edition 2017

Dierks Bohle Rechtsanwälte *Rechtsgutachten zur elektronischen Datentreuhänderschaft im Auftrag der Telematikplattform für Medizinische Forschungsnetze*, 2008 (cited: Dierks, in: Telematikplattform für Medizinische Forschungsnetze, Rechtsgutachten zur elektronischen Datentreuhänderschaft)

Dzida, Boris *Big Data und Arbeitsrecht*, NZA 2017, 541 et seq.

Ehmann, Eugen/Selmayr, Martin (eds.) *Datenschutz-Grundverordnung Kommentar*, 2nd edition 2018

Engels, Thomas Datenschutz in der Cloud-Ist hierbei immer eine Auftragsdatenverarbeitung anzunehmen?, *K&R* 2011, 548 et seq.

Ernst, Stefan Die Einwilligung nach der Datenschutzgrundverordnung, Anmerkungen zur Definition nach Art. 4 Nr. 11 GDPR, *ZD* 2017, 110 et seq.

Forst, Gerrit Bewerberauswahl über soziale Netzwerke im Internet?, *NZA* 2010, 427 et seq.

Geppert, Martin/Schütz, Raimund (eds.) *Beck'scher TKG-Kommentar*, 4th edition, 2013

Gersdorf, Hubertus/Paal, Boris P. (eds.) *Beck'scher Online-Kommentar Informations- und Medienrecht*, 17th edition, 1.8.2018

Gola, Peter/Pötters, Stephan/Wronka, Georg *Handbuch Arbeitnehmerdatenschutz unter Berücksichtigung der Datenschutz-Grundverordnung*, 7th edition, 2016

Gola, Peter/Schomerus, Rudolf (eds.) *Bundesdatenschutzgesetz Kommentar*, 12th edition, 2015

Grünwald, Andreas/Nüßing, Christoph Machine To Machine (M2M)-Kommunikation, Regulatorische Fragen bei der Kommunikation im Internet der Dinge, *MMR* 2015, 378 et seq.

Hoeren, Thomas/Sieber, Ulrich/Holznagel, Bernd (eds.) *Handbuch Multimedia-Recht, Rechtsfragen des elektronischen Geschäftsverkehrs*, 46th update, January 2018

Hofmann, Johanna M., Anforderungen aus GDPR und NIS-RL an das Cloud Computing, *ZD-Aktuell* 2017, 05488

Höinghaus, Christoph Daten: Das Öl des 21. Jahrhunderts, Big Data wirtschaftlich sinnvoll einsetzen, CIO, 28.8.2015, https://www.cio.de/a/big-data-wirtschaftlich-sinnvoll-einsetzen,3246278 (cited: https://www.cio.de/a/big-data-wirtschaftlich-sinnvoll-einsetzen,3246278)

IDC/DELL EMC Studie "Das digitale Universum", Bericht für 2014, http://germany.emc.com/leadership/digital-universe/index.htm (cited: http://germany.emc.com/leadership/digital-universe/index.htm)

Katko, Peter/Babaei-Beigi, Ayda Accountability statt Einwilligung? Führt Big Data zum Paradigmenwechsel im Datenschutz?, *MMR* 2014, 360 et seq.

Kilian, Wolfgang/Heussen, Benno (eds.) *Computerrechts-Handbuch, Informationstechnologie in der Rechts- und Wirtschaftspraxis*, 33rd update, February 2017

Kinast, Karsten/Kühnl, Christina Telematik und Bordelektronik-Erhebung und Nutzung von Daten zum Fahrverhalten, *NJW* 2014, 3057 et seq.

Klug, Christoph Der Datenschutzbeauftragte in der EU, Maßgaben der Datenschutzgrundverordnung, *ZD* 2016, 315 et seq.

Konferenz der unabhängigen Datenschutzbehörden des Bundes und der Länder "Zur Anwendbarkeit des TMG für nicht-öffentliche Stellen ab dem 25. Mai 2018" from 26.4.2018

Kühling, Jürgen/Buchner, Benedikt (eds.) *Datenschutz-Grundverordnung Kommentar*, 2nd edition 2018

Leistner, Matthias Die Landkarte als Datenbank, Überlegungen zum Datenbankschutz für topografische Karten und geografische Daten, *GRUR* 2014, 528 et seq.

Leistner, Matthias Was lange währt ...: EuGH entscheidet zur Schutzfähigkeit geografischer Karten als Datenbanken, *GRUR* 2016, 42 et seq.

Lindell, Yehuda/Pinkas, Benny Secure Multiparty Computation for Privacy-Preserving Data Mining, *Journal of Privacy and Confidentiality* 2009, 59 et seq. (cited: *Lindell/Pinkas*, in: The Journal of Privacy and Confidentiality, 2009, 59 et seq.)

Mantz, Reto/Spittka, Jan Anmerkung zu EuGH from19.10.2016-C-582/14, *NJW* 2016, 3582

Metschke, Rainer/Wellbrock, Rita Berliner Beauftragter für Datenschutz und Informationsfreiheit, Hessischer Datenschutzbeauftragter, *Datenschutz in Wirtschaft und Forschung*

Paal, Boris P./Pauly, Daniel A. (eds.) *Datenschutz-Grundverordnung*, Beck'sche Kompakt-Kommentare, 2nd edition 2018

Plath, Kai-Uwe (ed.) *Kommentar zum BDSG und zur DSGVO sowie den Datenschutzbestimmungen von TMG und TKG*, 3rd edition, 2018 (cited: editor, in: Plath, BDSG/DSGVO, 3rd edition 2018)

Rebmann/Säcker (eds.), *Münchener Kommentar zum BGB*, 7th edition 2017, to § 1004 BGB (cited: author, in: Rebmann/Säcker, MüKo, ...).

Roßnagel, Alexander Fahrzeugdaten – wer darf über sie entscheiden?, *SVR* 2014, 281 et seq. (cited.: Roßnagel, 52. Verkehrsgerichtstag 2014, p. 282.)

Roßnagel, Alexander/Scholz, Philip Datenschutz durch Anonymität und Pseudonymität, Rechtsfolgen der Verwendung anonymer und pseudonymer Daten, *MMR* 2000, 721 et seq.

Säcker, Franz Jürgen/Rixecker, Roland/Oetker, Hartmut/Limpberg, Bettina (eds.) *Münchener Kommentar zum BGB*, 7th edition, 2017

Schaffland, Hans-Jürgen/Wiltfang, Noeme (eds.) *Datenschutz-Grundverordnung, Bundesdatenschutzgesetz Kommentar*, update 4/17, Februar 2017 (cited: eauthor, in: Schaffland/Wiltfang, GDPR/BDSG)

Schild, Hans-Hermann (eds.) *Praxis der Kommunalverwaltung*, November 2015 (cited.: Schild/Ronellenfitsch/Arlt/Dembowski/Müller/Piendl/Rydzy/Schriever-Steinberg/Topp/Wehrmann/Wellbrock, in: Praxis der Kommunalverwaltung, Amendment November 2015)

Simitis, Spiros (ed.) *Bundesdatenschutzgesetz Kommentar*, 8th edition, 2014

Spindler, Gerald Text und Data Mining – urheber- und datenschutzrechtliche Fragen, *GRUR* 2016, 1112 et seq.

Thalhofer, Thomas Recht an Daten in der Smart Factory, *GRUR-Prax* 2017, 225 et seq.

Weisser, Ralf/Färber, Claus Rechtliche Rahmenbedingungen bei Connected Car, Überblick über die Rechtsprobleme der automobilen Zukunft, MMR 2015, 506 et seq.

Werkmeister, Christoph/Brandt, Ella Datenschutzrechtliche Herausforderungen für Big Data, *CR* 2016, 233 et seq.

Wójtowicz, Monika/Cebulla, Manuel Anonymisierung nach der DSGVO, *PinG* 2017, 186 et seq.

Wolff, Heinrich Amadeus/Brink, Stefan (eds.) *Beck'scher Online-Kommentar Datenschutzrecht*, 25th edition, 1.8.2018

Wybitul, Tim/Rauer, Nils EU-Datenschutz-Grundverordnung und Beschäftigtendatenschutz, Was bedeuten die Regelungen für Unternehmen und Arbeitgeber in Deutschland?, *ZD* 2012, 160 et seq.

Wybitul, Tim/Ströbel, Lukas/Ruess, Marian Übermittlung personenbezogener Daten in Drittländer, Überblick und Checkliste für die Prüfung nach der GDPR, *ZD* 2017, 503 et seq.

Zieger, Christoph/Smirra, Nikolas Fallstricke bei Big Data-Anwendungen, Rechtliche Gesichtspunkte bei der Analyse fremder Datenbestände, *MMR* 2013, 418 et seq.

Zoebisch, Michael Stimmungsanalyse durch Call-Center, Datenschutzrechtliche Zulässigkeit der Analyse der emotionalen Verfassung anhand der Stimme, *DuD* 2011, 394 et seq.

List of Figures

A. INTRODUCTORY REMARKS

I. Why Big Data?

1 *Big Data* refers to large amounts of data originating from different sources[1] which are stored, processed and analysed with special solutions for purposes of (inter-) dependency analysis, environmental and trend research, and for system and production control purposes. As in data mining, knowledge discovery is a priority for Big Data applications.[2]

2 Big Data as well as the individual data themselves are today often referred to as the *"oil of the 21st century"*, a statement made by Stefan Gross-Selbeck, former CEO of the business network *Xing*.[3]

3 The statement is supported by the EMC study *Digitales Universum*[4] as of 12 December 2012 (*Digital Universe*), in which a data volume of more than 8 Zettabyte from social networks, the IoT and services as well as numerous sensors on machines and products was already predicted for the year 2015. By 2013, the volume of data grew by an average of 22 %[5] compared to 2012; since that time, the speed of growth has continued to increase.

4 Big Data is now seen as a new source and a *reserve* of additional revenue. However, only those who not only have the necessary technical expertise and infrastructure but are also aware of the legal scope should exploit these reserves. As a result of the application of the EU General Data Protection Regulation since 25 May 2018 and the associated potentially substantial fines for data protection infringements, data protection supervisory authorities in particular will intensify their supervisory measures and also focus their attention on Big Data applications. Due to the economic effects of the drastically increased threat of fines for data protection infringements, this topic will also become relevant for the annual auditor of a company with Big Data applications.

II. Why must a party not established in the EU comply with GDPR with respect to Big Data applications?

1. General principles

5 Regardless of place of establishment, developing a Big Data application requires consideration of whether and to which extent such application and the activities needed to set it up must comply with the requirements of the EU General Data Protection Regulation 2016/679/EU (*GDPR*) as well as in any national data protection law of an EU Member State that applies in addition to the GDPR:

---

[1] For example the internet, mobile communications, the finance industry, the energy sector, health care, transport and sources such as intelligent agents, social media, credit and customer cards, smart metering systems, assistance devices, surveillance cameras as well as aircraft and vehicles.

[2] Definition from Gablers Wirtschaftslexikon as of 11/2017.

[3] www.cio.de/a/big-data-wirtschaftlich-sinnvoll-einsetzen,3246278, as of: 7/2018.

[4] https://www.it-daily.net/analysen/81-studie-der-woche/7084-neue-studie-zum-digitalen-universum-entdeckt-big-data-gap, as of: 7/2018.

[5] www.bitkom.org/Publikationen/2014/Studien/Studie-Big-Data-in-deutschen-Unternehmen/Studienbericht-Big-Data-in-deutschen-Unternehmen.pdf, as of: 7/2018.

6 The territorial scope set out in Art. 3 GDPR contains three different points of reference for the territorial application of the GDPR. In general, the GDPR applies if:

- Personal data are processed in the context of an establishment of a controller or processor in the EU, regardless of whether the processing takes place in the EU or not (Art. 3 (1) GDPR).
- A controller or processor not established in the EU processes personal data of data subjects in the EU to offer them goods or services or to monitor their behaviour (Art. 3 (2) GDPR).
- A controller not established in the EU processes personal data in a place where Member State law applies by virtue of public international law (Art. 3 (3) GDPR).

2. Companies established in the EU (Art. 3 (1) GDPR)

7 Pursuant to Art. 3 (1) GDPR, any processing of personal data in the context of the activities of an establishment in the EU is subject to the GDPR. The provision applies to data controllers and processors – as defined in Art. 4 (7) and (8) GDPR, respectively. Moreover, the GDPR will apply irrespective of whether the processing itself takes place inside or outside the EU.

8 Under the former Directive 95/46[6] (Data Protection Directive), a company is established in an EU Member State if they have a representative or a bank account in that Member State;[7] registration in that Member State is therefore not required.[8] In addition, according to recital 22 GDPR, an establishment implies the effective and real exercise of activity through stable arrangements. The legal form of the establishment, whether in form of a mere branch or a legal entity, is irrelevant in this respect. Likewise, Art. 3 (1) GDPR does not require the *main establishment* to be located in the EU; Art. 4 (16) GDPR defines the concept of a *main establishment.*

9 The wording of Art. 3 (1) GDPR and recital 22 are practically identical to Art. 4 (1) and recital 19 of the former Data Protection Directive. This suggests that the question whether, for example, letterbox companies or server locations suffice to constitute an establishment will continue to be a source of debate.[9]

3. Companies not established in the EU (Art. 3 (2) GDPR)

10 Art. 3 (2) GDPR expands the scope of the GDPR to the processing of personal data even by controllers and processors outside the EU where the processing activities are related to offering goods or services to EU data subjects, or to monitoring of their behaviour as far as their behaviour takes place within the Union. Unless a data controller located in a non-EU Member State only operates domestically, every entity which intends to establish and use a Big Data application cannot avoid the application of the GDPR as well as local data protection law of EU Member States (cf. Section 2 of this chapter A).

4. Offering of goods or services to data subjects in the EU

11 First, Art. 3 (2) (a) GDPR states that data processing is subject to the GDPR where the processing activities are related to the offering of goods or services, irrespective of whether a payment of the data subject is required, i.e. even if offered free of charge. This

---

[6] Directive 95/46/EC, OJ L 281, 23.11.1995, p. 31. The Directive has since been repealed by the GDPR.
[7] ECJ, 1 October 2015, C-230/14 – *Weltimmo*, para. 33.
[8] ECJ, 1 October 2015, C-230/14 – *Weltimmo*, para. 29.
[9] Cf. Wieczorek, in Taeger (ed.), *Law as a Service*, vol. 1, 2013, p. 5, 12.

also applies to Big Data applications in which the personal data of EU-based customers shall be processed, if such application is related to or the results of personal data processing within such application will be used in connection with the offering of goods or services, e.g. to prepare individualized offers based on the (potential) customers' preferences.

12 Recital 23 GDPR contains the underlying rationale, whereby application of the GDPR is intended to ensure that natural persons are not deprived of protection under the GDPR. Further, such an approach lays the groundwork for a level playing field for companies competing for customers in the EU. In practice, this means that the GDPR will apply to a company seated outside the EU and which targets EU-consumers. This has currently not been the case.

13 With respect to the former legal framework under the Data Protection Directive, the ECJ decision in *Google Spain*[10] had already paved the way to such an approach for the territorial scope of application. The Court stated that it is not decisive whether the establishment in the EU actually processes data itself as long as the establishment promotes the services of the data processing establishment and orientates its activities towards the inhabitants of EU Member States. The EU legislator has now implemented and further developed this case law in the GDPR thereby levelling the playing field in respect of data protection requirements for all companies competing for EU customers.

14 The decisive legal test is whether goods or services are offered to EU data subjects, i.e. to data subjects in one or more EU Member States. The term *goods* refers to tangible property while *services* mean any self-employed economic activity.[11]

15 The recitals to the GDPR provide helpful guidance as to whether such goods and services qualify as being *"offered to EU data subjects"* and, therefore, suffice to establish the required link to the EU. This requires more than merely providing access to a website or publishing an email address. Where a company provides EU customers the possibility of ordering the goods or services, a sufficient link may be established by use of language or currency generally used in EU Member States (cf. recital 23 GDPR). In particular, with respect to online services, further details may be drawn from the ECJ's case law regarding the notion of *directing commercial activities* to a Member State in consumer contracts.[12] Due to the similarity in content, it may be considered appropriate to use some indications as provided in that decision also in the present context:

16 In particular, the presentation of an offer (local vs. international) can serve as an overarching reference test. Services offered from outside the EU must at least have an *international character* and not just be domestic in scope. Otherwise they might not be considered as targeting EU users from the outset. Clearly, such foreign offers target EU-based users if they are provided on a European top-level domain (for example *.de* or *.fr* or *.eu*).[13]

17 On that note, the following criteria are relevant in assessing whether an online service targets EU citizens:

- language, currency, bank details;
- advertising and referencing services;
- country-specific presentation;
- reference to EU regulations;
- provider and business directories.

---

[10] ECJ, 13 May 2014, C-131/12 – *Google/AEPD.*

[11] Cf. the general definition in Article 4 (1) of Directive 2006/123/EC of the European Parliament and of the Council of 12 December 2006 on services in the internal market, OJ L 376, 27.12.2006, p. 36.

[12] Cf. ECJ, 7 December 2010, C-585/08 and C-144/09 – *Pammer and Alpenhof.*

[13] Cf. ECJ, 7 December 2010, C-585/08 and C-144/09 – *Pammer and Alpenhof.*

18 In a particular case, EU citizens are potentially not targeted by an online service where a provider points out explicitly that the service is excluded for use in the EU/in Europe or for EU-/European customers. However, there must not be any contradicting indications that the provider serves European customers nevertheless. The individual criteria must be considered in the individual context and within an overall assessment.

5. Monitoring the behaviour of subjects in the EU

19 The GDPR further applies to data processing for the purpose of monitoring the behaviour of EU data subjects by controllers and processors outside the EU. However, the monitored behaviour must take place within the EU (Art. 3 (2) (b) GDPR).

20 Such behavioural monitoring includes, for instance, the tracking of individuals on the internet including profiling techniques aimed at enabling decisions or predicting personal preferences, behaviours and attitudes (recital 24 GDPR). This includes all forms of web tracking (e.g. by way of cookies or social plug-ins such as *like buttons* etc.), profiling, targeted/programmatic advertising etc. Art. 3 (2) (b) GDPR thus likely covers almost all internet services as far as EU data subjects are concerned.

6. Data processing facilities in a place where Member State law applies (Art. 3 (3) GDPR)

21 The GDPR also applies to data processing by a controller without an establishment in the EU, but in a place where Member State law applies by virtue of public international law, such as in a Member State's diplomatic mission or consular post (Art. 3 (3) GDPR).

7. Limits of the scope of application – opening clauses

22 The Data Protection Directive was already meant to provide for a *"generally complete"*[14] level of harmonization of Member States' data protection regimes; nonetheless a significant number of differences between the national legislation implementing the Data Protection Directive (cf. recital 9 GDPR). To eliminate these differences, to *"ensure a consistent and high level of protection"* (recital 10 GDPR), and to promote the free movement of personal data within the EU (Art. 1 (3) GDPR) the EU legislator adopted the new data protection regime in the form of a regulation. According to Art. 288 of the Treaty on the Functioning of the European Union (*TFEU*), regulations have general application and are directly applicable. As a consequence of this change in legislative vehicle, unless explicitly required in a regulation, no national legislation is required to implement a regulation into national law. Conflicting and, in principle, identical national statute law must, therefore, be withdrawn by the Member States or will otherwise cease to apply.

23 Despite this basic principle, the GDPR leaves an important number of areas for specification by the Member States. These areas result from the trialogue negotiations between the EU Parliament, the EU Council and the EU Commission in which agreement on all open issues could not be reached in due course. Consequently, it was agreed to include approximately 50–60 so-called "opening clauses" that allow the Member States to enact more specific or deviating rules at the national level. While some opening clauses oblige the Member States to become active, other opening clauses give them the freedom to enact more specific or derogating national requirements (e.g. Art. 88 GDPR). It is for this reason that entities subject to GDPR under the aforemen-

[14] Cf. ECJ, 6 November 2003, C-101/01 – *Lindquist.*

tioned principles should always keep an eye not only on the GDPR but also on the applicable national data protection law. Therefore, the following guide not only explains the GDPR-relevance for Big Data applications but will also refer to the potential application of national data protection law. This guide uses German law to clarify the relevance of national data protection law.

The following three subchapters outline the most relevant opening clauses in the 24 GDPR; beside these examples there are many more opening clauses which may become relevant under the individual circumstances.

8. Most relevant opening clauses in the GDPR

a) Data processing in employment contexts (Art. 88 GDPR)

Any processing by electronic means of information about employees falls within the 25 scope of the GDPR. However, under Art. 88 GDPR rules on data protection concerning personal data of employees remain predominantly in the sovereignty of the Member States. More specifically, Member States may, by law or by collective agreements enact *"specific rules on the processing of employees' personal data in the employment context"* (recital 155 GDPR). It is somewhat unclear to what extent this gives Member States the authority to deviate from the rules provided in the GDPR. Based on the wording of Art. 88 GDPR (*more specific rules*), some commentators argue that the Member States are limited to only ratifying rules which comply with the spirit and purpose of the GDPR and in particular do not reduce the level of data protection as provided therein. Acknowledging that, the addendum *"within the limits set by this Regulation"* contained in a previous draft of the GDPR has been dropped in the final version. However, there is some indication that the Member States have the right to introduce stricter national levels of data protection.[15]

According to Art. 88 GDPR, national rules can in particular provide for specific 26 conditions under which employers may process employees' personal data:
- based on consent;
- for recruitment purposes;
- performance of the employment contract, including discharge of obligations laid down by law or by collective agreements;
- managing, planning and organising work;
- equality and diversity in the workplace;
- health and safety at work;
- protection of employer's or customer's property;
- for the purposes of the exercise and enjoyment, on an individual or collective basis, of rights and benefits related to employment; and
- for the purpose of the termination of the employment relationship.

It should be noted in this context that Art. 88 GDPR allows derogation from the 27 standards in the GDPR in respect of employment-related data processing for the above purposes not only by way of national laws but also by way of collective agreements, including works agreements (shop agreements, collective bargaining agreements). This gives companies more flexibility to act in a manner best suited to their own specific needs. Companies will, therefore, have to review and potentially amend their existing works agreements.

---

[15] Wybitul/Sörup/Pötters, *ZD* 2015, 559, 561.

28 Insofar as a Member State has not enacted any such specific laws and companies have not agreed on specific rules in their collective agreements, the standards stipulated in the GDPR apply.

b) Designation of a data protection officer in cases other than Art. 37 (1) GDPR

29 Art. 37 GDPR establishes an EU-wide concept of a data protection officer. Under certain conditions stipulated in Art. 37 (1) GDPR, controllers in all Member States are obliged to designate a data protection officer, even in EU Member States in which this obligation did not exist prior to the GDPR.

30 The trialogue negotiations reached the compromise which allows the Member States the possibility to specify national designation requirements (Art. 37 (4) GDPR). Accordingly, Member State law may require data controllers, processors or associations and other bodies representing categories of controllers or processors to designate a data protection officer also in cases other than those referred to in Art. 37 (1) GDPR. German data protection law, for instance, requires the appointment of a data protection officer if and as soon as 10 or more individuals are regularly processing personal data (§ 38 (1) BDSG).

c) Processing carried out in the public interest or in compliance with a legal obligation

31 The GDPR allows Member States in various instances to maintain or introduce national provisions to enact specific national rules with respect to situations where the controller processes personal data in order to comply with a legal obligation, to perform a task of public interest or to exercise official authority vested in the controller (recital 10 GDPR). Examples include: Art. 6 (1) (c) and (e) GDPR (concerning data processing that is necessary to comply with a legal obligation of the controller is considered lawful); Art. 6 (2) GDPR (for the determination of more precisely specific requirements for the processing and other measures to ensure lawful and fair processing); Art. 17 (3) (b) GDPR (exclusion of the right to erasure where the processing is necessary for the controller to comply with EU or Member State legislation or carry out public interests); Art. 49 (5) GDPR (stipulating that, in the absence of an adequacy decision by the Commission, Member States may for important reasons of public interest limit the transfer of personal data to a third country as well as international organizations); Art. 15, 16, 18–20 and 21 GRPR (in case of data processing for archiving purposes in the public interest right of the Member States under certain conditions to provide for derogations by law from the rights referred to therein).

9. Summary

32 Due to the GDPR's broad application by virtue of its Art. 3, unless a data controller located in a non-EU Member State only operates domestically, every entity intending to develop and use a Big Data application cannot avoid the need to conform to the GDPR as well as to the applicable national data protection laws of the EU Member States.

III. Which data are affected?

Data are values and findings about objects, events, persons and situations that are determined by observation and measurement and are technically recorded either electronically or physically in their formulation. 33

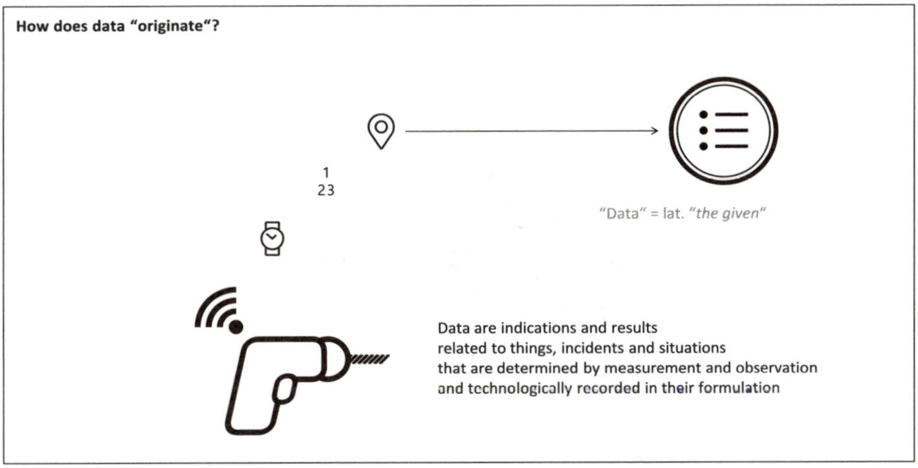

Figure 1: How does data "originate"?

Big Data analysis combines many different types of data from different sources: the larger the amount, the greater the likelihood of a precise and meaningful result from the analysis. Three types of data are used in the data to be merged; these also differ in their legal significance and treatment, which will be explained in the course of this guide. 34

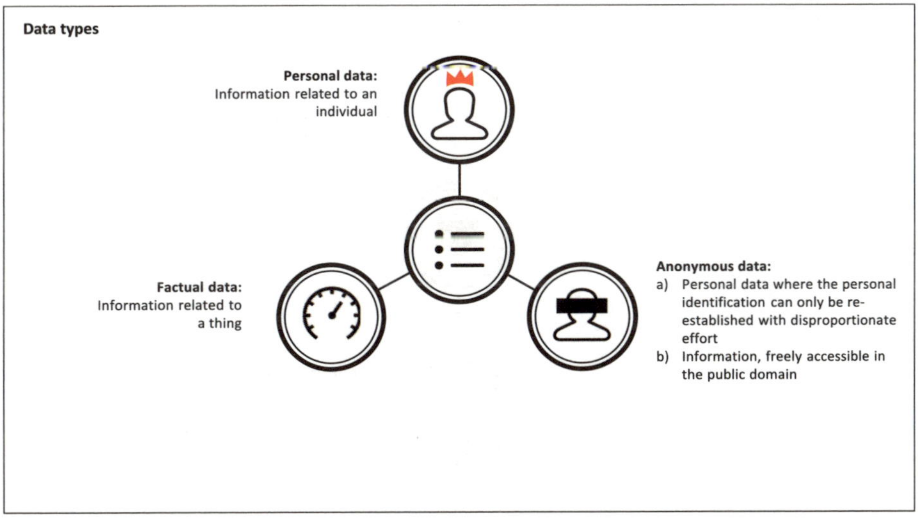

Figure 2: Data types

35 Databases play an important role in this context: Big Data applications are based on large databases in which the most diverse data from the most diverse sources are collected and stored in an orderly manner. Databases are collections of individual – personal, factual, and/or anonymous – data that are arranged systematically/methodically.

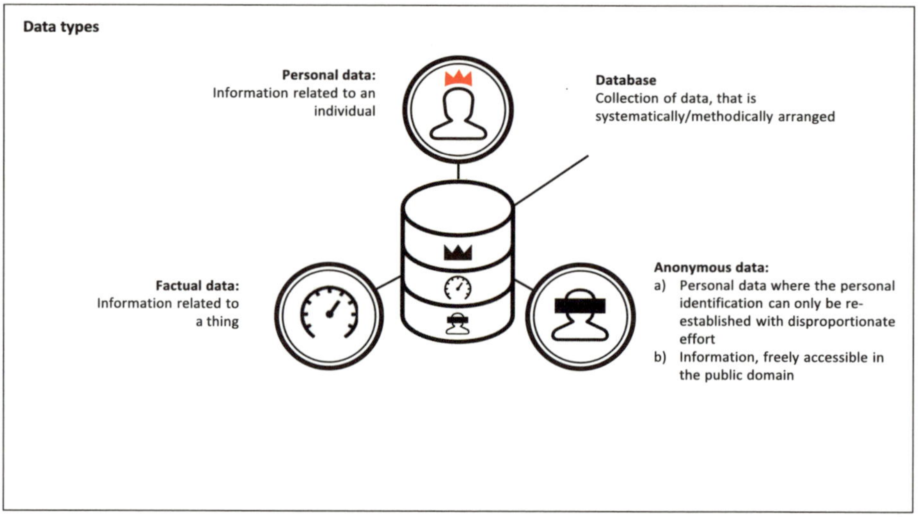

Figure 3: Data types and definitions

IV. What are the differences between the data types?

36 The different data have different right holders. As a consequence, the person who wants to work with these data has different partners.

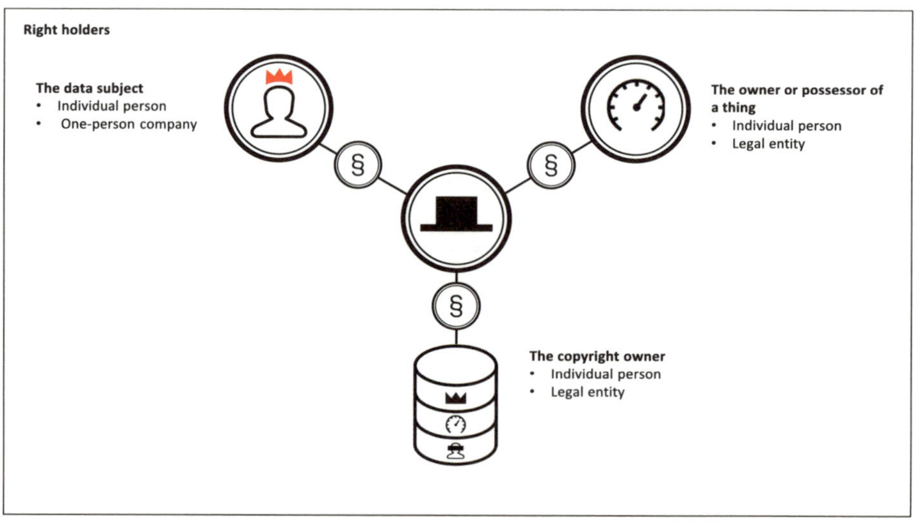

Figure 4: Right holders

The different right holders also enjoy different protection under the applicable laws. 37

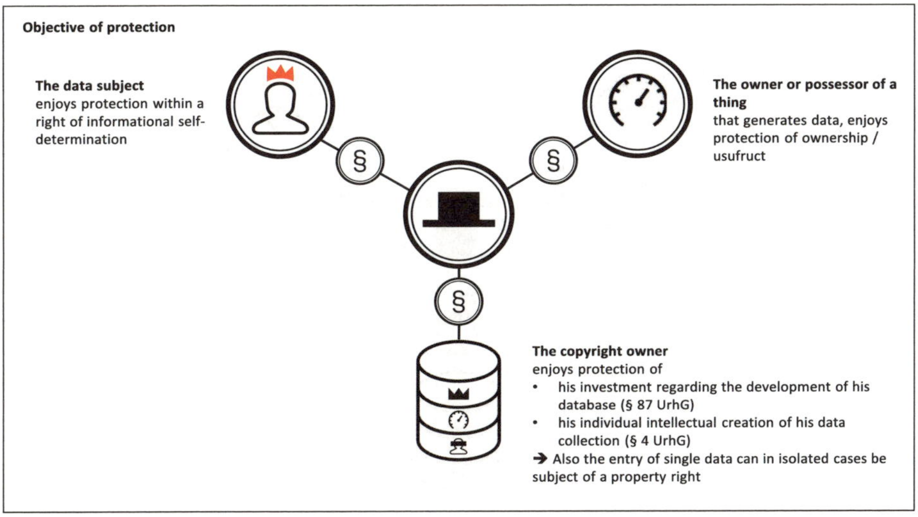

Figure 5: Objective of protection

The person/entity who intends to use the data (the *controller*) receives the data of the various right holders subject to different lawful grounds and legislation. 38

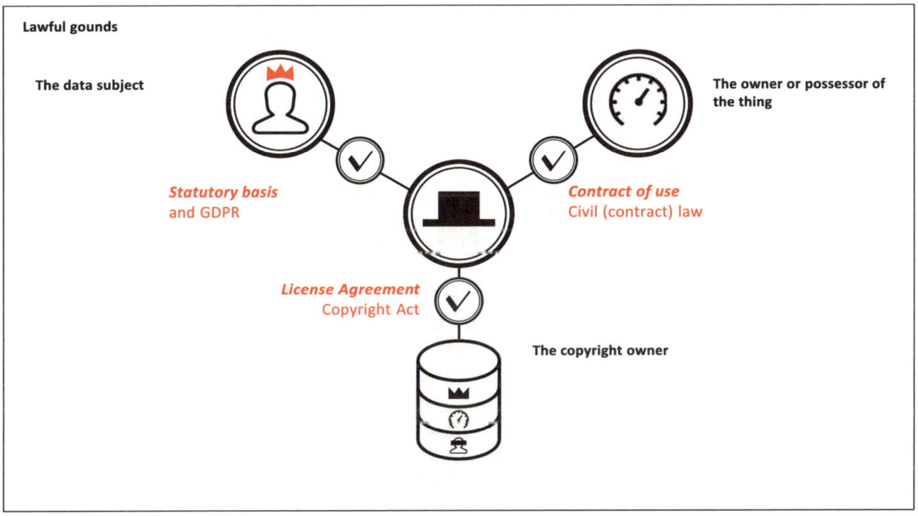

Figure 6: Lawful grounds

39 Due to the different underlying legislation, diverse prohibition rights are available to the various right holders in the absence of a lawful ground.

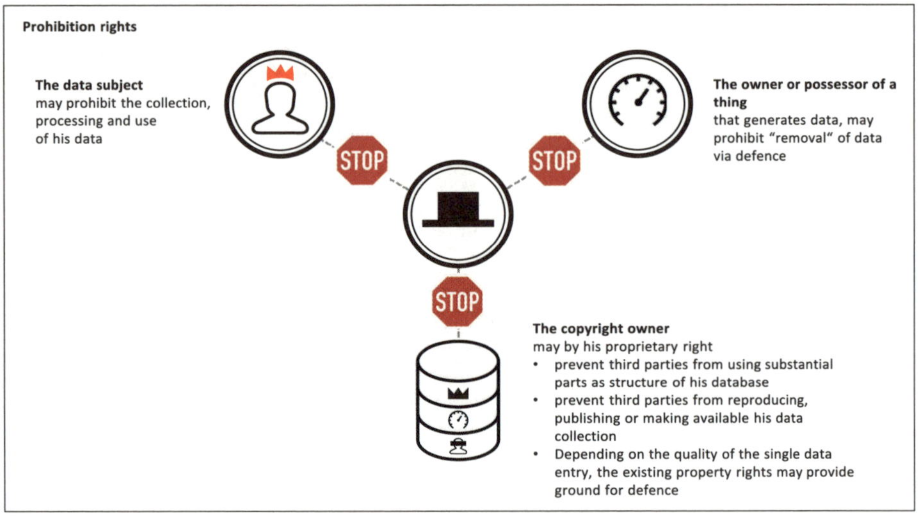

Figure 7: Prohibition rights

40 The variation in underlying legislation also results in differing legal consequences for processing data in the absence of a lawful ground.

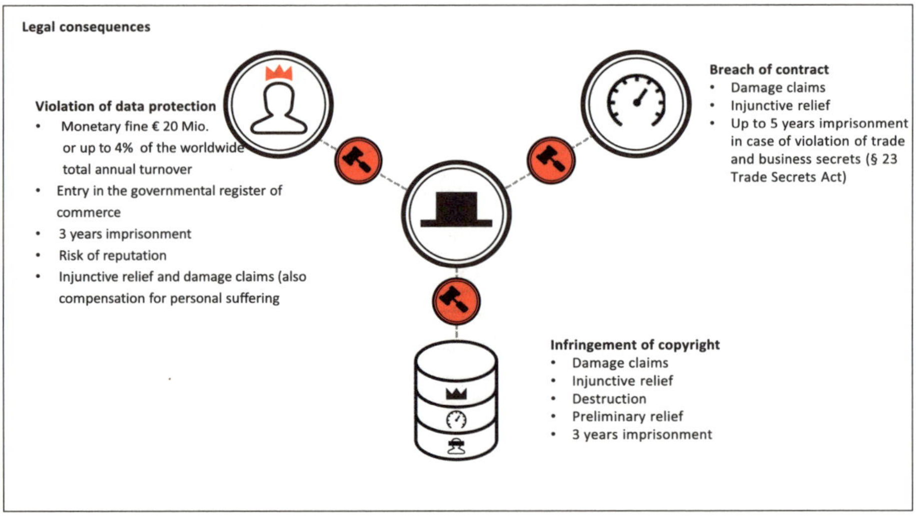

Figure 8: Legal consequences

V. Which verification steps need to be considered for a Big Data application?

Before developing a Big Data application, but also before adding any other category of data and undertaking any evaluation or analysis of data stored therein, it is necessary to examine the following: 41

- the categories of data (or types of data) to be collected, (additionally) stored and (also by means of evaluations or analyses) processed by the controller responsible for the Big Data application, i.e.
  - personal data,
  - purely factual data or
  - anonymized data

  (level of data content);
- the sources and thus, if applicable, from which right holders these data originate, i.e.
  - from a survey of the data subject,
  - from the device owner,
  - from a data provider or from a database,
  - from Open Data projects,

  (level of data retrieval); and
- whether these data have been lawfully acquired from both the source/data provider and the data provider, which must be assessed according to the location of the data source/data provider according to the national law applicable at its location,
  (level of applicable law); and
- whether the controller has concluded the necessary contractual agreements for the data concerned or whether he can also rely on sufficient lawful bases which entitle it to use this data at all in the context of a Big Data application
  (level of the lawful basis); as well as
- whether the data originally collected for operational purposes may also be processed in the Big Data application for the purposes of a specifically intended evaluation/analysis.
  (level of data purpose).

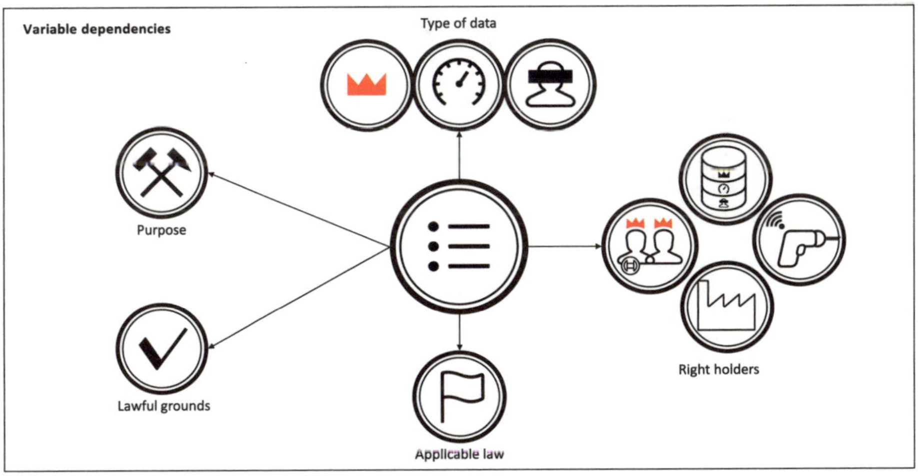

Figure 9: Variable dependencies

42 In any case, it is incumbent[16] upon the controller responsible for the Big Data application to record or otherwise document the results of these pre-audits in order to be able to demonstrate at all times that these data were lawfully collected, stored, and processed in the Big Data application.

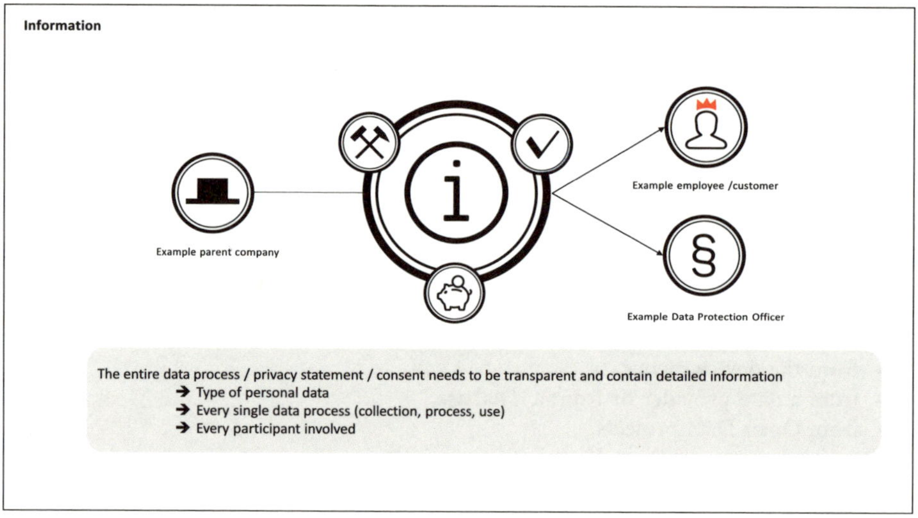

Figure 10: Information

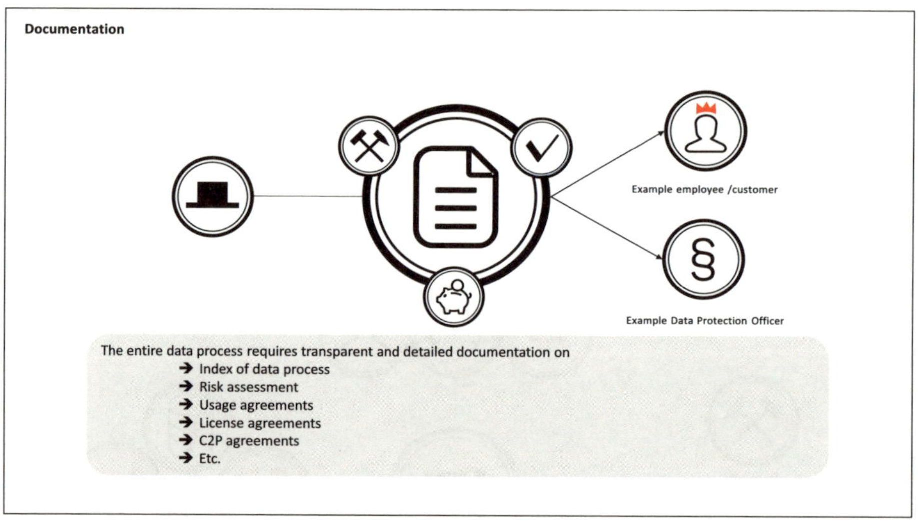

Figure 11: Documentation

[16] e.g., in German Civil law, "incumbent" in a contractual relationship means an obligation of a minor degree *(Obliegenheit)* whereby, if breached, the creditor cannot sue for performance and the debtor is not liable for damages. However, in the event of a breach of the obligations incumbent on him, the debtor must accept the disadvantages resulting from this breach in such a way that he loses or can no longer assert existing rights of his own or that he does not obtain rights which he would acquire upon performance of the obligation.

For personal data, this is even an explicit legal obligation under Art. 5 (2) GDPR: the controller responsible for the collection and processing of personal data must at all times be in a position to prove compliance with data protection obligations. A breach of this obligation is not only associated with legal consequences in individual cases, but as such – even in the case of lawful processing of personal data – an administrative offence which can be punished by a fine of up to EUR 20 million or 4 % of the worldwide annual turnover of the company or even the group to which the controller belongs (cf. mn. 514). In addition, there are other claims by those affected (cf. mn. 527) or risks of criminal liability (cf. mn. 522 *et seq.*). **43**

Although there is no comparable statutory documentation obligation for data not related to natural persons, factual or anonymous data, a preliminary examination of the aforementioned criteria is nevertheless necessary. This preliminary examination is required from general compliance aspects in order to prevent unlawful actions by a controller from the outset and at the same time to ensure that legal challenges by third parties upon the development and operation of a Big Data application are effectively counteracted, and that the undisturbed development and operation of the Big Data application be ensured for the benefit of the controller. **44**

In the case of infringement of other legal positions of third parties, e.g. infringement of virtual householder right of a system operator due to unauthorized tapping of data generated in this system or the infringement of database protection rights, the infringing party may be liable for injunctive relief and claims for damages, as well as risk criminal liability due to infringement of industrial property rights, e.g. § 106 UhrG for the violation of copyrights (for civil and criminal sanctions cf. mn. 527 *et seq.*). Legal consequences for the violation of data vary depending on which data and thus which laws are affected. These legal repercussions may also occur cumulatively. Such rights and claims can be demanded and/or asserted in court by the respective right holders. Under German law, it is precisely injunctive relief claims that can also be asserted and enforced in expedited judicial proceedings by way of an interim injunction, even without prior hearing of the legal entity responsible for infringing such legal positions of third parties. The imposition of such an injunction would typically result in an immediate obligation to cease any form of operation or use of the compromized Big Data application. Even an appeal against an interim injunction would not have a suspensive effect (for the consequences under procedural law cf. below under mn. 529 *et seq.*) While claims for injunctive relief can also be enforced in interim legal protection proceedings by an interim injunction, claims for damages can only be enforced in principal proceedings. The claim for damages under applicable law (e.g. in Germany under § 945 ZPO) for the defendant who has suffered damages as a result of an unjustified injunction, even though this is independent of fault, is of little use in the event of a temporary shutdown of a Big Data application: the benefit of a Big Data application lies precisely in the evaluation and analysis of data available almost in real time and the business opportunities created as a result are possibly irretrievably lost. The maintenance and further use of a Big Data application therefore rely upon the prior examination of aspects (which are to be further explained in detail below) and the documentation of the examination results as well as the agreements made with third parties. **45**

B. TYPES OF DATA

46 A distinction between different types of data is to be drawn with regard to Big Data applications:

47 It is of primary importance to determine whether the content of the datum concerns personal or non-personal data: personal data necessitate adherence to the legislative requirements of data protection law.

48 The processing of personal data is subject to the requirements of applicable data protection law. Even the processing of neutral, i.e. non-personal data, is not without restrictions as there may be industrial property rights, ancillary copyrights to databases or images, other rights, or the data may constitute business or trade secrets (cf. mn. 75–106 below). Of course, it is first necessary to determine the applicable law in each case, whereby the factors for this vary depending on the legal matter at issue.

49 Until 24 May 2018, national data protection provisions resulted from the applicable national data protection legislation, e.g. in Germany the Federal Data Protection Act (BDSG) in the version dated 14 January 2003 (BDSG a.F.) and the special data protection provisions applicable to individual fields, such as in the Telemedia Act (TMG)[17], and the Telecommunications Act (TKG). The provisions of the EU General Data Protection Regulation (GDPR) have been in force since 25 May 2018. These replace the existing national data protection laws of each EU Member State and only allow for national data protection regulations outside of the GDPR with regard to specific questions; e.g. the German legislator has excluded these possibilities in the form of the Federal Data Protection Act in the version of the EU Data Protection Adaptation and Implementation Act (DSAnpUG-EU) of 12 May 2016 (BDSG); for instance, the reformed BDSG goes beyond the GDPR with more detailed regulations for the processing of employees' personal data. Further relevant regulations are expected, such as the EU ePrivacy Regulation, a draft of which was published in January 2017 and which is to contain new regulations for the creation of user profiles (cf. mn. 66 below).

Guiding Principle:

The processing of personal data is subject to the requirements of data protection law; this will also include the future EU ePrivacy Regulation.
The processing of non-personal data, such as databases or images, may be subject to restrictions due to any existing industrial property rights or ancillary copyrights, the possible nature of the data to be used as company or trade secrets, and other existing rights. Determining which rights are available requires an examination of the applicable national law.

50 However, it is also necessary to distinguish according to the source from which the data is obtained. If the data is not generated by the company operating the Big Data application itself, it is obtained from a third party who may, for example, have copyrights or ancillary copyrights or other rights to this data that prevent its free exploitation. Here, it is often necessary to determine the right holder vis-à-vis such data

[17] According to the position of the Conference of the Independent Data Protection Authorities of the Federation and the of the Federal States of 26 April 2018 "On the applicability of the TMG to non public bodies from 25 May 2018, the data protection supervisory authorities are of the opinion that the data protection provisions of the TMG are no longer applicable due to the precedence of the GDPR."

and whether the entitled party has acquired sufficient rights to allow the operator of the Big Data application to use this data within the framework of the Big Data application. Even if data is made freely available by third parties, this provision – comparable to open source software – is often subject to conditions which, if not complied with, make the use of the data legally inadmissible (cf. mn. 71–104 below).

I. Personal data

51 The inclusion and evaluation of data in a Big Data application is always relevant under data protection law if the data to be evaluated are personal data. In contrast to complete databases or database extracts, which are often acquired in their entirety, personal data are typically (although not necessarily) collected as data from or in connection with an individual case (e.g. a sales transaction or a customer-satisfaction survey of individual customers) in order to be further evaluated by means of a Big Data application. Utilization of personal data is only permitted within the framework of the requirements of the applicable data protection law; any use of personal data outside these data protection limits is not permitted and is therefore subject to varying legal consequences (cf. mn. 510 *et seq.*) depending on which data and thus which laws are affected. These legal consequences may also occur cumulatively. Accordingly, it is necessary to ask at the beginning of every examination of the admissibility of a Big Data application whether personal data should be included and evaluated.

Guiding Principle:
The inclusion and evaluation of personal data must be determined at the beginning of each examination of the admissibility of a Big Data application.

1. Definition of "personal data" pursuant to Art. 4 (1) GDPR

52 Pursuant to the definition in Art. 4 (1) GDPR, *personal data* are any information relating to an identified or identifiable natural person (hereinafter *data subject*). An identifiable natural person is one who can be identified directly or indirectly, in particular by reference to an identifier such as a name, an identification number (e.g. a personnel number, a registration number, documented serial number of a machine sold to the customer, etc.), location data, an online identifier (e.g. the IP address) or one or more specific characteristics expressing the physical, physiological, genetic, mental, economic, cultural or social identity of that natural person. Personal data is only such information which also refers to a natural person, i.e. an individual living human being.

53 Legal entities or pluralities of persons are therefore excluded. However, in the case of legal entities (such as, in particular, a one-person limited liability company) or pluralities of persons (such as a partnership under civil law) or a commercial partnership (such as a general partnership or a limited partnership), it may arise that information relating to a group of persons is passed on to individual members. This can be the case, for example, with information about the financial situation of a group of persons, with the consequence that this data is also to be regarded as personal. In the case of the typical one-person limited liability company, information with reference to this company is formally with regard to a legal entity, but in fact it always refers to the individual natural person who constitutes this company.

Figure 12: Personal or factual data

> **Guiding Principle:**
> Personal data is only information relating to a natural person, i.e. an individual living human being. Information relating to a group of persons or to legal entities can affect individual members depending on the circumstances of the individual case.

Data of deceased persons are in theory not personal data (cf. recital 27 GDPR). However, if such data also contain a reference to living persons, the matter must be assessed differently; such data will qualify as "*personal*". An example of this would be information about a hereditary disease of the deceased which indicates that potential living descendants of the deceased also suffer from this disease. **54**

> **Guiding Principle:**
> Data of deceased persons are in theory not personal data, unless its use would indirectly result in a reference to living persons.

The definition of the concept of personal data in Art. 4 (1) GDPR is to be interpreted broadly and includes any type of information that may be identify a person. There are no "irrelevant" data for the collection and collection of personal data and their automated processing[18]. Qualifying data as personal does not require a balance of interests or a distinction based on the subjective perception of the data's sensitivity. Thus, even apparently "harmless" data such as name, address, telephone number or the fact of having an employment relationship with a particular company or sending a letter or email are personal data; collecting and processing such data is thereby subject to the restrictions of data protection law. **55**

[18] Cf. BVerfG, 15 December 1983, BVerfGE 65, 1/45.

2. Identifiability of personal data (Examples)

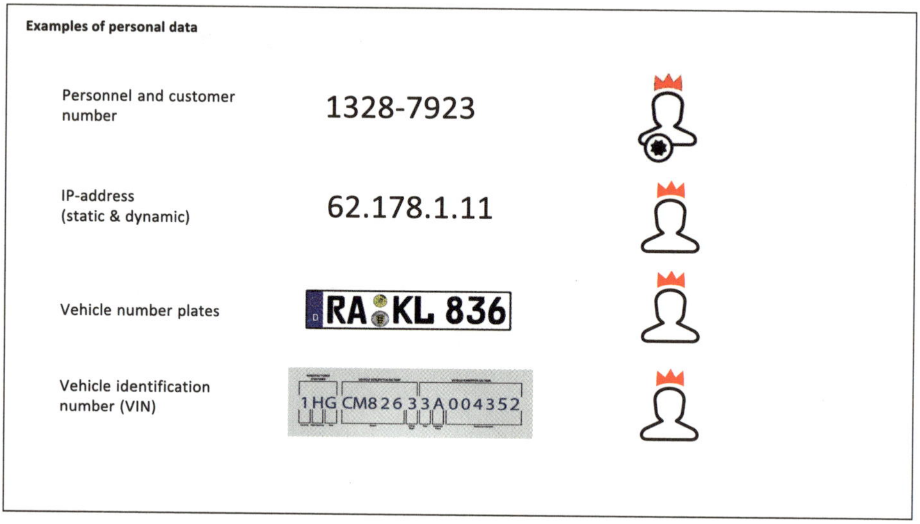

Figure 13: Examples of personal data

a) Dynamic IP addresses

56 Static as well as dynamic IP addresses are, for example, person-related data for the provider of online services when a person accesses a website that this provider makes generally accessible, since in turn at least the access provider of the subscriber knows in each case to which person it has assigned a dynamic IP address at which time. This information can be used to at least identify the user of the online service. There is thus the possibility for the service provider to use the stored protocol data to draw conclusions about the online behaviour of the owner of the connection to which the IP address is assigned.[19] This naturally also applies to any other IP-supported transmission of data: as soon as this is transmitted or collected together with an IP address assigned to a natural person, this combination of information and IP address becomes personal data. The IP address, from which data is transmitted to a data collecting point, thus forms the link, especially in M2M communication in IoT applications, which is why only factual or machine-related information about the IP address or a mobile phone number can initially be assigned to a natural person again.

> **Guiding Principle:**
> IP addresses and any information relating to an IP address must always be treated as personal data. This applies in particular to data exchanged in the course of M2M communication in IoT applications, where the IP address is the "sender's address".

b) Personnel or customer numbers

57 Personnel and customer numbers allow one to draw conclusions about the persons in question, since they are assigned to a specific person by the employer or principal. For this reason, they always represent personal data for the employer/principal. Other data processing entities are not privy to this additional information, which enables the

[19] Cf. BGH, 16 May 2017, *ZD* 2017, 424.

employer to assign a personnel number to the employee. As these third party entities also cannot claim the disclosure of this additional information, such information referring to a personnel number is highly unlikely to be person-related.

> **Guiding Principle:**
> Personnel and customer numbers at least allow the employer/principal to draw conclusions about the employee/customer concerned; information with reference to such personnel or customer numbers is therefore personal data.

c) VIN/Vehicle registration numbers

Vehicle Identification Numbers (VIN) and vehicle registration numbers and the data collected together with them, for example on driving behaviour, performance or consumption values of the vehicle, etc., are also personal data. If a legitimate interest is shown, it is possible without disproportionate effort to determine the owner of a particular vehicle by means of an ownership enquiry including the vehicle data on record. For example, this is taken into account in the rule in § 45 sentence 2 Road Traffic Act (StVG), in which the registration number of a vehicle and the vehicle identification number are qualified as data that enable a reference to a specific or identifiable person. 58

> **Guiding Principle:**
> Information with reference to vehicle identification numbers and vehicle registration plates shall also be treated as personal data; the collection and further processing of such data is subject to data protection law.

d) Special categories of personal data

Special categories of personal data are merely a type of personal data with particularly sensitive content. The specific types of personal data already include information on racial and ethnic origin, political opinions, religious or philosophical beliefs, trade union membership, any kind of health data and information on sex life.[20] 59

With the application of the General Data Protection Regulation from 25 May 2018, special categories of personal data also include genetic data, biometric data for the unique identification of a natural person and data relating to the sexual orientation of a natural person.[21] 60

Special categories of personal data may only be collected and processed in specific cases; otherwise their collection and processing are also prohibited. The cases in which special categories of personal data may be collected and processed are specifically listed numerically for these special categories of personal data in the legislation.[22] 61

[20] Definition according to § 3 (9) BDSG a.F.
[21] Art. 9 (1) GDPR.
[22] Art. 9 (2) and 3 GDPR as well as based on Art. 9 (4) GDPR, in addition § 22 BDSG.

62 The main legal grounds for the collection and processing of special categories of personal data are as follows:
- the consent of the data subject for one or more purposes specified in the consent;[23]
- processing is necessary to enable the controller or data subject to exercise his rights under employment law and social security and social protection law and to fulfil his obligations thereunder[24]
- processing is necessary for the purpose of establishing, exercising or defending legal claims or whenever courts are acting in the course of their judicial capacity[25]

63 There are numerous other legal grounds, however these are usually not relevant for Big Data applications.

> **Guiding Principle:**
> Special categories of personal data have a particularly sensitive content (in particular racial and ethnic origin, political opinions, religious or philosophical beliefs, trade union membership, health data, sex life, sexual orientation, genetic and biometric data). They may only be processed in limited cases.

e) Location, traffic and usage data

64 Location data obtained from the use of publicly accessible telecommunications services may typically only be used in accordance with the provisions of the applicable telecommunication law, e.g. in Germany § 98 Telecommunications Act (TKG). Pursuant to § 98 (1) first sentence TKG, location data used with regard to users of public telecommunications networks or publicly accessible telecommunications services may only be processed to the extent and within the period necessary for the provision of value-added services if they have either been rendered anonymous or if the subscriber has given his consent to the provider of the value-added service. According to § 3 (5) TKG, such a *value-added service* is any service that requires the collection and use of traffic data or location data to an extent that goes beyond that required for the transmission of a message or the billing of the charges for this process. Examples include advertising tailored to the individual location, road traffic reports or telematics services and navigation aids, or the location of children via their mobile phones.[26]

> **Guiding Principle:**
> Location data resulting from the use of mobile networks in particular may only be used in limited cases pursuant to § 98 TKG for the provision of services with additional benefits which the data subject has booked. This does not apply to location data determined with the aid of a satellite-based positioning system (e.g. GPS system).

65 The collection and use of traffic data from the telecommunications sector are also subject to specific restrictions under telecommunications law; for traffic data, these are the provisions in § 96 TKG. Traffic data includes the number or identifier of the connections involved or of the terminal equipment, personal authorization identifiers, the card number if customer cards are used, the location data if mobile, the start and end of the individual connection by date and time as well as the data volumes transmitted, the telecommunications service used by the user, the end points of fixed

---

[23] Art. 9 (2) (a) GDPR.
[24] Art. 9 (2) (b) GDPR as well as§ 22 (1) No. 1 (a) BDSG.
[25] Art. 9 (2) (f) GDPR.
[26] Braun, in: *Beck'scher TKG-Kommentar*, 4th ed. 2013, § 3 mn. 14.

connections, their start and end by date and time and the data volumes transmitted as well as other data required for establishing telecommunications and for billing. This traffic data may only be used insofar as is necessary for the purposes listed in §§ 91–107 TKG or for establishing further connections. In addition, traffic data must be deleted immediately by the service provider after termination of the connection; collection using traffic data that goes beyond the aforementioned purposes is not permitted.[27] Furthermore, the collection and processing of traffic data in the telecommunications sector is again only permitted with the consent of the data subject, whereby the personal reference may only then be maintained with regard to the consenting subscriber to telecommunications services; the data of the party called, on the other hand, must be made anonymous without delay.[28]

Guiding Principle:
Traffic data are also specific categories of personal data originating from the use of telecommunications services; in Germany, they may only be used in accordance with the provisions of § 96 TKG.

A group of personal data comparable to the category of traffic data is the usage data generated by the use of telemedia (in particular websites), which includes, in particular, characteristics for the identification of the user, information about the beginning and end as well as the scope of the respective use and information about the telemedia used by the user.[29] According to the applicable national telemedia law, such usage data from the use of telemedia may only be collected and used insofar as this is necessary to enable and account for the use of telemedia. However, the service provider may also create user profiles for the purposes of advertising, market research or for the demand-oriented design of the telemedia if he creates pseudonyms for this purpose and technical and organizational measures are taken to ensure that the user profiles are not combined with data about the bearer of the pseudonym.[30] The user has the right to object to the creation and use of user profiles. The user must be made aware of his right to object.[31] With the entry into force of the GDPR, its lawful grounds shall take precedence over those of the applicable national telemedia law, i.e. as a rule the balance of interests pursuant to Art. 6 (1) (f) GDPR. **66**

Guiding Principle:
Usage data, which is generated by the use of telemedia (in particular websites), may be used as pseudonymized data to set up user profiles insofar as the data subject does not object. The user must be informed of his right to object.

f) Characteristics of specific data sources

aa) Social Media. Where Big Data applications are concerned, the data generated on social media platforms are particularly considered relevant in order to be able to predict **67**

---

[27] § 96 (1) sentence 3 as well as (2) TKG.

[28] § 96 (3) sentence 2 TKG.

[29] § 15 (1) TMG; according to the Konferenz der unabhängigen Datenschutzbehörden des Bundes und der Länder from 26.4.2018 "Zur Anwendbarkeit des TMG für nicht-öffentliche Stellen ab dem 25. Mai 2018" the data protection authorities are of the opinion that the data protection regulations of the TMG are no longer be used because of the overriding application of the GDPR.

[30] Cf footnote 13: § 15 (3) TMG which is, however, pursuant to the German data protection supervisory authorities no longer applicable; rather Art. 6 (1) (f) GDPR applies.

[31] Cf. footnote. 13: § 15 (3) sentences 1 and 2 TMG no longer apply; rather Art 6 (1) (f) GDPR applies.

customer requirements and customer behaviour, and to determine who, when, and on which occasion opinions concerning a product, a service or a brand are announced and published online. From a legal perspective, prior to 24 May 2018, the specific provisions of the applicable national telemedia law (described in mn. 66 *et seq.* above) were primarily applicable to such data; from 25 May 2018 onwards the provisions of the GDPR apply, whereby the position of the German Conference of the Independent Data Protection Authorities of the Federal Government and the States "On the Applicability of the TMG to Non-Public Bodies from 25 May 2018" showed that the data protection supervisory authorities were of the opinion that the GDPR's data protection provisions took precedence over the TMG, thereby rendering the latter inapplicable.

68 If the data in question have been provided by the data subject himself, the general prohibition with reservation of permission also applies. However, the purposes of the use of the data posted by individual persons (e.g. application documents, comments in blogs or on fan pages) for their analysis in Big Data applications can also be described within the data protection declaration, so that the data subject can anticipate on the basis of this information the purposes for which his data will be used – as a rule this is based on a balance of interests[32].

> **Guiding Principle:**
>
> Postings in social media may be used by the operator of the social media platform for his own Big Data applications if the data subject has been informed of this use in the context of the data protection declaration.

69 If a Big Data application uses personal data which have been stored on websites independently operated by a third party, the users who have posted their data on such websites shall as a rule only be subject to the third party's terms of the data protection declaration and terms of use. The transfer of personal data by the operator of a Big Data application from a third party's social media platform to his own Big Data application is therefore not covered in any case by the original declaration which the user may have made as part of his registration or posting on the third party's social media platform. The collection of such data from such social media platforms was only permissible in Germany within the scope of the provisions in § 29 (1) sentence 1 No. 2 BDSG a. F. (e.g. data from a publicly accessible source),[33] now it is permissible within the scope of a balance of interests pursuant to Art. 6 (1) (f) GDPR. Publicly accessible data may be collected if no legitimate interests of the data subject implicated in the exclusion of the processing or use outweigh the legitimate interest of the data controller. Within the meaning of § 29 BDSG a. F., all sources of information are publicly accessible if, in terms of both their technical design and their objectives, they are suitable for communicating information to an individually indeterminable group of persons. Data is therefore only public if it can be accessed by anyone without access control or without overcoming technical access restrictions such as logins or similar. The complexity of such technical access restrictions does not require high standards. As soon as it is clear that the operator of a social media platform wants to prevent completely uncontrolled distribution or accessibility for everyone, the data is no longer publicly accessible. In this case, the regulation in § 29 (1) sentence 1 (2) BDSG a. F. did not apply. In the context of the balancing of interests pursuant to Art. 6 (1) (f) GDPR, the existence of access

---

[32] Art. 6 (1) (f) GDPR; see mn. 201 et seq. E.I.2.

[33] Also § 29 BDSG a. F. is a substantiated and modified balancing of interests, whose values can be used in the context of Art. 6 (1) (f) GDPR.

restriction or the question of public accessibility of data is an essential aspect in the recording and evaluation of the data subject's interests worthy of protection.

> **Guiding Principle:**
>
> Postings on social media platforms operated by third parties may only be used in Big Data applications if the relevant social media platform is publicly accessible, i.e. without any access control, and there is no prevailing protection of the data subject which excludes the processing or use in the Big Data application.

In its position statement of 26 April 2018 *"On the applicability of the TMG to non-public bodies from 25 May 2018"*[34] the German Conference of Independent Data Protection Authorities of the Federal Government and the States took the view that the prior consent of the data subject is required for the creation of user profiles as well as for the use of tracking mechanisms that make the conduct of data subjects on the internet traceable (cf. mn. 197 *et seq.*). **70**

bb) Open Data. *Open data* refers to data stocks that, in the interest of the general public, are made freely accessible for unrestricted use as well as further distribution and use. These are often public data. Such data can be data relating to natural persons or legal entities as well as purely factual or anonymized data. However, open data can also be made available in the field of science by private commercial enterprises or non-governmental organizations, e.g. geodata, statistics, traffic information or scientific publications. **71**

As with open source software, open data projects generally contain license information that, for example, prescribes the labelling of open data or contains other restrictions on use. In particular, data from German authorities is often subject to approval by the data provider. Open data can therefore not be tapped and used in Big Data applications in a completely unrestricted manner or without regard for any legal requirements. Each source of open data must rather be examined to see whether there are any license notices and which requirements and/or usage restrictions they contain. If these requirements and/or restrictions on use are not observed, the right to use the data published as *Open Data*, which would otherwise belong to everyone, will lapse and the use of the data in a Big Data application can be prohibited by the data provider and punished with claims for damages[35]. **72**

> **Guiding Principle:**
>
> Although open data is also available to everyone for use in Big Data applications, lawful use of open data requires compliance with the conditions and requirements of the license notices applicable to each open data project.

cc) Data acquisition through Apps. There are no special features for data retrieval using applications operated on mobile devices (*apps*) compared to the data described above. Whereas the declarations of consent and/or data protection notices or information on data subjects[36] must each be in a transparent and easily accessible form, and use **73**

[34] Positionsbestimmung der Konferenz der unabhängigen Datenschutzbehörden des Bundes und der Länder of 26 April 2018 "Zur Anwendbarkeit des TMG für nicht-öffentliche Stellen ab dem 25. Mai 2018".

[35] Hackenberg, in: Hoeren/Sieber/Holznagel, *Multimedia-Recht*, 46th update January 2018, Part 16.7 mn. 33–34.

[36] Art. 13, 14 GDPR.

clear and plain language,[37] the limited display space on the screen of a mobile device require special consideration.

74 Location and sensor data are particularly relevant for apps –the aforementioned data protection requirements apply equally to them as well as to the collection and processing of personal data by any other means. If data are to be obtained and processed from the use of apps, it is particularly advisable in Germany to observe the recommendations of Art. 29 Data Protection Working Party (G29) in its Opinion 2/2013 on Apps on intelligent terminal devices of 27 February 2013.[38]

II. Non-personal data

75 Non-personal data are usually either factual data, data with reference to an anonymous person, or data with reference to a legal entity (for example, consumption values of a heating system that is located in the building of property company X). Factual data refers exclusively to one thing (for example, consumption values of a heating system that cannot be assigned to an owner of this system). It does not matter whether a person is identified if the information does not refer to the person. An example of this would be the statement that the city of Stuttgart lies at an altitude of 247m above sea level. Even if the person responsible here knew that a certain person had been in Stuttgart once, this statement does not contain any information relating to this person.

76 A piece of information refers then to a natural person and not to a certain thing, if one of three elements is given: a content element, a purpose element or a result element.[39]

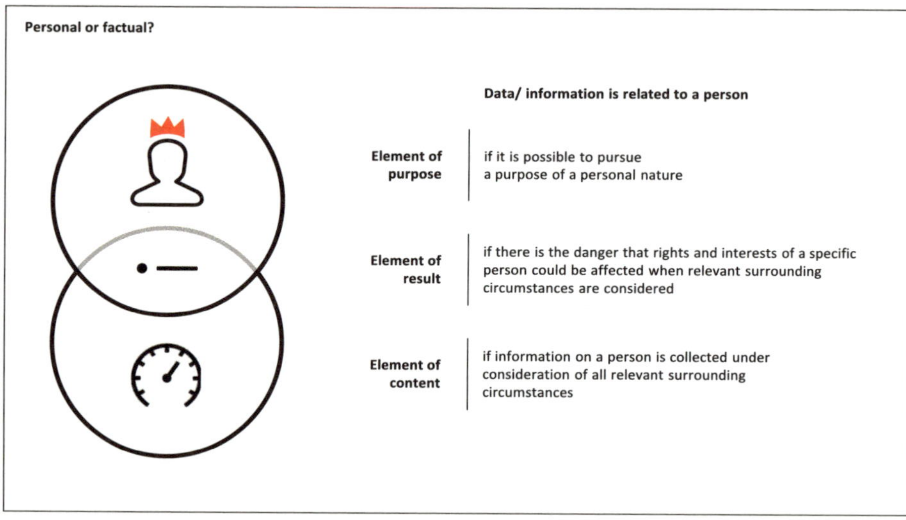

Figure 14: Personal or factual data

77 A content element exists when information about a person is collected using all relevant circumstances and with exemption from purpose on the part of the controller or a third party or from the effects on the data subject.

[37] Art. 12 GDPR.
[38] To be found at www.lda.bayern.de/mobileapplikationen/wp202 _ de.PDF, edition of 7/2018.
[39] Cf. Art.-29-Working Party, Opinion 4/2007, “Personenbezogene Daten”, WP 136, 10 *et seq.*

A purpose element applies when it is possible to use the information for a particular purpose, be it assessment, treatment or influence. 78

The result element refers to a situation where there is a risk that the information may affect the rights and interests of a particular person, taking into account all relevant circumstances. 79

Guiding Principle:

Information refers to a natural person and not to a particular matter if, from an abstract view, information is collected about a person where there is the possibility to use them for a particular purpose which may affect that person's rights and interests, taking into account all relevant circumstances.

Statistical data, for example, also do not contain any personal references, provided they do not focus on a specific person, but – as is usually the case – on a group of persons. Seemingly purely factual data, however, can still be regarded as personal data in the large number of cases that occur in practice, simply because they are transmitted to the entity collecting such data, for example via the internet or by mobile phone. The transmitted IP address or mobile phone number is the element in the data record collected which allows for the identification of the natural person from whom or from whose installations/devices this data was transmitted. This form of transmission therefore makes data protection law relevant in almost all cases. However, special regulations or protection standards for certain categories of data also apply to purely factual data or information relating to a legal entity: 80

Guiding Principle:

Purely factual data as well as statistical data do not contain personal references, unless a reference to a natural person can be established via their "sender information" (IP address, mobile phone number).

III. Databases and collections

Databases and collective works can both enjoy copyright protection. 81

However, copyright protection for databases as such can only be considered if the particular way in which the database entries are arranged and structured is an expression of a personal intellectual creation. In the case of collective works, the criterion justifying copyright protection also lies in the order and structure of the individual entries in the collective work. Both protective rights can be applied cumulatively because they have a different object of protection. Both do not contain any protection with regard to the individual datum or the protection of the software used to operate a database. 82

For databases, the ancillary copyright of the database manufacturer can also be considered, which merely requires a substantial investment in the structure and order of their contents, but no personal intellectual creation. 83

These criteria also apply to user-generated content.[40] The criterion of personal intellectual creation becomes relevant above all in the case of so-called computer-generated content, in which copyright protection can only be considered if the creative process used in the computer program is itself the result of a personal intellectual 84

[40] Hassemer, Nutzergenerierte Inhalte zwischen Urheberrecht und Datenbankschutz, in: Conrad/Grützmacher, *Recht der Daten und Datenbanken im Unternehmen*, 2014, p. 234 *et seq.*

creation – independent of the respective software development service – which is then reflected in the respective workpiece.

85 Both the copyright and the database protection right for databases grant the respective owner the exclusive right to use, modify and exploit a copyrighted collective work or database and to enable third parties to use, modify or exploit it in whole or in part. An appropriate right of use (= license) must always be acquired in order to be able to use copyrighted collective works or databases of third parties.

86 The owners of collective works/databases protected by copyright or ancillary copyright may also decide whether they wish to grant such licenses upon payment or gratuitously. Thus, collective works or databases marketed as open source products are also subject to the corresponding legal protection and the conditions set out in the individual license agreements must be observed for open source products as well as for licenses. In the case of open source products, the right of use typically lapses with non-compliance with the license's conditions linked to the use of such products.

Guiding Principle:

A database is a collection of individual pieces of information that are structured and ordered in a particular way; the acquisition, verification or presentation thereof requires a substantial investment in terms of type or size. The use of databases or extracts thereof by saving the database elements to individual data records in a Big Data application is therefore only permitted if the right holder has acquired the corresponding rights of use (= licenses). Individual information as such is not protected.

87 Differences exist in the subject-matter and the duration of protection. While database protection law protects the time-consuming acquisition, verification and presentation of data – i.e. investment protection for 15 years (§§ 87a *et seq.* UrhG) – copyright law protects the creative selection or order of data in a collective work or database – i.e. individual intellectual creation up to 70 years *post mortem auctoris* (§ 64 UrhG)

1. Collections of works, data or other independent elements, § 4 German Copyright Act

88 Under German law, collections of works, data of any content category or other independent elements which are a personal intellectual creation solely on the basis of the selection or order of the individually and independently accessible elements (*Collections*) shall be without prejudice to any copyright or related right which may exist in the individual elements (such as the database protection right, cf. §§ 87a and 87b UrhG) are copyrightable as independent works (§ 4 (1) UrhG). The subject matter of collective works can therefore be protected by copyright on the basis of the corresponding level of creativity and quality; however, unprotected designs may also be considered, such as works whose copyright protection has expired or which do not meet the criteria of individual intellectual creation and the level of copyright protection pursuant to § 2 (2) UrhG.[41] Data, i.e. formalized representations of facts, concepts or instructions suitable for human or machine communication, can also be the subject of collective works. The subject of collective works may also be websites, emails or articles in newsgroups and even collections of real objects such as minerals, coins or automobiles.

---

[41] Auer-Reinsdorff, Schutz von Datenbanken und Datenbankwerken, in: Conrad/Grützmacher, *Recht der Daten und Datenbanken im Unternehmen*, 2014, p. 205 *et seq.*; Leistner, Die Landkarte als Datenbank, Überlegungen zum Datenbankschutz für topographische Karten und geographische Daten, *GRUR* 2014, 528; Leistner, Was lange währt…: EuGH entscheidet zur Schutzfähigkeit geographischer Karten als Datenbanken, *GRUR* 2016, 42.

For copyright protection as a compilation, however, it is crucial that **89**
- the selection or arrangement of the elements of the collection is itself an individual, personal intellectual creation based on human action within the meaning of § 2 (2) UrhG. This is not the case if the selection or design is
  - known and common,
  - is based solely on specialist knowledge, laws of thought or technical necessities, or
  - is largely predetermined by the purpose of the data collection[42]
- the selection and arrangement are considered original when, in selecting and arranging the data contained in a database, the author expresses his creative abilities in an independent manner by making free and creative choices, thereby giving it a *personal touch*. The criterion of originality is not met if the creation of the database is determined by technical considerations, rules or constraints which leave no room for artistic freedom.[43]

In a collective work, *selection* describes the process of collecting and recording, **90** viewing, evaluating, and assembling elements on a particular subject with regard to particular selection criteria.

The term *order* means the classification, presentation and accessibility of the elements **91** selected according to one or more classification systems. The order may be of a systematic or methodological nature.

Intellectual content must manifest itself in the selection or arrangement which goes **92** beyond the mere sum of the contents of the individual elements. The resulting investment expenditure is irrelevant for copyright protection, as is the expertise involved. Copyright protection of collective works is limited to the selection and order of data. It does not extend to the individual works or data collected.

Guiding Principle:
Collected works are protected by copyright as independent works, without prejudice to any copyright or related right that may exist with regard to the individual elements (§ 4 (1) UrhG). Their use in Big Data applications is therefore only permissible if the right holder has acquired the corresponding rights of use (= licenses).

2. Database protection rights

Data base protection rights, such as §§ 87a and 87b UrhG, constitute performance **93** protection standards in favour of a database manufacturer and are intended to protect his investments in the development of databases from external access. A database in the sense of § 87a UrhG is a collection of works, data, individual information or other independent elements which is systematically or methodically arranged and individually accessible by electronic means or by other means.[44]

[42] Auer-Reinsdorff, Schutz von Datenbanken und Datenbankwerken, in: Conrad/Grützmacher, *Recht der Daten und Datenbanken im Unternehmen*, 2014, p. 205 *et seq*.

[43] ECJ, 1 March 2012, C-604/10 – *Football Dataco Ltd.*

[44] As Art. 1 (2) EU-Database Directive [...]; Lehmann, Daten als rechtliches Schutzgut, Verfügungsbefugnis an Daten, Herausgabeansprüche, in: Conrad/Grützmacher, *Recht der Daten und Datenbanken im Unternehmen*, 2014, p. 138; Auer-Reinsdorff, Schutz von Datenbanken und Datenbankwerken, in: Conrad/Grützmacher, *Recht der Daten und Datenbanken im Unternehmen*, 2014, p. 205 et seq.; Leistner, Die Landkarte als Datenbank, Überlegungen zum Datenbankschutz für topographische Karten und geographische Daten, *GRUR* 2014, 528; Leistner, Was lange währt...: EuGH entscheidet zur Schutzfähigkeit geographischer Karten als Datenbanken, *GRUR* 2016, 42.

- Independent elements are individual elements that can be separated from each other without affecting the value of their informative content. They must have a self-contained, independent and inherent value as they provide relevant information to third parties, which remains undiminished even in separate access. Whether extracted data combinations qualify as independent individual elements rests on whether the extraction of such combination corresponds exactly to the conception of the database. This applies, for example, to the extraction of data combinations from a methodically-arranged topographic map. In the case of pieces of music, on the other hand, this does not apply because the individual elements are clearly fused in a uniform design (= database), because at least certain melodic combinations (i.e. parts) can be extracted, but the concept of a uniform design form and typical listening behaviour do not correspond to the criteria for such elements.
- A systematic or methodological arrangement exists when there is a medium, such as an index, a table of contents, an outline or a particular type of classification, which makes it possible to locate each element contained in the collection.[45]

94 The collection of database entries in a database may be related to a natural person or a legal entity or may consist of purely factual or anonymized data. The decisive factor to qualify as a database is that the individual database entries are structured and ordered in a certain way, whereby their acquisition, verification or presentation requires a significant investment in terms of type or scope. The protection of databases therefore depends on the protection of the underlying investment, while creative performance is irrelevant. Conversely, the copyright protection of collective works protects the creative performance and the investment costs for this are irrelevant. A significant investment is made when, from an objective point of view, substantial expenses that could not easily be incurred by anyone were necessary to create the database.

95 Small and simple databases are therefore not subject to these standards. Furthermore, the database must be arranged systematically and methodically. Raw data alone are not systematically-arranged data and are therefore not subject to §§ 87a or 87b UrhG. Also, the database is always only protected as a whole and not individual data.[46]

96 An investment must have flowed into the collection and order of existing data and their presentation; investments in the provision, maintenance, servicing and servicing of the hardware and software infrastructure necessary for this, i.e. in particular the provision and ongoing operation of a database system and/or data extraction tools or tools for the preparation and presentation of data, can also be considered. The expenditure going into an examination of the individual database entries is only considered an investment if the expenditure refers to the verification of the procured data and not to the production and addition of incomplete data, which are or become part of the database. However, the effort involved in updating required to justify protection does not have to be reflected in externally recognisable or otherwise comprehensible changes, even if a comprehensive, costly examination as such is sufficient.

97 The mere generation of data without it being subsequently collected and ordered in a systematic and methodical manner is not an investment leading to database protection. Nor does an investment lead to database protection rights when already existing data are used a second time if they have not been systematically or methodically processed, or

---

[45] Leistner, Die Landkarte als Datenbank, Überlegungen zum Datenbankschutz für topographische Karten und geographische Daten, *GRUR* 2014, 528; Leistner, Was lange währt…: EuGH entscheidet zur Schutzfähigkeit geographischer Karten als Datenbanken, *GRUR* 2016, 42.

[46] Cf. Thalhofer, *GRUR-Prax* 2017, 225 (226).

unless there have been other specific investments in the presentation of the database.[47] The human, financial and technical resources required to collect and examine individual data in order to create a database as an independent usable asset must be separately demonstrable and provable in each individual case.[48] The disclosure of expenses, time, money and/or personnel services and the economic value of all these expenses is therefore required.

Without corresponding investments in the development of a database, the protection of data collections is only possible if the selection and arrangement of the individual elements of a database contain a creative achievement capable of copyright protection in the sense of a personal intellectual creation (in this case copyright protection can be considered as a collective work, cf. above mn. 88). **98**

The protection of works, data of any content category or other independent elements which are a personal intellectual creation solely on the basis of the selection or order of the individually and independently retrievable elements shall be without prejudice to any copyright or related right which may exist in the individual elements (such as, for example, the database protection right, cf. §§ 87a and 87b UrhG) and shall constitute performance protection standards in favour of a database producer and shall protect its investments in the development of databases from external access. **99**

Guiding Principle:

The database protection right of §§ 87a, 87b UrhG is based on the investments made by the database producer for collecting and organising existing data and their presentation as well as for the provision, maintenance, care and servicing of necessary hardware and software infrastructure. Investments for generating data to be entered into a database are not investments leading to database protection.

3. Protection of individual elements of a database or a collection

Databases as well as collections consist of different elements, which can enjoy different types of protection: **100**

a) Database model

The database model is the model that is to be implemented in a database. There are essentially four database models: **101**

- Hierarchical database model: a hierarchical tree structure in which each record has precisely one predecessor and exactly one record forms the root. Links between different trees or across several levels within a tree are not possible.
- Network database model: a strict hierarchy is not required. A data record can have several predecessors. Several data records can also be at the top. There are usually different search paths to get to a specific data record.
- Relati onal database model: The data is managed in the form of two-dimensional tables that can be linked together using keys.
- Object-oriented database model: the contents are objects in the sense of object-oriented programming. An object is a combination of associated attributes. Data and methods are not stored separately.[49]

---

[47] Auer-Reinsdorff, Schutz von Datenbanken und Datenbankwerken, in: Conrad/Grützmacher, *Recht der Daten und Datenbanken im Unternehmen*, 2014, p. 205 et seq.

[48] See ECJ, November 2004, C-338/02 – *Fixtures Marketing*.

[49] Schmidt, in: Auer-Reinsdorff/Conrad, *Handbuch IT- und Datenschutzrecht*, 2nd ed. 2016, p. 33 et seq.

102 Each database model has different phases from the abstract to the concrete, in which different types of protection can be granted[50]

- Conceptual data modelling: The objects of the real world that are to be represented in the database, together with their attributes and their relationships to each other, are mapped here. This is typically done in graphical form, in which the objects (entities) and their relations (relations) are illustrated, for example, by boxes and connecting lines. A conceptual data model can enjoy the protection of collective works (§ 4 UrhG) because the author is given a certain amount of discretion with regard to the concrete conception related to a certain data set both in terms of the selection decision and of arranging the attributes, allocation criteria and links and not the entire design is already given technically or materially by the database. Copyright protection may be considered where the database creator uses this discretion in an individually creative manner.
- However, the effort required for data modelling is also relevant for performance protection under §§ 87a *et seq.* UrhG, since all costs associated with the creation of the data model serve the structural design of the data in the database.
- Logical data model: This is the subsequent phase. Here, the data is prepared to be acquired by a database system by differentiating and naming the object relationships (data fields) used for storage, mapping object relationships in tabular form, and adjusting information that has been mentioned several times. This step is already largely determined by the technical requirements. The logical data model does not provide any protection according to § 4 UrhG due to the lack of an individual creative act, but it does provide a right to ancillary copyright according to §§ 87a *et seq.* UrhG, since all costs associated with the creation of the data model serve the structural presentation of the data in the database.
- Physical data model: Here the data is brought into the syntax of the database management system. This requires the data records to be translated or supplemented in a form that can be read by the database management system. The dataset is also now supplemented by indexing to make it easier to locate the data. This step is largely automated by the database management system. Furthermore, the physical data model justifies no protection following § 4 UrhG for lack of individually creative acts; the expenditure justifies however an ancillary copyright in accordance with §§ 87a *et seq.* UrhG.

b) Data format

103 Data format refers to the syntax and semantics of data within a file.[51] File formats can be publicly available and freely usable as industry standards, but they can also be kept under lock and key by individual manufacturers in order to bind users to their own programs. The data format is seen as part of the database management system. Therefore, protection as a computer program would at best be considered and ultimately enjoys no copyright protection because the data format ultimately consists of instructions for the creation of compatible files, which must inevitably be contained in every file to be processed.

[50] Hoppen, Wirtschaftliche und technische Grundlagen Teil 2, in: Conrad/Grützmacher, *Recht der Daten und Datenbanken im Unternehmen*, 2014, p. 7 et seq.; Metzger, Urheberschutz von Datenmodellen, Dateiformaten und Schnittstellen, in: Conrad/Grützmacher, *Recht der Daten und Datenbanken im Unternehmen*, 2014, p. 245 et seq.

[51] Metzger, Urheberschutz von Datenmodellen, Dateiformaten und Schnittstellen, in: Conrad/Grützmacher, *Recht der Daten und Datenbanken im Unternehmen*, 2014, p. 245 et seq.

Guiding Principle:
The data format does not enjoy copyright protection due to its inevitable technical requirements.

c) Interface

The interface[52] is part of the database management system, which ensures that external application programs can read and change data from the database. Legal protection of interfaces can only be considered with regard to computer programs: if it is a matter of programming the interface or of principles underlying the interface, the concrete implementation of the idea in the form of the source code and the binary code can be protected by copyright insofar as it is a personal, intellectual creation in which the developer has exploited creative scope beyond the technical requirements, specifications and standardizations in individual cases. On the other hand, ideas and principles underlying an element of a computer program, including the ideas and principles underlying the interfaces, are not protected. Interfaces do not enjoy copyright protection if the scope for design is restricted by technical requirements, standardized specifications and standardizations and therefore there is no scope for individual creative achievements. **104**

Guiding Principle:
Interfaces allow external application programs to access data from the database. For interfaces, legal protection can be considered for computer programs.

IV. Protection as business or trade secret

Business or trade secrets are often protected by applicable national law. For example, in Germany, the German Trade Secrets Act (*GeschGehG*) contains requirements for protection of business or trade secrets under both civil and criminal law. With regard to Big Data, the industrial espionage offence of § 23 (2) GeschGehG is of particular importance. Accordingly, **105**

> *"a custodial sentence of up to three years or a pecuniary fine shall be imposed on any person who, in order to promote his own or another's competition, for his own benefit, in favour of a third party or with the intention of causing damage to the owner of a business,*
> *1. […],*
> *2. […] or*
> *3. contrary to § 4(2) no. 3 discloses, as a person employed by an undertaking, a trade secret which has been entrusted to him or has become accessible to him in the course of his employment, during the period of validity of the employment relationship.*
> *(2) Likewise penalized shall be anyone who uses or discloses a trade secret which he has acquired through a third-party act pursuant to § 23 (1) No. 2 or No. 3 in order to promote his own or another's competition, for his own benefit, for the benefit of a third party or with the intention of causing damage to the owner of an enterprise."*

[52] Metzger, Urheberschutz von Datenmodellen, Dateiformaten und Schnittstellen, in: Conrad/Grützmacher, *Recht der Daten und Datenbanken im Unternehmen*, 2014, p. 245 et seq.

106 The subject matter of a business or trade secret may be personal data, data not relating to natural persons, purely factual data or anonymized data. Requirements to classify data as alleged trade or industrial secrets are: a connection to a business operation, lack of disclosure of the relevant information, interest in secrecy and subjective willingness to maintain secrecy on the part of the trade or industrial owner, which is, however, recognisable from external objective circumstances thus allowing for the assignment of a company owner as *owner* or also *holder* of a license or right of use.[53] Not all categories of data that are to be summarized and analysed in a Big Data application satisfy the requirement of a trade secret: for example, the temperature of a heating rod in a production plant may be part of a chemical production process subject to secrecy because the manufacturing temperature of the product in question is relevant for subsequent product properties (taste, storage life, molecular structure), whereas the temperature of the heating rod in a heating system is consumption-relevant but not subject to secrecy and is therefore not a trade or industrial secret of the building owner.

Guiding Principle:

Individual factual data may in turn be monopolized in the interest of a business owner as part of business or trade secrets so that their use by adding them to individual data records in a Big Data application is only permissible if the business owner has acquired corresponding rights of use.

V. Householder's right with regard to the collection of factual data

107 It is questionable whether, with regard to data from equipment installed in a property, a right exists to prevent the collection of factual data if and to the extent that such collection takes place within the normal scope of the exercise of the householder's right. In Germany, immunity of the home (i.e. the right to determine who shall be allowed or denied access) is derived from §§ 858, 903, 1004 BGB and is to be understood as a product of the inviolability of a home pursuant to Art. 13 GG. It is right conceded to the owner or entitled possessor (e.g. tenant, lessee) of premises and is not an independent legal institution, but only a bundle of powers assigned to the owner or entitled possessor of the premises in general. According to § 903 BGB, the owner of an object has only such powers that presuppose possession or are at least structured according to the model of possession. As § 903 BGB does not provide for a separation of data from the specific object where they are stored, data ownership does not follow ownership of physical objects under German property law.

108 The absence of property data ownership under German property law, however, also leaves the householder's right as the regulatory location of a general right of defence against the free exploitation of property data in the lurch since a householder's right is based on and arises from the concept of property ownership under property law. A possible householder's right to defend against collecting factual data is therefore not suitable as a regulatory connecting factor for an assignment of factual data to the asset group of the owner, possessor or user of the system or device that generates such factual data. In addition, in its direct application it only provides a link to the ownership or legitimate possession of premises and thus excludes all non-real-estate-related data sources from the outset.

[53] Cf. Thalhofer, *GRUR-Prax* 2017, 225 (227).

VI. Virtual householder's right

With regard to online services such as internet forums[54], websites[55] or online games[56], some courts have invoked a virtual householder's right derived not from the direct application of ownership or possession rules but from an analogous application of those rules. A prerequisite for the virtual householder's right is therefore, on the one hand, that a system operator be the owner or at least the lawful possessor or – for example on the basis of a rental or other cloud service contract – the lawful user of the hardware on which certain information is stored and, on the other hand, that the scope of the right can be clearly defined. The data is then assigned to the authorized user of a system or IT system, regardless of the legal basis. This scope of a virtual householder's right is clearly limited by the IP address of the server on which the relevant information is stored. Whether the stored information is ultimately information that belongs to the plot of an online game, or whether it is other information, for example with reference to the equipment, of which the respective storage location is merely an element, can ultimately not be relevant to the existence of such a virtual householder's right. **109**

One could still ask the question whether the – automated – transfer of such information from the equipment to a storage location of the operator or user of a Big Data application or the access of the operator of a Big Data application to the data of such equipment could infringe a virtual householder's right. This is clear if merely a copy of such data is transmitted to or *extracted* from the operator of the Big Data Application and the *original* data is simultaneously deleted from the storage location in the right holder's equipment. However, if the *original data* are still present on the right holder's equipment even after transmission to or access by the operator of the Big Data application, then there is no impairment of the physical substance of that data. The value of this data lies not in its physical substance, which is ultimately formed by only one byte of a binary code, but in its originality and uniqueness. Creating a copy of the data impairs its value because the data is consequently deprived of its originality and uniqueness. Accordingly, the intention of the LG Munich I in its judgment of 12 August 2014 on the virtual householder's right of the operator of online games can also be applied to situations in which data are created and stored in an IT system. Just as the owner or operator of an online game is authorized in the aforementioned decisions to prevent the effects of access to its server by applying §§ 1004 (1), 903 sentence 1 BGB accordingly, the authorized user of an IT-supported system also has the sole right to exclude third parties from the use of this server by copying or otherwise *extracting* data. In the case of rented or otherwise lawfully-used systems, a corresponding right of exclusion results from the analogous application of the property protection rules according to §§ 858, 862 BGB.[57] **110**

It should therefore also be noted for factual data that these are not in the public domain either and can be readily *extracted* or the purposes of their transmission and evaluation in a Big Data application; indeed, the authorized user of an system during the operation of which such factual data are generated would also have the possibility and **111**

---

[54] Cf. LG Bonn, MMR 2000, 109; OLG Köln, MMR 2001, 52.

[55] Cf. LG Ulm, MMR 2016, 31; OLG Hamburg, MMR 2008, 58; OLG Hamm, MMR 2009, 269.

[56] Cf. LG München I, 12 August 2014, BeckRS 2014, 121728; OLG München, Decree of 2.7.2015, BeckRS 2015, 119932; critical though Baldus, in: *Münchener Kommentar BGB*, 7th ed. 2017, § 1004 BGB mn. 28.

[57] Cf. Conraths/Krüger, *MMR* 2016, 310 et seq.

the right here to prevent the *extraction* of such data on the basis of the defensive rights to which he is entitled by virtue of ownership or possession. Whether legitimate use is based on ownership or any other legitimate use (e.g. rent, leasing, cloud contract) is irrelevant for applying the principles of virtual householder's right; the right holder is the respective legitimate user of the installation/IT system whose use ultimately leads to the creation of the relevant data: the tenant of an apartment with a fitted kitchen may serve as an example – the data generated in the appliances of the fitted kitchen are the property of the tenant and not of the owner of the apartment or building. The virtual householder's right understood in this way is entitled to each operator of an installation or an IT system, regardless of whether this operator is a natural person or a legal entity; if the operator is a natural person, virtual householder's rights stand independently alongside the rights of the data subject arising from data protection regulations.

112 Accordingly, in order to acquire the authority to extract such data, appropriate data procurement and usage agreements must be entered into between the operator of a Big Data application and the owner, operator or other authorized user of an installation or system that generates such factual data.

Guiding Principle:

A virtual householder's right assigns the sole right of use to the data generated in a system/IT system to the authorized user of the installation/IT system, irrespective of whether these data are personal. It is irrelevant whether authorized use is based on ownership or other authorized use (e.g. rental, leasing, cloud contract) of the relevant installation/IT system. The use of such data in a Big Data application therefore requires the conclusion of a corresponding user agreement with the authorized user of the installation/IT system, which also includes the (intra-group or external) transfer of this data.

VII. Factual data linked to IP addresses or other identifying characteristics

113 Even with machine-to-machine communication (*M2M communication*), the data exchanged can be linked not only to a system that sends this data but also to the owner of an IP address. If the owner of this IP address is a natural person, the data in question is *personal data* as described above (mn. 51 *et seq.*), whereby their collection and processing in a Big Data application is subject to the restrictions of the applicable data protection law. Examples would be the location of vehicle occupants in connected cars or patient data from machine-to-machine medical devices.[58] If the owner of the IP address is a legal entity, a data usage agreement with the owner of the system sending an M2M communication will nevertheless be necessary for the aforementioned reasons (mn. 109 *et seq.*).

114 The same applies to factual data linked to other identifying characteristics, such as vehicle identification numbers or personnel numbers, where the holder of such data has access to the means to identify the data subject.

115 In many cases, M2M communication initially generates data without a personal reference since the content of the information collected and transferred is data of a respective *machine*. In the vast majority of cases, these data nevertheless allow conclusions to be drawn about the user or the person responsible for the creation of data.[59]

[58] Cf. Grünwald/Nüßing, *MMR* 2015, 378 (382).

[59] OLG Naumburg, 27 August 2014, 6 U 3/14, juris, Hoeren, Dateneigentum, *MMR* 2013, 486 (488); Welp, *jur* 1988, 443 (447).

Supposedly non-personal communication data and technical records must not be viewed in isolation in M2M communication. The various data must rather be considered in combination with other data, which in their entirety lead in most cases to a personal reference.[60] In purely technical terms, a personal reference is made via the IP address through which the machine communicates with the recipient of the data and which, as the *sender* of the data, can provide information about the owner of this IP address and thus the natural person behind the machine.

With regard to connected cars, for example, a motion profile of the user can be created from the navigation system's data. Even supposedly only *technical data* on tyre pressure or brake wear allow conclusions to be drawn about human driving and maintenance behaviour,[61] where the personal reference can usually be established using the vehicle identification number. **116**

Guiding Principle:
Factual data, especially in the area of M2M communication in IoT applications, is related to a person solely via their *sender information* (IP address, mobile phone number), which allows for a natural person to be identified.

VIII. No data ownership

With regard to property issues, a distinction must be made in accordance with German civil law between physical and intangible objects. Property rights can only exist in *things* as defined in § 90 BGB, namely physical objects. In the absence of physicality, data therefore cannot be regarded as physical objects; no property from a civil law perspective can result. In legal transactions, data are classified as intangible assets. Nevertheless, the ownership status of a person as defined in property law is always linked to the material quality of the object. According to the basic concept of the German Civil Code, there is no civil law notion of ownership of data. Data therefore do not belong to anyone as immaterial information,[62] but in view of the applicability of the principles developed in case law on virtual householder rights of a system operator, the formal ownership position is of no importance. **117**

The aforementioned comments also apply to data from publicly accessible sources (e. g. telephone directories, address lists, commercial registers). In the case of purely factual data without reference to a natural person, such data may be freely used subject to any restrictions on use imposed by the person who published the data. **118**

A further restriction applies to personal data from publicly accessible sources: pursuant to § 28 (1) No. 3 BDSG a. F., the collection, storage, modification or transmission of personal data and their use as a means of satisfying one's own business purposes was permitted under data protection law if the data were generally accessible or if the controller was permitted to publish them, unless the legitimate interest of the data subject in excluding processing or use manifestly outweighs the legitimate interest of the controller. It was therefore necessary to examine whether an exceptional scenario existed in which there were special interests of the data subject worthy of protection which, despite the public accessibility of his data, prevented the processing of the data and thus the pursuit of the data controller's legitimate interests and, moreover, **119**

[60] Cf. Kinast/Kühnl, *NJW* 2014, 3057 (3058).
[61] Cf. Weisser/Färber, *MMR* 2015, 506 (508).
[62] Cf. Roßnagel, *52. Verkehrsgerichtstag* 2014, p. 282.

manifestly outweighed these interests. If and to the extent that these criteria allowing for an exception were not met, the use of publicly accessible personal data was already permissible under the former data protection law.

120 Although the GDPR does not contain any comparable wording, this does not mean that the processing of personal data available from public sources would be permissible without any limitation. In fact, the points described above, derived from § 28 (1) No. 3 BDSG a. F., are to be taken directly from the balance of interests pursuant to Art. 6 (1) (f) GDPR.

121 Any rights of use required under civil law for such publicly accessible data (e.g. on the basis of database protection rights of the publisher of such data) remain of course unaffected by their fundamental permissibility under data protection law, so that such rights of use must still be obtained before such data can be used in Big Data applications.

Guiding Principle:

The use of personal data obtained from generally accessible sources may be permitted unless the legitimate interest of the data subject in excluding their processing or use clearly outweighs the legitimate interest of the controller. The necessity to obtain rights of use required for other reasons remains unaffected.

C. THE CONTROLLER

According to Art. 4 No. 7 GDPR, *controller* within the context of the GDPR is a natural or legal person, authority, institution or other body that alone or jointly with others decides on the purposes and means of the processing of personal data. The definition of the term in § 3 (7) BDSG a. F. was already similar; according to which, *data controller* was any person or entity who collected, processed or used personal data for himself or had such data processed or used by others on his behalf. For Big Data applications, this means that the *controller* of a Big Data application is the body which collects, processes or uses personal data for itself in or for that Big Data application, or which commissions other processors to do so. The body which collects, processes or uses personal data for its own Big Data application shall also decide accordingly on the purposes and means of processing personal data. 122

The controller responsible for a Big Data application, as determined by these criteria, is subject to all data protection regulations as well as other legal obligations mentioned in this guide and, accordingly, to all legal liabilities (fines, claims for damages, risks of criminal liability, etc.). It is therefore also the responsibility of this controller to take appropriate organizational measures to ensure that the data protection and other legal obligations listed in this guide are identified and complied with in each individual case. 123

Guiding Principle:
The controller of a Big Data application is the body that collects, processes or uses personal data in or for the Big Data application on its own behalf and in so doing decides on the purposes and means of processing personal data.

For the sake of simplicity, the term controller is also used below for the holder of non-personal data. In the area of non-personal documents/data, different legal concepts can be considered for designating a *controller* of non-personal data in the sense of assigning all rights and obligations associated with such non personal documents/data and their life cycle. Examples of such objects are: 124
- copyright protection for individual works of authorship such as, in particular, written works or drawn representations,
- copyright protection for collections of works in which the creative nature is limited to the particular way in which the contents are arranged and presented,
- an ancillary copyright of the database producer pursuant to §§ 87a and 87b UrhG for collections of individual information which are structured and arranged in a certain manner, whereby their acquisition, verification or presentation requires substantial investments in terms of type or scope;
- purely factual data or also anonymized (originally personal) data which are the subject of a trade or business secret and are assigned to the owner of the trade or business (§ 2 No 1 GeschGehG); or
- a virtual householder's right analogous to §§ 1004 (1), 903 sentence 1 BGB for IT systems and the data created and/or stored therein.

If data from different data controllers are combined in a common database under one responsible controller, it must of course first be verified whether there may be a permitted transfer of the personal data concerned by the entity which initially collected 125 the data to the other data controller subsequently operating the shared Big Data application (cf. mn. 310 *et seq.*).

> **Guiding Principle:**
> If data are combined in a shared database, the legality of the transfer of the affected personal data to the operator or operators of the shared Big Data application must be verified. This shall also apply if the Big Data Application is operated by several parties as shared data controllers.

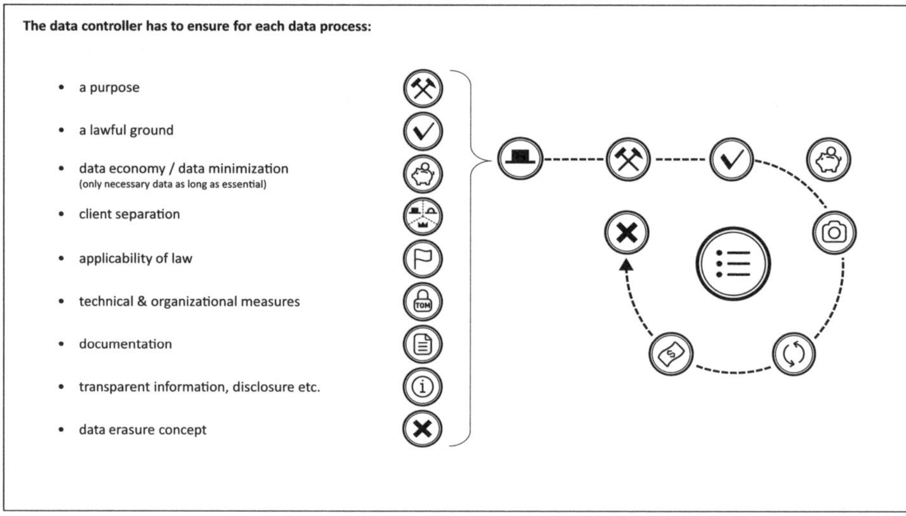

Figure 15: Responsibilities of a data controller

I. Processor

126 An entity which only operates a Big Data application on behalf of and in accordance with the instructions of another controller will usually be regarded as a processor in the sense of Art. 28 GDPR. With regard to the permissibility of the processing of the data supplied for the Big Data application, the commissioned processor can generally rely on the controller providing the data to have examined the lawfulness of the use of the data supplied within the framework of the Big Data application and having been given a positive decision accordingly. If an entity operates a Big Data application as a processor on behalf of another and if, in this function, data acquired by such other bodies from third parties (regardless of whether such data is personal data, factual data or anonymous data or not relating to natural personal data) is made available to it by a controller for additional storage and further processing in the Big Data application, the processor in such a case must have the necessary data usage or other licensing rights granted to it by its principal. In the sense of such data use or other license agreements, the entity acting as processor would be a sub-licensee of the entity or entities issuing the processing and evaluation order. If it subsequently transpired that the controller placing the order had no corresponding right to use or license such data in relation to the entitled party, the continued retention of the acquired data in a Big Data application would be inadmissible so that the data concerned would have to be erased (cf. mn. 365 *et seq.*).

Guiding Principle:

An entity operating a Big Data application solely on behalf of and in accordance with the instructions of another data controller is a processor in accordance with Art. 28 GDPR. The legal grounds for the processing services of a commissioned processor must be vested in his principal, the controller. The client must also provide the commissioned processor with the necessary rights of use for any existing industrial property rights.

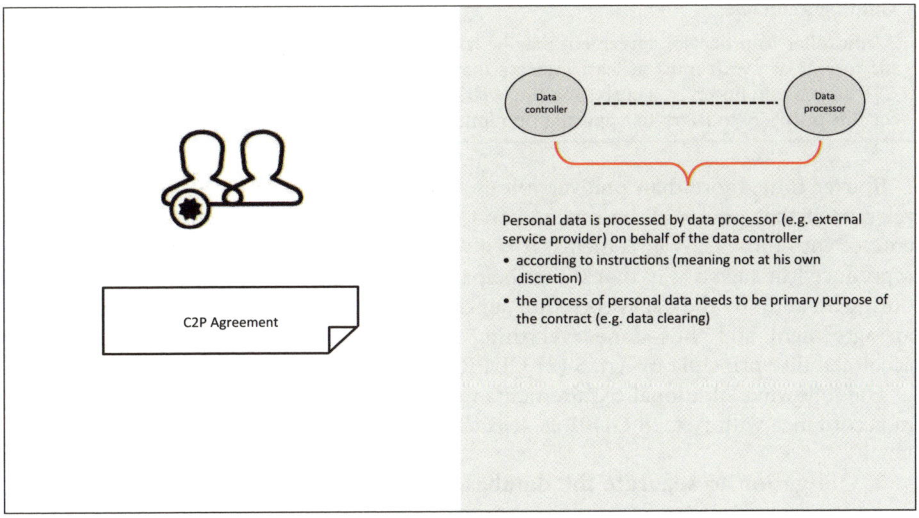

Figure 16: Controller-to-processor agreement (C2P)

Order processing is the collection, processing, or use of personal data by a service provider on behalf of the controller. The data must therefore only be collected, processed or used by the third party following the instructions and detailed guidelines of the data controller (as in the case of an *extended workbench*). **127**

A mere provision of data or a sharing of data with others, on the other hand, is not considered to be order processing within the context of the GDPR if no further processing is carried out in accordance with the controller's detailed guidelines. **128**

1. Controller-to-processor agreement (C2P)

If processing exists, the controller and the commissioned processor must conclude an agreement which, at a minimum, is to contain the contents listed in Art. 28 (3) GDPR. **129**

This agreement may be concluded in writing or electronically. A physical copy of the controller-to-processor agreement in the form of a printout is therefore not mandatory. However, not every electronic form satisfies the requirements of Art. 28 (9) GDPR because in terms of the form requirement, the legislator still pursues purposes for securing both documentation and evidence as well as authenticity. The electronic form is therefore intended to guarantee that the contracting parties are aware of the obligations they have entered into and that these are listed in the document as part of its content. According to some authors, electronic form can only be considered equivalent to the written form if the electronic format satisfies these requirements, in particular if it ensures the authenticity of the obligations mentioned in the document, particularly with regard to the risk of subsequent changes or forgeries. A simple email is usually not sufficient; in **130** some cases, the conclusion of a C2P agreement with an electronic signature is also required.[63] Other authors do not consider the very strict formal requirement of an electronic signature to be necessary[64] The fact that the parties acknowledge that the obligation of a C2P agreement can also be documented, for example, by placing a corresponding mark in a check box to indicate their agreement to the specified conditions of a C2P agreement and also by including the name and designation of the position in the company of the person who agrees to the C2P agreement.

> **Guiding Principle:**
> A controller-to-processor agreement may be concluded in writing or electronically, the electronic format of which must at least indicate that the parties have accepted the obligations of a C2P agreement; however, a corresponding mark in a check box as a sign of consent is sufficient for this purpose, contrary to opposing opinions.

131 If, over time, more than one version of a C2P agreement exists, all versions that are relevant at that time shall be retained and made available for review by the entity that entered into those C2P agreements. It is also important that the C2P agreements can be reproduced in such a way that the principal, as the controller, can prove beyond doubt during an audit by the data protection supervisory authority that he has concluded such an agreement and thus done everything legally required (legal consequence of the accountability principle in Art. 5 (2) GDPR).

132 The following additional requirements must be met where the concept of processing in accordance with Art. 28 GDPR is selected for a pooling of the Big Data application:

2. Obligation to separate the databases

133 The obligation to separate data stocks applies with regard to the data stocks of various controllers. If the data stocks are not strictly separated, this constitutes a transfer to the other bodies involved in a pooling which requires justification.

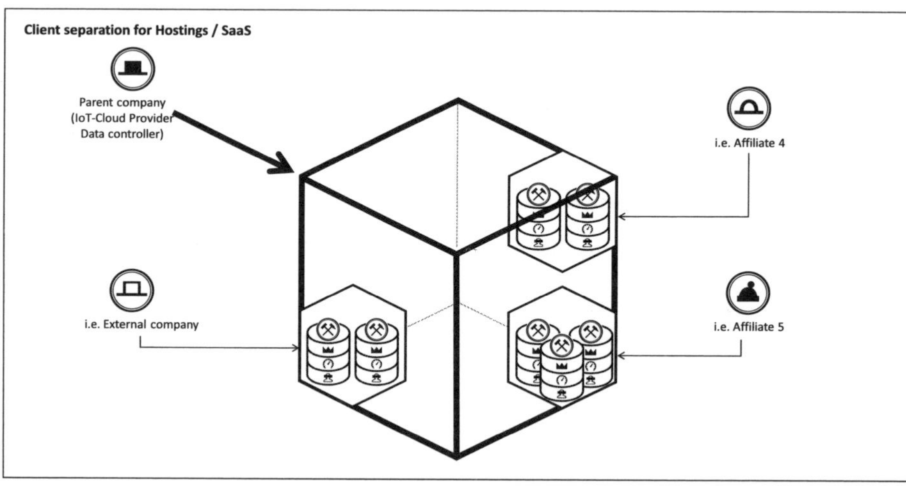

Figure 17: Client separation for Hosting/SaaS

[63] Martini, in: Paal/Pauly, *GDPR*, 2nd ed. 2018, Art. 28 mn. 75.

[64] Hartung, in: Kühling/Buchner, *GDPR*, 2nd ed. 2018, Art. 28 mn. 96; just as: Bertermann, in: Ehmann/Selmayr, *GDPR*, 2nd ed. 2018, Art. 28 mn. 9.

It also follows from Art. 4 (11) GDPR that a consent as the legal ground justifying the initial collection of personal data must include the recipient of the permission. Only the specific processing by this controller is covered by any consent given. For this reason, the data must be treated separately by the central body so that the personal data is not available to any other controller. Under these conditions, making the data available to a subsidiary, for example for the purpose of cross-selling, would not be covered by consent. **134**

Guiding Principle:

If a Big Data application is operated centrally for processing by several controllers, the databases made available by each individual controller are to be kept technically or logically separate from each other.

3. Other obligations of the processor

If a central controller operates a Big Data application for several entities as a processor on behalf of several entities, all other obligations of a processor must be fulfilled in addition to the obligations expressly set out in a C2P agreement (cf. minimum content pursuant to Art. 28 (3) GDPR), i.e. in particular to **135**

- maintain an independent record of processing activities (Art. 30 (2) GDPR),
- cooperate with the competent supervisory authority on request in the interest of the contracting controller (Art. 31 GDPR), or
- appoint a data protection officer (Art. 37 GDPR in conjunction with § 38 BDSG).

Guiding Principle:

If an entity operating a Big Data application continues to physically or logically separate the databases made available to it by individual entities and further processing and evaluation/analysis of this data is carried out separately for each entity on behalf of and in accordance with the instructions of this entity, the authorization to perform these analyses shall be sanctioned by the controller. The controller and the processor must conclude a C2P agreement which must meet the requirements of Art. 28 (3) and (9) GDPR with regard to content and form.

4. Securing instruments for compliance with data protection obligations of a controller of Big Data Applications with regard to the processor

If a third party is employed as processor, the requirements of Art. 28 GDPR with regard to the C2P agreement must be considered in addition to the requirements set out in mn. 126–135 above. **136**

a) Selection and prior checking

137 Firstly, the controller must diligently select the processor according to whether it offers sufficient guarantees for proper processing (Art. 28 (1) GDPR). This obligation also applies beyond the contractual relationship[65], which must be ensured in particular through the technical and organizational measures to be agreed upon with the processor.

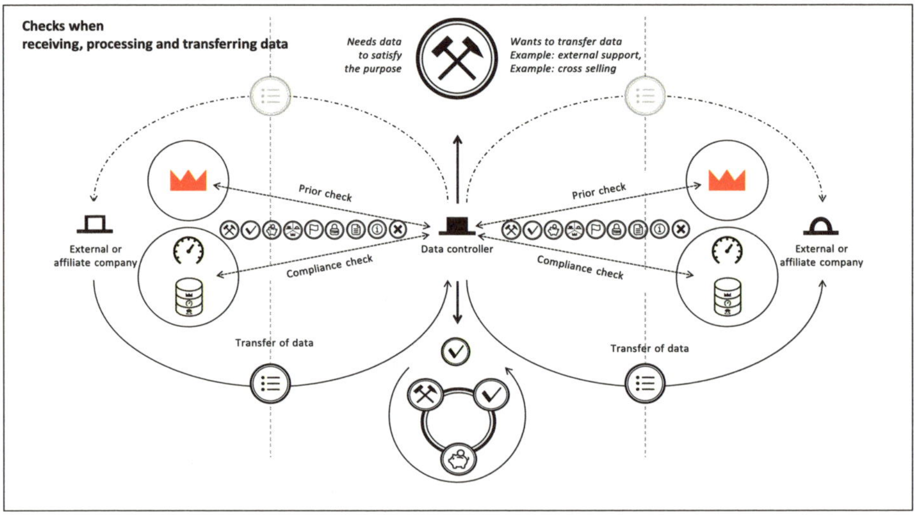

Figure 18: Checks when receiving, processing and transferring data

138 It is also possible for the processor to make use of other subcontractors. However, this requires the consent of the controller either on a case-by-case basis or, in general, as per Art. 28 (2) GDPR. The performance of these prior checks as well as the ongoing checks during the contractual relationship with the processor and, of course, their results must be documented in each case so that the controller can prove compliance with the data protection provisions (Art. 5 (2) GDPR on accountability). A breach of this obligation is not only associated with legal consequences in individual cases, but as such – even in the case of materially lawful processing of personal data – an administrative offence that can be punished with a fine (for the possible amount, cf. mn. 4 *et seq.* and 513 *et seq.*).

Guiding Principle:

The use of subcontractors by the processor requires the prior general or specific consent of the controller; this consent as well as the prior and ongoing checks carried out during the contractual relationship must be documented in each case.

b) C2P agreement

139 Furthermore, Art. 28 (3) sentence 1 GDPR provides that a contract be concluded by and between the controller and processor on a standard basis. Art. 28 (3) GDPR contains (minimum) content requirements for such agreements:

- subject-matter, duration, nature and purpose of processing; type of personal data; categories of data subjects; obligations and rights of the controller (Art. 28 (3) sentence 1 GDPR);

[65] Spoerr, in: Wolff/Brink, *BeckOK DatenSR*, 25th ed., from 1.8.2018, Art. 28 DS-GVO mn. 35.

- the obligation of the processor to process data only in accordance with documented instructions (Art. 28 (3) sentence 2 (a) GDPR);
- the persons to be entrusted with the data processing by the processor must be under an obligation of confidentiality (Art. 28 (3) sentence 2 (b) GDPR);
- the processor must ensure that data security requirements are met pursuant to Art. 32 GDPR (Art. 28 (3) sentence 2 (c) GDPR);
- in view of the aforementioned risk-based approach (cf. mn. 485 *et seq.* and 374), measures are required – in the context considered here – which relate specifically to the storage of large data sets;
- the processor must undertake to comply with the obligations relating to the use of subcontractors (Art. 28 (3) sentence 2 (d) GDPR);
- in connection with the assertion of data subjects' rights by data subjects (e.g. the erasure of data), the processor must undertake to assist the controller in responding to the data subject (Art. 28 (3) sentence 2 (e) GDPR); if a retention concept involves a backup, the processor must be obliged to enable erasure of individual personal data from the backup, too;
- assist the controller in ensuring compliance with his obligations under Art. 32–36 (Art. 28 (3) sentence 2 (f) GDPR), for instance with regard to notification obligations in the event of data protection violations or the performance of data protection impact assessments or necessary consultations with data protection supervisory authorities;
- an agreement is required regarding the handling of personal data after completion of the processing services concerning deletion or return of the data (Art. 28 (3) sentence 2 (g) GDPR);
- finally, information and cooperation obligations must be expressly agreed upon in the case of audits (including inspections) by data protection supervisory authorities and by the contracting authority itself (Art. 28 (3) sentence 2 (h) GDPR).

Furthermore, by analogy with what has been stated in Chapter G of this guide on **140** transfers to third countries, due consideration is necessary with regard to whether the processor operates in a third country.

Guiding Principle:

An effective C2P agreement must contain the minimum content pursuant to Art. 28 (3) GDPR. The award of a processing order without the prior conclusion of such an agreement is an administrative offence by the controller and punishable by a fine.

II. Joint controllers, Art. 26 GDPR

In theory, the GDPR also allows several parties to define the purposes and means of **141** the processing. In contrast to processing under the authority of a sole controller, however, there is an equal cooperative relationship between the joint controllers. In connection with Big Data applications, shared responsibility can arise, for example, in the use of data pools. If this is the case, Art. 26 GDPR stipulates that the joint controllers must reach an agreement so that individual responsibilities, which the joint controllers have to fulfil as an overall responsibility towards the data subjects, be assigned to the individual participants within the group. The absence of such an agreement results in an administrative offence punishable by a fine.[66]

[66] Martini, in: Paal/Pauly, *GDPR*, 2nd ed. 2018, Art. 26 mn. 22.

142 The need for a legal ground underpinning the transfer of personal data also applies if all data controllers whose person-related data are to be jointly processed, evaluated and analysed in a common Big Data application, act jointly in such a way that they only ever decide as a whole on the manner in which their person-related data are to be processed and evaluated/analysed. In this case, within the framework of joint controllership pursuant to Art. 26 GDPR, a transfer to all other controllers, who participate in the joint data pool, requires a legal ground. According to Art. 26 (1) sentence 2 clause 1 GDPR, an agreement on the processing of personal data must be concluded between the participating controllers. This agreement lays out the performance of data protection obligations to the various parties in the most transparent manner possible. In accordance with the recitals to the provision, the aim of such an agreement is to create legal certainty and clear stipulations as to which data controller fulfils which obligation under the GDPR.

Guiding Principle:

If the Big Data application is operated by several responsible entities as joint controllers, they must conclude an agreement in accordance with Art. 26 GDPR which contains the minimum contents listed therein.

143 Art. 26 GDPR specifies certain minimum contents of such an agreement:

144 The agreement must specify the purposes and means on which the controllers base their agreement. Furthermore, the parties involved in a joint controllership must regulate which party must comply with which information obligations pursuant to Art. 13, 14 GDPR. Furthermore, the agreement must specify the party responsible for internal processing and exercising of the rights of data subjects. According to Art. 13 (1) (a) GDPR, the name and contact details of this representative must be indicated. The agreement must also reflect the obligations of those responsible with regard to the satisfaction of data subjects' rights pursuant to Art. 15–22 GDPR. The minimum requirement here would probably be a tabular overview stating which obligations apply to a particular controller mentioned by name and in which situation.

145 According to recital 58 GDPR, the content of the agreement must be concise, easily accessible and easy to understand, written in clear and plain language and, where appropriate, include additional visual elements.

146 Pursuant to Art. 26 (1) sentence 3 GDPR, the agreement may specify a point of contact for the data subjects. Although such a point of contact is not absolutely necessary, specification would mean that ambiguities on the part of the data subjects with regard to the internal division of the legal tasks and duties of a controller could then be resolved immediately. The point of contact must be one of the parties involved in the processing. A third party cannot be involved here.

Guiding Principle:

A point of contact for the data subjects should also be indicated in the agreement of the joint controllers required pursuant to Art. 26 GDPR in order that all communication between the data subjects and the joint controllers be channelled uniformly. However, Art. 26 GDPR does not impose any obligation in this regard.

1. Internal relationship between the joint controllers

147 In their agreement pursuant to Art. 26 GDPR, the controllers are required to specify in a transparent manner who meets which obligations under the GDPR and who fulfils which obligations, as outlined in Art. 13 and 14 GDPR.

Nevertheless, several entities responsible for a Big Data application are jointly and severally liable in an external relationship. Therefore, according to general principles of German civil law, there is an internal obligation to compensate according to the share of responsibility.[67] Against this background, in particular, the internal division of tasks should be clearly defined and all related procedures documented. 148

2. Provision of the internal agreement

As can be seen from Art. 26 (2) sentence 2 GDPR, *the essence* of this agreement must be made available to the data subjects of a Big Data application. This information can, for example, be made available on a website. However, the GDPR does not regulate what is *essential* in this context. It is argued in the literature that this duty to provide information serves to enable those affected to assert their rights so that at least the following information should be made available:[68] 149

- the entities, their registered office or place of business;
- the purposes pursued by the controllers responsible for a Big Data application;
- the data stocks being managed and, where appropriate, their location;
- the allocation of shared responsibility;
- the regulations on how to deal with the data of the Big Data application in case of termination of joint controllership.

3. External Relationship Between the Joint Controllers and the Data Subject

Even if a separate provision has been made internally as to who has to comply with what obligations and even if a contact person has been determined for the data subjects (Art. 26 (1) sentence 3 GDPR), a data subject may assert his rights vis-à-vis all controllers involved (Art. 26 (3) GDPR). 150

All controllers are jointly and severally liable to the data subjects for claims for damages (Art. 82 (4) GDPR). 151

III. Dynamic matrix structures

1. Participation in projects of multiple responsible entities

If, on occasion, individual controllers work together on a project-by-project basis to establish a Big Data application, some aspects must be clarified with regard to the project structure: 152

- if the entity responsible for the content of the Big Data application collects data from different data sources according to its own criteria and at its own discretion and stores it in the Big Data application and, if necessary, combines it with other data of its own, or
- whether that controller does so solely on behalf of and under the direction of one or more other controllers, and
- whether, in the latter case, the contracting controllers decide individually or jointly on the manner in which personal data are to be processed in the Big Data application, the procedures and systems to be applied and the design of the corresponding processes.

In the first case, the entity responsible for the Big Data application is itself the controller for this Big Data application. In order for other responsible bodies to make 153

[67] Werkmeister/Brandt, *CR* 2016, 233 (236).

[68] Spoerr, in: Wolff/Brink, *BeckOK DatenSR*, 25th ed., as at 1.8.2018, Art. 26 GDPR mn. 35.

personal data available for this Big Data application, there must be a corresponding lawful ground under data protection law which can justify the transfer of the personal data to be entered into the Big Data Application by these other controllers.

154 In the second case, the entity responsible for the Big Data application is more likely to be regarded as the processor for the other controllers. However, a distinction will then have to be made between the two subcases,

- whether each of the other controllers involved has a separate contractual relationship with the controller operating the Big Data application, on the basis of which contract instructions can be given to that entity concerning the manner in which the data in the Big Data application are to be processed and analysed,
  or
- whether there is only a contractual relationship between the controller operating the Big Data application and the other controllers as a whole.

155 In the first subcase, each of the other controllers would have to conclude a C2P agreement with the controller operating the Big Data application in accordance with Art. 28 (3) GDPR (cf. mn. 129 *et seq.*).

156 In the second subcase, the other controllers are jointly responsible in accordance with Art. 26 GDPR, for which case the requirements set out above in mn. 141 *et seq.* must be met. These controllers in their entirety as joint creditors must conclude a single C2P agreement pursuant to Art. 28 (3) GDPR with the entity operating the Big Data application.

Guiding Principle:

Even if several affiliates cooperate on a project-by-project basis to establish and operate a Big Data application, it must be determined which company is responsible for the Big Data application and how the provision of personal data for this Big Data application by other affiliates is to be grounded under data protection law. There is no intra-group doctrine in data protection law. C2P agreements may have to be concluded if the companies providing data for the Big Data application have the right to issue instructions regarding the manner in which the data provided by them is to be processed.

2. Employee secondment/supply of temporary staff

157 If a controller transfers his own employees to another controller operating the Big Data application for the purpose of establishing or developing a Big Data application and/or its continuous operation, the transferred employees shall be deemed to be employees of the controller operating the Big Data application. In this case, however, the functional authority to issue instructions to the transferred employees would no longer lie with the transferring controller, but with the controller operating the Big Data application to which these employees were transferred. It must be examined on the basis of these criteria whether in the individual cases there is the actual participation in a project involving different controllers (as explained above under mn. 152 *et seq.*) a case of a transfer of employees resulting in the controller operating the Big Data application bearing sole responsibility.

Guiding Principle:

If employees of a controller are ceded to another controller operating the Big Data application, they shall be deemed to be employees of the controller operating the Big Data application for the duration of the secondment. In this case, no additional data protection agreements or measures need to be taken.

3. Joint controllers within the meaning of Art. 26 GDPR with regard to project participations

The provisions of mn. 141 *et seq.* of this guide shall apply accordingly. 158

IV. Cloud computing

The term *cloud computing* is not legally defined in data protection law, at least not according to the GDPR and BDSG. Art. 4 (19) Directive (EU) 2016/1148 on the Security Level of Network and Information Systems defines *cloud computing service* as a digital service that enables access to a scalable and elastic pool of shareable computing resources. This shows that cloud computing goes beyond mere storage services. In the following explanation, however, consideration will be limited to such storage services since Big Data applications are often not operated on the company's own cloud platforms, but on platforms of third-party providers within or outside the group. 159

An examination on a case-by-case basis is necessary to determine who is subject to which obligations in the relationship between cloud provider and cloud customer; particular attention is to be paid to the question of who is responsible. According to Art. 4 (7) GDPR, this is the entity which alone or jointly with others decides on the purposes and means of processing personal data. With regard to cloud computing, this can mean the cloud customer, the cloud provider or both together in accordance with Art. 26 GDPR (cf. also mn. 161 *et seq.*).[69] Since only storage services are being considered here, it generally remains the case that the cloud provider does not offer any services of its own beyond the provision of storage and is therefore to be regarded as an authorized processor pursuant to Art. 28 GDPR.[70] 160

Guiding Principle:
Where the Big Data application uses the cloud platform of a third party, that third party is to be regarded as the processor so that a C2P agreement must be concluded pursuant to Art. 28 (3) GDPR.

1. Storing in your own cloud

If the data is stored in a cloud of the entity also responsible for the content of the Big Data application (so-called private cloud), the general legal data protection requirements apply – provided the associated servers are located in the EU[71]. The controller remains *master of the data* to this extent[72]. Of course, all server locations must be considered, even if they are backup servers. 161

[69] Hofmann, *ZD-Aktuell* 2017, 05488.

[70] Cf. Arbeitskreise Technik und Medien der Konferenz der Datenschutzbeauftragten des Bundes und der Länder as well as Arbeitsgruppe Internationaler Datenverkehr des Düsseldorfer Kreises, in Orientierungshilfe – Cloud Computing, Version 2.0, from: 10/2014, p. 9; Schild, in: Wolff/Brink, *BeckOK DatenSR*, 25th ed., from: 1.8.2018, § 3 mn. 111; Gola, in: Gola/Schomerus, *BDSG*, 12th ed. 2015, § 11 mn. 8; emphasising the concrete design Art.-29-Working Party, in WP 196, p. 9–10.; equally differentiating Hofmann, *ZD-Aktuell* 2017, 05488. objecting to this Engels, *K&R* 2011, 548 (549), who considers that an own service like creating a backup is a requirement for a processor.

[71] For now, the EEA Member States have not declared the GDPR to be applicable. To that extent, the storage of data in these states still has a reference to third countries.

[72] Hackenberg, in: Hoeren/Sieber/Holznagel, *Multimedia-Recht*, 46th update, January 2018, part 16.7 mn. 46.

162 The principles on the transfer of data to third countries (below under mn. 248 *et seq.*) also apply if the servers can be attributed to the controller but are located outside the EU.

2. Use of third-Party cloud storage

163 In the following passage, the term cloud storage is to be understood as the provision of cloud-based storage space by an entity other than the controller (Art. 4 (7) GDPR) in contrast to a private cloud. This distinction depends solely on whether the operator of the cloud platform is a different natural or legal person than the controller for the content of the Big Data application; whether both belong to the same group is not relevant from a data protection point of view, as there is no standard definition of *intra-group privilege* in data protection law. A company belonging to a group is thus also a third party within the meaning of Art. 4 (10) GDPR. In the case of a processor being used – which will in general be the case of a cloud storage provider – it is not a third party in this sense according to Art. 4 (10) GDPR. Nevertheless, the processing in Art. 4 (2) GDPR is defined so broadly that a transfer does not have to have a third-party reference in order to fall within this area of application.[73]

[73] Cf. Spoerr, in: Wolff/Brinck, *BeckOK DatenSR*, 25th ed., from: 1.8.2018, Art. 28 GDPR mn. 108; in detail and with note on the legitimate interests that can be used as justification according to Art. 6 (1) (f) GDPR; Schaffland/Holthaus, in: Schaffland/Wiltfang, *GDPR/BDSG*, Lfg. 4/17, Art. 28 mn. 2 with further references.

D. SPECIFIC REQUIREMENTS AND TASKS OF THE DATA PROTECTION OFFICER WITH REGARD TO BIG DATA APPLICATIONS

The controller of the Big Data application and the appointed processor must each designate a data protection officer if and to the extent that, as a rule, they continuously deal with the automated processing of personal data by at least ten persons, not only in connection with the Big Data application in question, but generally with all personal data (§ 38 (1) sentence 1 BDSG in conjunction with Art. 37 (1) (b) and (c) GDPR). 164

I. Specialist knowledge

With an increasing number and scope of processing operations using Big Data analyses, the knowledge required of the data protection officer to be appointed as well as of his department within the company of the controller for a Big Data application also increases accordingly. The data protection officer requires this knowledge in order to be able to competently answer enquiries from the department(s) responsible for the Big Data application, to train the relevant employees and to be able to answer enquiries from data subjects. Since it is only possible to appoint a data protection officer who has the necessary expertise and ability (Art. 37 (5) GDPR), it must be continuously checked whether the data protection officer has sufficient personnel and resources at his disposal, especially with regard to developing new Big Data applications. Should this examination show that such resources are lacking, it must be ensured that the data protection officer and his staff can acquire and maintain the necessary specialist knowledge (Art. 38 (2) GDPR). 165

II. Organizational and operational involvement of the data protection officer

The data protection officer reports directly to the highest management level and is independent of instructions (Art. 38 (3) GDPR). He must be properly and in a timely manner involved in all matters relating to the protection of personal data (Art. 38 (1) GDPR). "*Properly*" means that the data protection officer receives comprehensive information on data processing operations. "*In a timely manner*" means that the data protection officer is involved as early as possible in the planning phase and can therefore act in an advisory capacity in this phase.[74] This corresponds in particular to the task of the data protection officer to inform and advise the controller. Finally, the data protection officer must be granted access to personal data and processing operations (Art. 38 (2) GDPR). 166

Particularly this early and comprehensive integration will not always be easy in connection with Big Data applications. In many cases, the nature of the future use of the data will not be clear at the beginning of the data collection. The entity responsible for the Big Data application would therefore do well to discuss the intended use of Big 167

[74] Klug, *ZD* 2016, 315 (318).

Data applications or the inclusion of new data categories or data from previously unused data sources in an existing Big Data application with its data protection officer at an early stage and to establish common guidelines (e.g. in the form of a *Big Data guideline*) for this purpose. At the same time, relevant plans for the analysis – including preliminary steps such as collection and storage – of personal data should be disclosed as fully as possible to the data protection officer.

III. Communication with data subjects

168 Data subjects may contact the data protection officer on all matters relating to the processing of their personal data and the exercise of their rights under the GDPR (Art. 38 (4) GDPR). This also applies to the processing of their personal data and to the exercise of their rights in connection with Big Data applications used in the company concerned.

169 However, this must not be understood to mean that enquiries regarding the rights of data subjects (cf. mn. 431 *et seq.* below) are to be addressed directly to the data protection officer (even if the latter can be named externally as the contact person for this purpose); in this respect, the responsibility of the controller to address the claim remains unchanged.[75]

170 The greater the amount of data – as it is typically the case with Big Data applications – the greater the need for information on the part of those affected, at least potentially. In order for the data protection officer to be able to perform his duties nevertheless, it is important to ensure that he has sufficient personnel and resources.

IV. Information and monitoring obligations

171 As part of his duties to provide information and advice, the data protection officer must inform and advise the controller of the Big Data application and his employees about their data protection obligations (Art. 39 (1) (a) GDPR). This creates an interdependency with the fact that resources must also be made available to the data protection officer to maintain his expertise (Art. 38 (2) clause 2 GDPR).

172 With the increasing importance of Big Data applications, the data protection officer must be provided with the appropriate resources so that he can train himself accordingly. In addition, the data protection officer will also define an appropriate group of employees as part of the training concept, who will regularly be involved with Big Data applications and design and carry out the relevant training courses. At the same time, it is also in the interest of the controller of the Big Data application to ensure that its data protection officer has the appropriate expertise, as the number of requests for advice is likely to increase.

173 The supervisory duties of the data protection officer pursuant to Art. 39 (1) (b) GDPR are closely related to this acquisition of knowledge. Accordingly, he must not only check for compliance of relevant data protection provisions, but also of the internal strategy of the controller of the Big Data application and/or its processor with regard to protection of personal data. At the same time, he can define responsibilities with regard to monitoring and must review said defined responsibilities. It is recommended that the data protection officer carries out regular checks which he documents.[76] For reasons of

---

[75] Moos, in: Wolff/Brinck, *BeckOK DatenSR*, 25th ed., as at 1.8.2018, Art. 38 GDPR mn. 19.

[76] Moos, in: Wolff/Brinck, *BeckOK DatenSR*, 25th ed., as at 1.8. 2018, Art. 38 GDPR mn. 8.

synergy, it may be advisable to build on the existing controls of an internal audit department that may already exist at the entity responsible for the Big Data application.

In view of the special relevance of Big Data analyses to fundamental rights (mn. 476 *et seq.*), it will often be appropriate to create a special task for monitoring in this area. Ultimately, this area of responsibility includes checking whether training is carried out in the above sense and whether the employees identified for this purpose have also taken part. **174**

The involvement of the data protection officer described in this way must be taken into account in particular in cases where a data protection impact assessment is to be carried out. In this respect, the data protection officer must advise the controller (Art. 35 (2) GDPR). **175**

V. Cooperation and control obligations

As a technically competent body, the data protection officer should also act as a point of contact for the competent data protection supervisory authorities, Art. 39 (1) (d) and (e) GDPR. **176**

It is expressly regulated that the data protection officer is to be the contact person of the supervisory authority if a data protection impact assessment reveals a high risk that has not been contained by appropriate measures and accordingly a consultation procedure must therefore be carried out in accordance with Art. 36 GDPR. For Big Data applications, it cannot be ruled out that a data protection impact assessment will arrive at such a result simply because of the quantity of data to be processed and the system of comparisons. This result and his position in relation to the data protection supervisory authorities lead to the fact that the data protection officer more frequently serves as the first point of contact for data protection supervisory authorities, who may also impose a fine on the controller of the Big Data application. It is therefore in the controller's best interest to support the data protection officer in the points mentioned here in such a way that he can provide targeted and skilled answers to the authorities and thus positively influence the criteria for calculating a fine in accordance with Art. 83 (2) sentence 2 GDPR in favour of the controller for the Big Data application. **177**

VI. Internal procedure in the event of a data protection violation

Two notification obligations can arise if a breach of data protection occurs within the framework of a Big Data application: on the one hand, to the data protection supervisory authority (Art. 33 GDPR) and, on the other hand, to the data subjects affected by the Big Data application (Art. 34 GDPR). This notification must be made by the controller of the Big Data application itself. Probably the most common case in practice is of course that an internal process is designed in such a way that the data protection officer is internally responsible for all relevant processes and is therefore not excluded from the notification process in question. **178**

The data protection officer shall be named with contact details when notifying the data protection supervisory authority (Art. 33 (3) (b) GDPR). As a rule, this will lead the authority to communicate with the controller via this contact, i.e. by means of the data protection officer of the controller for the Big Data application. Here, too, the circle relies on the necessary expertise of the data protection officer; it can only be ensured that the data protection officer acts as a competent contact person for the data **179** protection supervisory authority where such expertise is guaranteed. Ultimately, any fines can be avoided or at least reduced in this way.

Guiding Principle:

If a data protection officer is to be appointed according to the generally applicable criteria within the structure of the controller for a Big Data application (Art. 37 GDPR in conjunction with § 38 (1) BDSG), he is likewise responsible for the Big Data application. It must be ensured that the data protection officer appointed has or can obtain the relevant knowledge needed for Big Data applications. All rights and obligations of the data protection officer also apply with regard to the Big Data application.

E. LAWFUL GROUND FOR DATA PROCESSING (COLLECTION, ACQUISITION, TRANSMISSION, EVALUATION AND COMMERCIALIZATION)

For each type of data processing, a distinction must be made between personal data (as described in mn. 51–74) or data not relating to natural persons, factual data or anonymized data which are then to be collected in the Big Data application for the purposes of the application: **180**

In the case of personal data **181**

- the restrictions of data protection law must first be observed (cf. mn. 184 *et seq.* below), and
- subsequently, when obtaining such data, the requirements applicable at this level for the conclusion of data use contracts and/or license agreements (cf. mn. 256 *et seq.* below).

In the case of data not relating to natural persons, factual data and anonymized data, only compliance with the requirements at data procurement level (conclusion of data use and/or license agreements) set out in mn. 256 *et seq.* is required. **182**

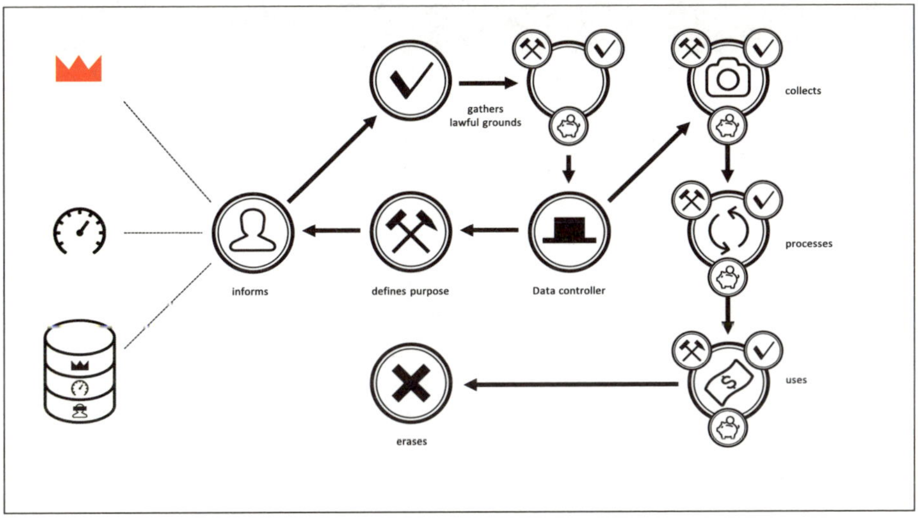

Figure 19: Examination order when processing data

In order to enable the reader to examine these lawful grounds at each stage of data processing in a Big Data application, without being forced to switch back and forth to the appropriate references, and to be able to discuss the problems specific to each stage on the spot, the typically relevant lawful grounds are explained for each stage. **183**

I. Statutory lawful grounds for personal data

184 Generally speaking, the collection, processing, use and storage of personal data is prohibited.

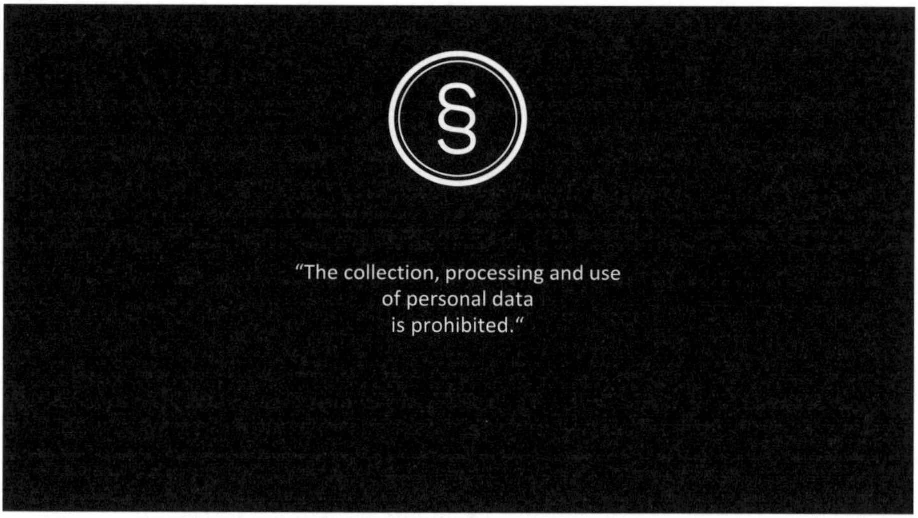

Figure 20: Prohibition subject to permission

185 Exceptions are made whenever the law expressly stipulates the conditions permitting such activities or the data subject has given consent.

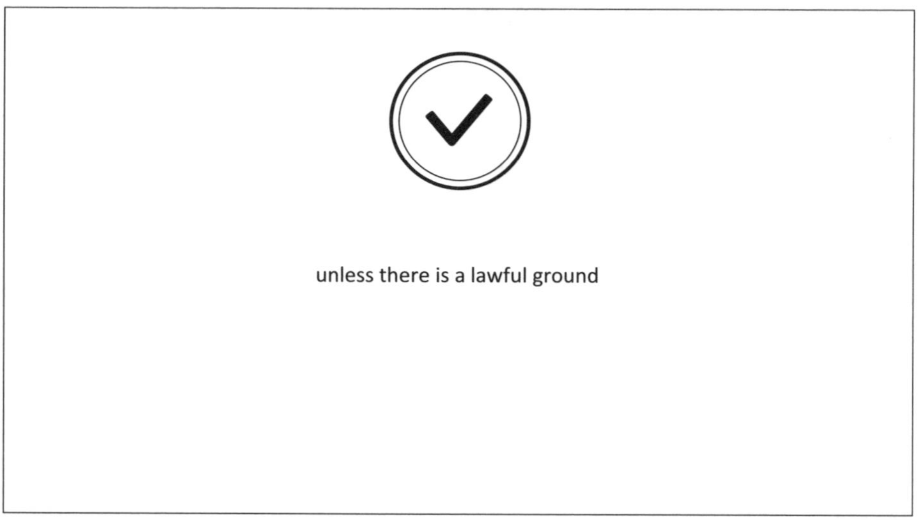

Figure 21: Prohibition subject to lawful ground

Guiding Principle:

The collection, processing, storage, transmission and analysis of personal data and their use can be permissible pursuant to Art. 6 (1) GDPR only if and to the extent that this specific processing operation is necessary for the creation of processing operations as well as being in such a case permitted or even ordered by a legal provision in the GDPR or in other legislation, or if the data subject has consented to this collection and processing.

This applies to each stage of the processing of personal data. When examining the statutory permissibility of the use of personal data in these individual phases of data processing, the relevant facts of the legality shall be examined for each stage of processing. 186

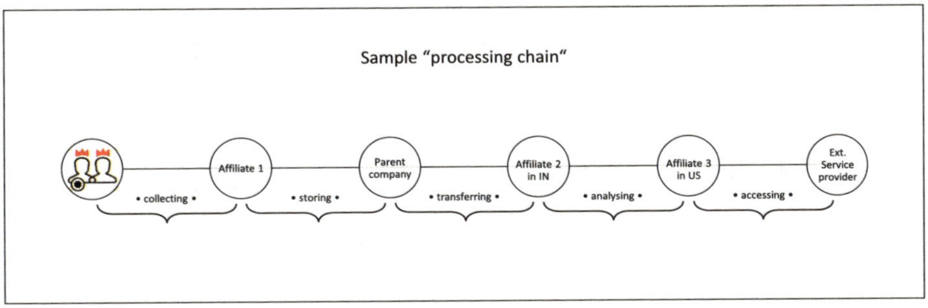

Figure 22: Lawful grounds required per processor in a "sample processing chain"

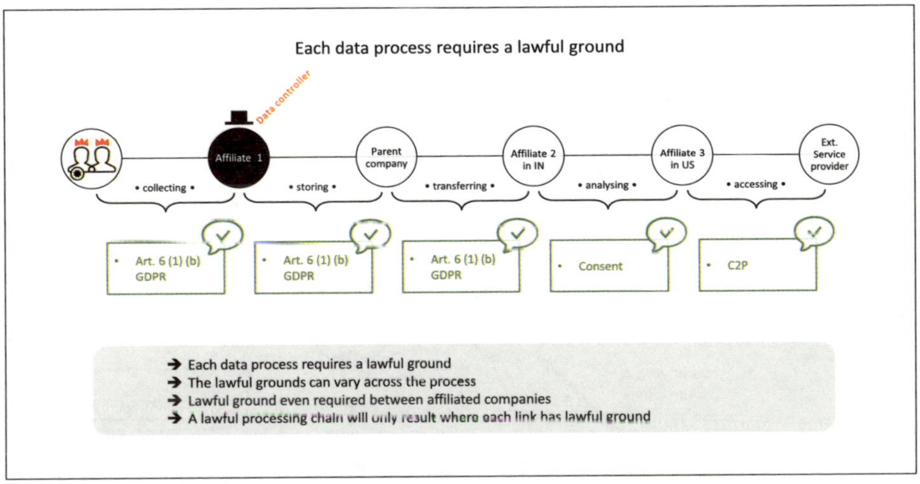

Figure 23: Lawful grounds in a sample processing chain

In addition to consent (cf. mn. 197 *et seq.*), the GDPR lists the following conditions as lawful grounds for the lawful collection – and later further processing, storage and transmission – of personal data: 187

- the processing is necessary for the performance of a contract to which the data subject is party or in order to take steps at the request of the data subject prior to entering into a contract (Art. 6 (1) (b) GDPR);

- the processing is necessary for compliance with a legal obligation to which the controller is subject (Art. 6 (1) (c) GDPR);
- the processing is necessary in order to protect the vital interests of the data subject or of another natural person (Art. 6 (1) (d) GDPR);

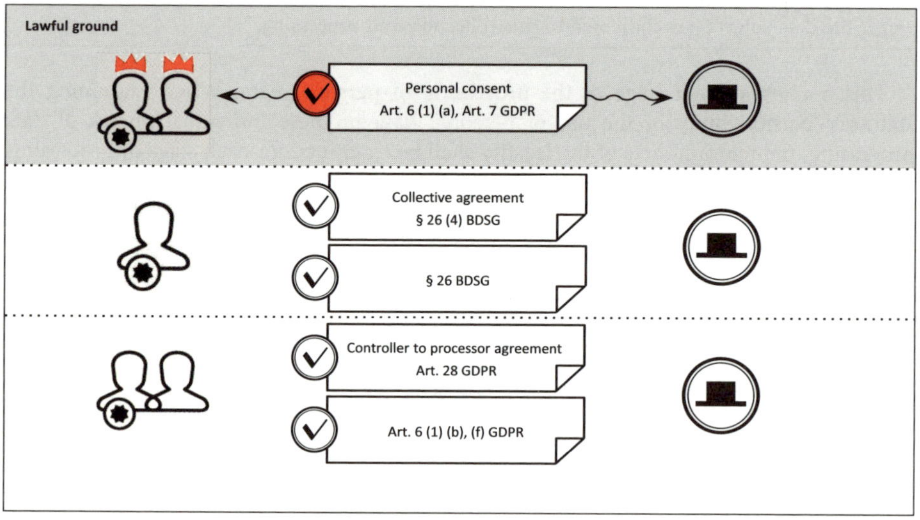

Figure 24: Lawful grounds

- the processing is necessary for the performance of a task carried out in the public interest or in the exercise of official authority vested in the controller (Art. 6 (1) (e) GDPR); and
- the processing is necessary for the purposes of the legitimate interests pursued by the controller or by a third party, except where such interests are overridden by the interests or fundamental rights and freedoms of the data subject which require protection of personal data, in particular where the data subject is a child (Art. 6 (1) (f) GDPR).

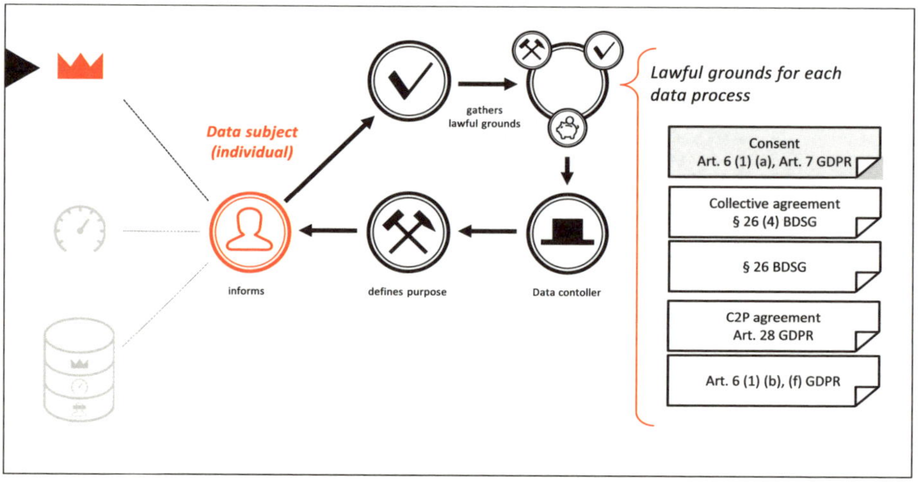

Figure 25: Examination order when processing personal data

Even if the wording of Art. 6 (1) GDPR might initially give the impression that all the lawful grounds listed in Art. 6 (1) GDPR are of equal value and can be used alternatively or even cumulatively, the view of the data protection supervisory authorities, at least under the application of the former version of the BDSG, was that recourse to statutory grounds for permission is no longer possible and permissible if the data subject has already been asked for his consent in relation to a specific data collection or processing. The reason for this, however, was not directly a matter of data protection law; rather, in the opinion of the data protection supervisory authorities, it is deceptive with regard to the data subject and therefore unfair if a request for consent gives the impression to the data subject that he can control the collection and processing of his data solely by granting or refusing consent, whereas in the event of refusal of consent, statutory justifications can then be used. Once a request for consent has been made, it results in a blocking effect on the other lawful grounds, which can then no longer be invoked. This also applies if consent has been obtained but is invalid due to deficiencies in content or form (cf. mn. 197 *et seq.*). **188**

> **Guiding Principle:**
> Once a request for consent has been made, it blocks the other lawful grounds, which can then no longer be used. This condition also applies if consent has been obtained but is invalid due to content or formal defects.

In addition to consent, the following lawful grounds set out in Art. 6 (1) GDPR are also of particular interest: the contractual performance in Art. 6 (1) (b) GDPR and the balancing of interests in Art. 6 (1) (f) GDPR: **189**

1. Performance of a contract

According to Art. 6 (1) (b) GDPR, the collection, processing, storage and transmission of personal data is permissible whenever and to the extent that it is necessary and not merely expedient for the performance of a contract concluded by the controller with the data subject in question. When initiating or performing a contract with the data subject, no more data may be collected than is absolutely necessary for the performance of this contract (principle of data minimization in Art. 5 (1) (c) GDPR). **190**

> **Guiding Principle:**
> The collection, processing, storage and transmission of personal data is permitted if and to the extent that it is necessary for the performance of a contract concluded by the controller with the data subject.

§ 26 (1) sentence 1 BDSG contains a special legal basis for the collection and subsequent processing, storage and transmission of personal data of employees (cf. the remarks under mn. 318 *et seq.*). According to this provision, personal data of an employee may be collected for the employment-related purposes and may later also be processed or used if this is necessary for deciding on the establishment of an employment relationship or, after its establishment, for the performance or termination of an employment relationship. Personal data of employees of the company which then also wishes to process the personal data of these employees are thus subject to the same legal restrictions as the collection and subsequent processing, storage and transfer of personal data of other third parties. Data of the employee of a company that is not identical with the company collecting and/or processing the personal data, but is only linked to the **191** company as a group, are considered as "simple" personal data in the sense of Art. 4(1) GDPR, for which the general lawful ground in Art. 6 (1) (b) GDPR can be applied.

> **Guiding Principle:**
> The collection, processing, storage and transfer of an employee's personal data is permitted if and to the extent it is necessary for deciding on the establishment of an employment relationship between the controller and the data subject or, after its establishment, for the performance or termination of such an employment relationship.

2. Balance of interests

192 According to Art. 6 (1) (f) GDPR, the legitimate interests of the controller or a third party in the collection of a specific piece of data are to be determined and set in relation to the data subject's interests worthy of protection and his fundamental freedom rights, which could be affected by the collection and processing of the respective personal data. Art. 6 (1) (f) GDPR reads:

> *"processing is necessary for the purposes of the legitimate interests pursued by the controller or by a third party, except where such interests are overridden by the interests or fundamental rights and freedoms of the data subject which require protection of personal data, in particular where the data subject is a child."*

193 In view of the fundamental right of informational self-determination of the data subject, which is to be safeguarded and protected by the provisions of data protection law, it is to be assumed that the individual has a fundamental interest that his personal data is not being collected and processed.[77] A three-step test can be determined on the basis of this provision:

- First, there must be a legitimate interest in the processing through evaluation and analysis. This legitimate interest is to be understood broadly. The interest may also be of an economic or immaterial nature. This can, for example, be seen as an interest of the controller in direct advertising to the customer.
- Furthermore, processing by evaluation and analysis must be necessary to safeguard the legitimate interest in question. Any necessity must also be measured against the purpose limitation and the principle of data minimization.
- Finally, the legitimate interests of the data subject must not prevail. Processing by evaluation and analysis is excluded in particular if the interests, fundamental rights or freedoms of the data subject outweigh the opposing legitimate interests of the data controller in the evaluation and analysis.

> **Guiding Principle:**
> The collection, processing, storage and communication of personal data shall be permitted where and to the extent that it is necessary to safeguard the legitimate interests of the controller or of a third party and where the interests or fundamental rights and freedoms of the data subject, which require protection of personal data, do not prevail.

[77] Cf. Buchner/Petri, in: Kühling/Buchner, *GDPR*, 2nd ed. 2018, Art. 6 mn. 146 et seq.

3. Works council agreements

Collective agreements between the employer and the works council can only regulate the collection and processing of personal data of employees of the company for which the works council is responsible. 194

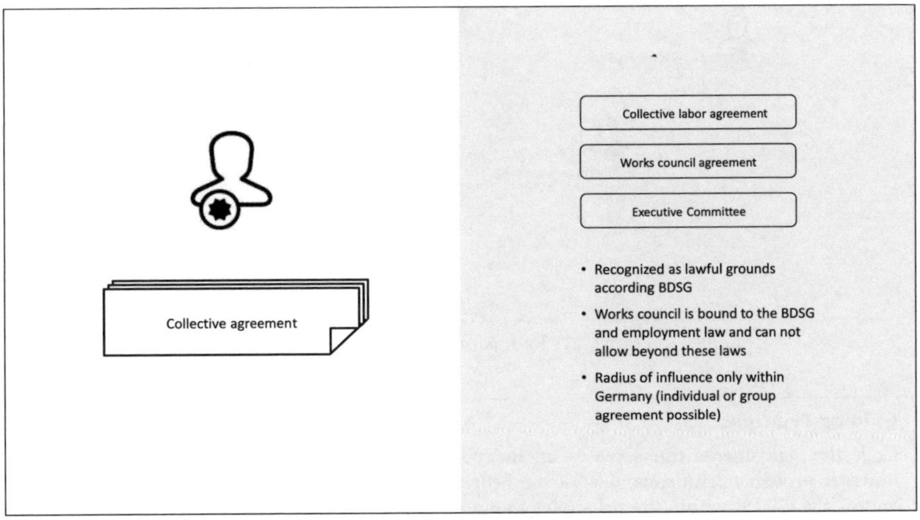

Figure 26: Collective agreement

According to prevailing opinion in Germany, collective agreements are included in the legal provisions as described in § 26 (4) BDSG. However, it is disputed whether collective agreements only work within the margin implied in the applicable data protection law in question, thus not alone but always together based on a particular lawful ground and from this form a legal basis for data collection, processing or transmission. Conversely, as the German Federal Labour Court represents in a decision, the question is asked whether in a collective agreement as independent lawful ground can deviate from the regulations of the GDPR even to the disadvantage of the employees. In § 26 (4) BDSG, a collective agreement qualifies as a lawful ground for the collection, processing, storage and transmission of personal data. However, the above-mentioned issue however is not settled. § 26 (4) sentence 2 BDSG refers to the principles in Art. 88 (2) GDPR in which only the general order to the data protection right is mentioned, namely to take measures for the protection of human dignity, the entitled interests and the fundamental rights of the data subject in particular with regard to the transparency of the processing and the transmission of personal data to third parties. In addition, a comparison with the absolutely individual character of a consent to be given by the data subject shows that, if a certain collection, storage or processing of personal data cannot have a lawful ground, the works council cannot replace the consent of the data subject by its consent to a collective agreement within the framework of the mandate given to it by the Works Council Constitution Act (BetrVG) (cf. also mn. 194 *et seq.).* 195

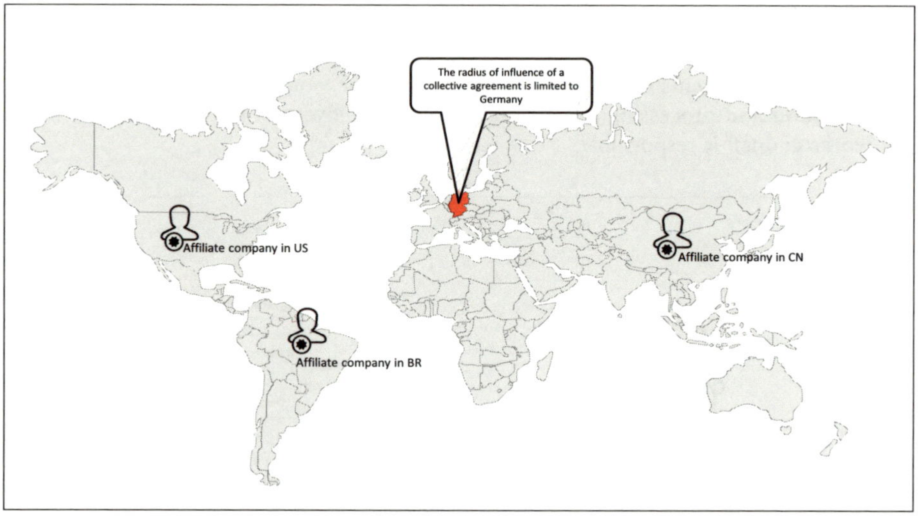

Figure 27: Radius of collective agreement

Guiding Principle:

Collective agreements can serve as an independent legal basis in which – according to the however probably erroneous view of the Federal Labour Court – the regulations of the BDSG and/or the GDPR within the principles found in Art. 88 (2) GDPR can be deviated from even to the disadvantage of the employees.

196 For the limitation of a collective agreement as a lawful ground for the collection and processing of personal data cf. also mn. 318–351.

4. Consent

197 Consent comes into play whenever the collection, storage and processing of personal data is not permitted or expressly ordered by law. In this case, the collection, storage and processing of personal data may still be permissible if the data subject has given prior consent. As the use of the term *consent*[78] shows, this permission must be given prior to the collection, processing and storage of personal data;[79] subsequent consent cannot subsequently or retrospectively change the unlawful nature of the data collection, storage or processing operation at the time of collection, storage or processing of personal data due to lack of consent.

[78] Stemmer, in: Wolff/Brink, *BeckOK DatenSR*, 25th ed., as at 1.8.2018, Art. 7 GDPR mn. 55.

[79] Cf. only Simitis, in: Simitis, *Bundesdatenschutzgesetz*, 8th ed. 2014, § 4a mn. 94 with numerous further references.

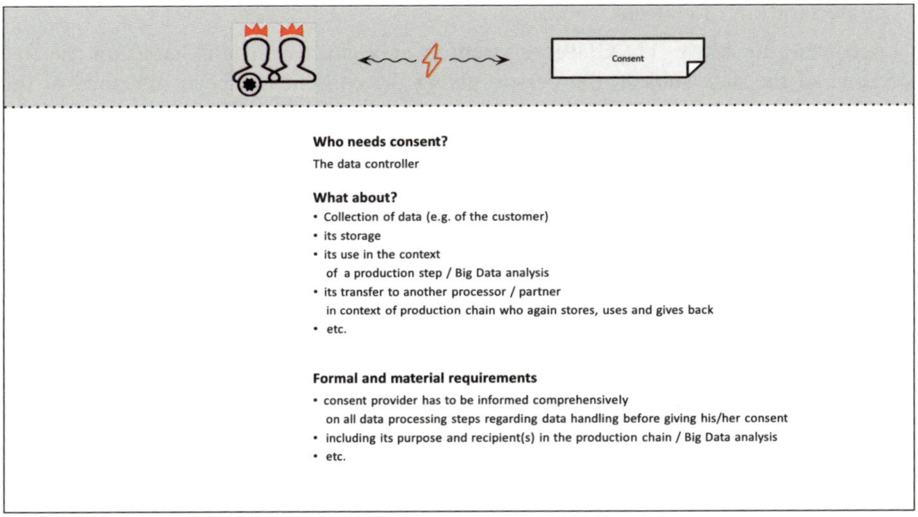

Figure 28: Content of a consent

Consent in the sense of Art. 6 (1) (a) in conjunction with Art. 7 GDPR is freely given, specific (i.e. meant for the case in question), and an informed declaration given unmistakably in the form of a statement or another unambiguous affirmative action with which the data subject gives to understand that he agrees with the processing of the personal data relating to him (cf. Art. 4 (11) GDPR). Regarding the possibilities of an opt-in or opt-out solution, cf. mn. 216. The consent is therefore a declaration of intent and as such therefore subject to interpretation under civil law (§ 133 BGB). In addition, the consent is usually pre-formulated by the controller so that general terms and conditions are given and must therefore meet the relevant requirements.[80] **198**

Guiding Principle:

Obtaining the consent of the data subject only comes into consideration if the collection, storage and processing of personal data has not been permitted or expressly ordered by law. Effective consent is only given if its content and formal requirements are met. Minors can only give their effective consent after reaching the age of 16.

The question, whether a minor can deliver a consent effectively or needs the consent of a legal guardian, has been decided in the meantime by the GDPR: minors are able to give their own consent where they are at least 16 years old (Art. 8 (1) sentence 1 GDPR). The Member States can allow a lower age limit according to Art. 8 (1) sentence 3 GDPR for the purposes of the consent ability, which however may not be below 13 years of age; the German legislator made no use of it in the BDSG, however, so that the age limit of 16 years according to Art. 8 (1) sentence 1 GDPR remains in use in Germany. **199**

[80] Cf. only Simitis, in: Simitis, *Bundesdatenschutzgesetz*, 8th ed. 2014, § 4a mn. 94 with numerous further references.

a) Declaration of consent

200 According to Art. 4 (11) GDPR, consent is only effective if it is based on the free decision of the data subject, the person giving the consent has been informed of the intended purpose of the collection, processing or use, and the consequences of the refusal of consent have also been pointed out. These requirements in terms of content result from Art. 4 (11) and Art. 7 GDPR.

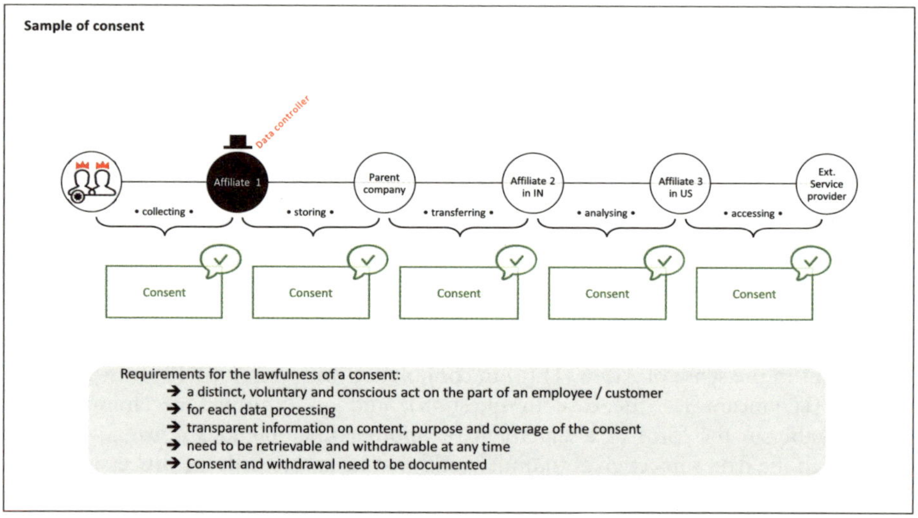

Figure 29: Consent in a sample processing chain

b) Formal requirements

201 In addition, consent pursuant to § 4a (1) sentence 2 BDSG a.F. was required in writing, while from 25 May 2018 it may also be given electronically or in another form. Due to the accountability principle anchored in Art. 5 (2) GDPR, the data controller must be able at any time to be able to prove that consent was given by the data subject.

202 If the consent is to be given together with other explanations in writing, according to Art. 7 (2) sentence 1 GDPR it is to be presented in a manner that is clearly distinguishable from the other matters. Furthermore, the following criteria must be kept cumulatively:

- Consent must be given by the data subject through a clear, affirmative and voluntary act. These are satisfied, for example, by the active placement of a mark in a tick box next to a consent text on a website or a form (opt-in). A pre-ticked box, which the consenting party must first reset in order not to declare consent (opt-out), does not constitute consent.[81]
- The consent must not have been given indiscriminately. It must state which personal data are to be processed, for what purpose and by whom and, if applicable, to which (specifically identified) third parties they are to be transmitted.
- The consent of the data subject must be given with his full awareness of the circumstances. The data subject must have the opportunity to take reasonable notice of the contents of the declaration. Hidden, incomprehensible or inaccessible information is not suitable.

[81] Recital 32 GDPR.

- The corresponding declaration must be formulated in a comprehensible manner in the light of the requirement of transparency; otherwise, informed consent cannot be assumed.
- Consent must have been given unequivocally. This means that consent must be given in the form of a declaration or other unambiguous act. In principle, a declaration can be made in any form. Even consent in the form of an oral declaration is possible, but not recommendable since the data controller carries the burden of proof (in particular on the basis of demonstrating compliance pursuant to Art. 5 (2) GDPR).
- The processing of special categories of personal data as stated in Art. 9 (1) GDPR, from which racial and ethnic origin, political opinions, religious or philosophical beliefs, or a trade union membership emerge, as well as the processing of genetic data, biometric data for the unambiguous identification of a natural person, health data or data to the sex life or the sexual orientation of a natural person, is only permissible on the basis of a consent if the data subjects have expressly consented to the processing of the aforementioned personal data for one or more ascertained purposes. However, this does not apply if, according to EU law or Member State law, a general prohibition according to Art. 9 (1) GDPR applies and the consent of the data subject does not suffice to lift the prohibition.

c) Free Will

A declaration of consent is only valid if it is based on the free decision of the data subject. There is no such voluntary action if the data subject is placed in a situation in which, for various reasons, he is prevented from seriously considering giving his consent, e.g. due to lack of time, or where there is such a strong relationship of dependence between the consenting party and the recipient of the consent that the consenting party considers himself (morally) obliged to give consent (often the case in an employment-based relationship[82]). Linking a service (e.g. the granting of favourable conditions, discounts or gifts) with consent to ensure the use of data can also lead to an invalid consent, in particular if the consenting party cannot obtain the same or an equivalent service from the recipient of the consent or a third party without said permission, or if this is not absolutely necessary for the use of the service. 203

When obtaining consent for an employment relationship, it is generally questionable whether the employer can effectively obtain the employee's consent because, due to a relationship of dependency, it is questionable whether consent given to the employer is voluntary. While some authors even take the view that the special employer–employee relationship excludes the grant of effective consent by the employee due to their lack of free will, the supervisory authorities[83], in particular, take a more nuanced view which takes account of the circumstances of the individual case. This has now been followed by the legislator as reflected in the provision of § 26 (2) BDSG. 204

A clear decision whether consent can be given voluntarily in an employment relationship is not to be found either in the GDPR or the BDSG. According to recital 43 GDPR, whether consent has been freely given depends on whether there is a *clear imbalance* between the data subject and the data controller and whether it is therefore unlikely in view of all the circumstances that the consent was given voluntarily. Under the scope of the GDPR, the voluntary grant of consent in the employment relationship is therefore certainly possible; it depends on the circumstances under which the signing of a declaration of consent was explained to the employees concerned. 205

---

[82] Cf. Recital 43 GDPR.

[83] Art 29 Working Party, Guidelines on Consent, WP 259 rev. 01, as of 28 November 2017, section 3.1.1.

> **Guiding Principle:**
> Consent is only effective if given voluntarily. In particular, the criterion of free will must be examined particularly critically in the case of employment-based relationships or the where there is counter-performance in exchange for granting of consent.

d) Indication of the purpose of the collection and processing

206 According to Art. 7 (2) sentence 1 GDPR as interpreted in recital 42 sentence 3 GDPR, informed consent from the data subject requires information in particular about the purposes of the processing for which his personal data are intended.

207 However, especially with Big Data applications, analysis purposes are typically subject to continuous further development. Consequently, future analyses cannot be included in the declaration of consent with the effect that as the number of analyses performed increases, the actual analyses will become increasingly distanced from the content of the analyses described in the original declaration of consent. As a result, the declaration of consent will therefore become increasingly inadequate. Using a data protection consent thus carries the latent risk that it cannot keep up with the dynamics of the further development of a Big Data application.

> **Guiding Principle:**
> In the context of the consent to be given, the data subject shall be informed in particular of the purposes for which the personal data are to be processed. Especially in the case of Big Data applications, analysis purposes are typically subject to continuous further development.

208 This dynamic situation requires that with each new purpose of processing, the statement of consent would have to be revised and, in case of doubt, a corresponding supplementary statement of consent would have to be obtained from those data subjects who have already signed an earlier version thereof. This in turn carries the risk that different versions of declarations of consent would have to be administered at the same time and stored in the data model in order to ensure that data once collected would only be processed and analysed to the extent that the consent given by the data subject is sufficient. At least insofar as the data are not completely anonymized, but only pseudonymized (i.e. can still be traced back to the individual data subject), the link between the version of consent given by the data subject and the data collected from that data subject must be maintained in order to ensure that the data subject's data are always processed and analysed only to the extent that the consent given by that data subject is sufficient.

e) Transmission to third parties, in particular to countries outside the EU

209 Although Art. 4(11) or Art. 7 GDPR do not expressly require the data subject to be informed of the transfer of his personal data to third parties, in particular if that third party is not established in an EU or EEA Member State, that requirement is derived from the need to inform the data subject of the purpose of use and from the fact that the grant of consent is the essence of the right to informational self-determination. If and insofar that Big Data analyses are to be carried out by a company located in another EU country, the data subject must also be informed of this in the consent text. Nevertheless, the legal necessity of such a reference results from the fact that the data subject already has to be informed about the intention of the data controller to transfer personal data to a third country and about the legal situation in this third country entirely independently of a consent which can be obtained from him according to Art. 13 (1) (f) GDPR.

Accordingly, one can draw the conclusions that, where consent is concerned, this condition must apply even more so with regard to information about a transfer of personal data to a third country.[84]

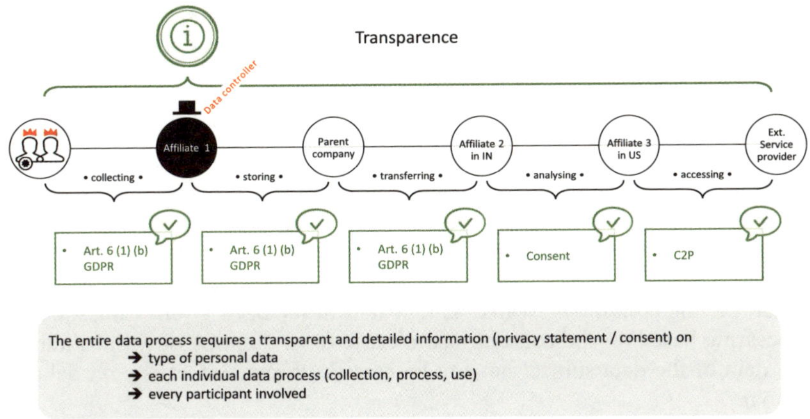

Figure 30: Requirement of transparency in a sample processing chain

According to Art. 13 (1) GDPR, the data subject must also be informed about the categories of recipients to whom his personal data are transferred. This applies even more so in the context of consent on the basis of which the data subject must be able to estimate which personal data are transmitted to which recipients. In order to make a declaration of consent effective and to enable the data subject to fully assess the processing consequences, the declaration of consent must indicate the potential recipients.[85] The potential data recipients must be listed explicitly although they can still be identified under a category term such as *companies of the X group*, a blanket term *third party* or *business partner* can ultimately mean any third party, no matter where they are located. This would make it impossible for the data subject to assess the purposes of use and the consequences of processing, since he is completely unaware of the potential recipients of the transfer. This aspect, too, shows that the concept of consent is not practicable in view of the dynamics in the further development of a Big Data application. 210

Guiding Principle:
Within the framework of the consent to be given by the data subject, he shall be informed of any transfer of personal data relating to him to a third country and of the level of data protection in force in that country on the basis of that country's legal system and of the measures taken by the data controller to establish an equivalent level of data protection.

[84] Cf. Stemmer, in: Wolff/Brink, *BeckOK DatenSR*, 25th ed., as at 1.8.2018, Art. 7 GDPR mn. 58.
[85] Cf. only Simitis, in: Simitis, *Bundesdatenschutzgesetz*, 8th ed. 2014, § 4a mn. 72 with numerous further references.

f) Right to withdraw consent

211 Generally, any declaration of consent can subsequently be withdrawn. While the former version of the BDSG allowed for the possibility to withdraw consent only in limited cases, the fundamental possibility to withdraw each consent was however generally recognized.[86] The possibility to withdraw consent at any time is even expressly stated in Art. 7 (3) sentence 1 GDPR. According to Art. 7 (3) sentence 3 GDPR, the data subject is to be informed – prior to giving the consent – of his right to withdraw. Such an instruction and/or obligation to indicate the right to withdraw consent corresponds, however, to a common practice.

212 According to the principles developed under § 4a BDSG a. F., it is not so straightforward to simply withdraw the given consent where the data processing has already begun. Rather, the data subjects are in theory only entitled to withdraw their consent if they can no longer objectively be expected to accept continued processing. This applies, for example, if the contractual relationship on which the consent is based, e.g. an employment relationship, no longer exists. In this case, the withdrawal must have an *ex tunc* effect, i.e. the consent is treated as if it had never been given. Consequently, the data processing based on the consent has to cease from the time of withdrawal and the personal data of the data subject have to be erased (cf. mn. 365 *et seq.* on data erasure obligations).

213 The right to withdraw consent in accordance with Art. 7 (3) sentence 1 GDPR must also be limited in the case that it was granted within the framework of a more extensive contractual relationship, otherwise the withdrawal of the consent would make further performance of the contract impossible. In this case, the possible withdrawal of consent presupposes additionally that the continued processing of the data subject's personal data is no longer to be expected or the circumstances relevant for the data processing have substantially changed. A significant change can also be seen, for example, in the fact that the data controller processing the data was interested in collecting the data prior to the conclusion of the contract, but later ceased to be so. If these exceptional conditions are not met in a specific case, the withdrawal of consent would not only be unlawful but possibly even irrelevant.

214 If the relevant data controller had previously made the personal data public to an unlimited number of third parties, and if the data were now to be erased as a result of a withdrawal of consent, the controller of the Big Data application would have to inform these third parties (further) processing personal data that the data subject had requested the erasure of all links to this personal data or of copies or replication of this personal data (Art. 17 (2) GDPR, *right to be forgotten*). This requires that (i) the identities of the recipients of such data (personal data *per se* or personal evaluations and/or analyses of such data) and the categories of data transmitted to them be documented by the controller of the Big Data application and (ii) that appropriate procedures and/or technical processes be implemented to handle the withdrawal of consent and its technical consequences. However, the obligation of the controller of the Big Data application is limited to the duty to inform; Art. 17 (2) GDPR does not imply any obligation to guarantee the actual erasure of links, copies or replications of the personal data affected by a withdrawal on the part of these third party data recipients or for them to be responsible for this in any other way.[87]

---

[86] Cf. only Simitis, in: Simitis, *Bundesdatenschutzgesetz*, 8th ed. 2014, § 4a mn. 94 with numerous further references.

[87] Paal, in: Paal/Pauly, *GDPR*, 2nd ed. 2018, Art. 17 mn. 32.

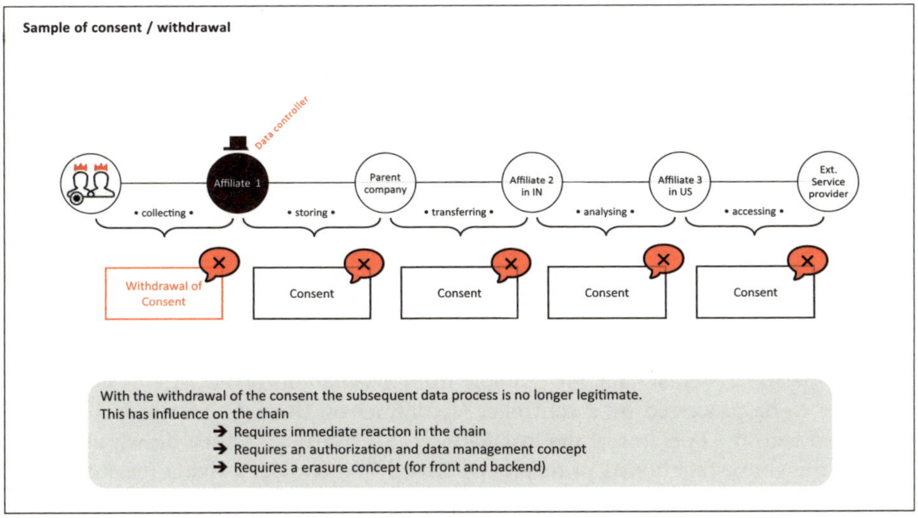

Figure 31: Consent and withdrawal in a sample processing chain

Accordingly, the entity collecting the initial personal data is not obliged to verify that each third party has implemented an effective data erasure policy, regardless of whether the data is to be used in a Big Data application of the originator or by another entity operating the Big Data application, 215

> **Guiding Principle:**
>
> Consent can be withdrawn by the data subject at any time with effect for the future, taking into account the principles of good faith. From the time of receipt of the declaration of withdrawal, data processing based on the consent must cease and the personal data of the data subject, in case of doubt, must be erased. The data subject's right to be *forgotten* must also be observed.

g) *Opt-in* and *opt-out* solutions

Consent could be given both by an explicit declaration or a correspondingly affirming declaration of intent, for example by actively checking a tick box (so-called opt-in solution); but it could also be requested by a declaration of consent that has already been prefilled and checked-off in advance, in which the data subject must actively remove a mark already set in a tick box by the controller for the Big Data application in order to expressly refuse or not even give a corresponding declaration of consent (so-called opt-out solution). Indeed, it is clarified in the GDPR (recital 42) that only an opt-in solution results in a lawful consent of the data subject but the matter is not explained, however, in an explicit regulation in the GDPR or in the BDSG. 216

> **Guiding Principle:**
>
> The grant of consent requires an expressly affirmative declaration of will, for example by actively checking off a box (opt-in solution); a pre-set declaration which the data subject would have to delete or change (opt-out solution) does not result in effective consent.

II. Processing of non-personal factual data

217 If factual or anonymized data is to be processed for a Big Data application that cannot be assigned to a natural person via an IP address or other factors – for example, because they were obtained from an M2M communication – no data protection restrictions apply to their use. However, this does not necessarily mean that such data may be used completely without the need for further measures, in particular at the level of data retrieval, which is explained in detail below under mn. 256 *et seq*.

1. Processing of factual data

218 If non-personal factual data, for example from installations or IT systems in installations, are to be processed by a controller, a contract on the use of such data shall be concluded with the operator of the installation. This contract shall be drawn up on the basis of the above-mentioned principles of virtual householder's rights (cf. mn. 109 *et seq*.). If applicable, a contract must also be concluded if the nature of such data can be viewed as business or trade secrets of the operator of the installation (cf. mn. 105 *et seq*.). Such a contract would allow the controller to process the data in each case and to use it (as freely as possible) in the Big Data application.

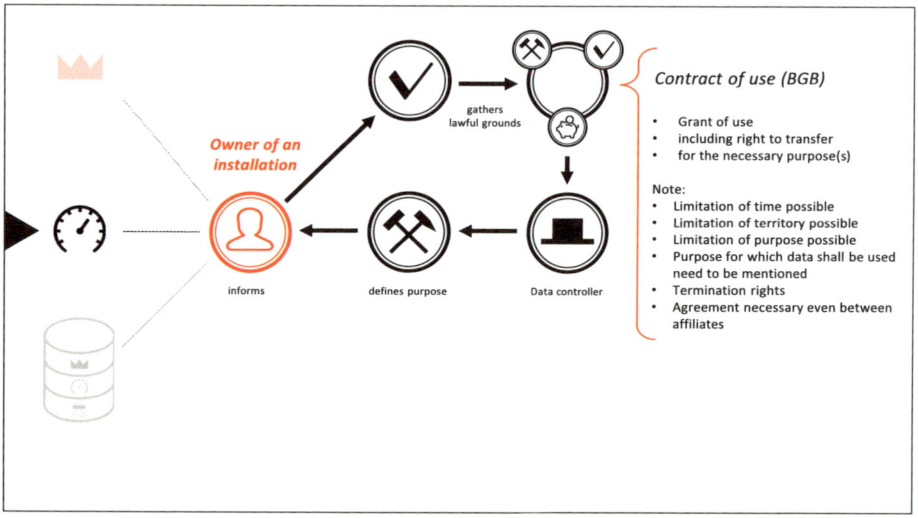

Figure 32: Examination order when processing factual data

2. Obtaining data from data collections/databases

219 Third party rights may also exist with regard to data collections or databases containing data not relating to natural persons, non-personal factual data or anonymized data, namely, in the case of collective works, copyrights of the person who selected or arranged the elements of a collective work (cf. mn. 88 *et seq*.) and, in the case of databases, ancillary copyrights of the person who invested in the collection and arrangement of existing data and their presentation as database producers (cf. mn. 95 *et seq*.). Contracts shall be concluded with the holders of such industrial property rights for the provision and use of such data within the scope of the intended Big Data

application. Without the conclusion of such agreements, the use of the data extracted from such collective works or databases would be unlawful due to infringement of these industrial property rights (for sanctions in this case, cf. mn. 527 *et seq.*).

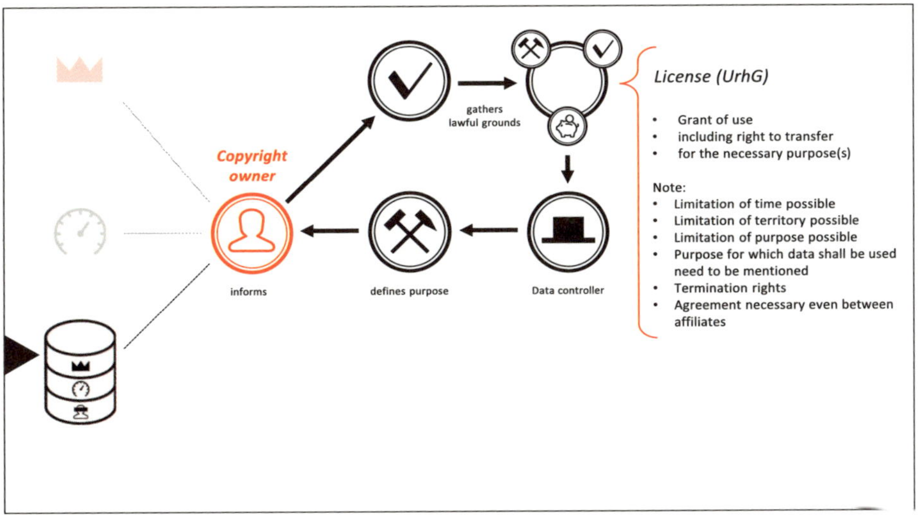

Figure 33: Examination order when processing databases

3. Obtaining data from Open Data projects

220 License notices are usually published for open data projects, which can provide data of any content category. These notices, for example, prescribe the labelling of open data as such to be used in other applications or contain other usage restrictions. For each source of open data used, it must therefore be checked whether there are any license notices and which requirements and/or usage restrictions are contained therein. Both when using such data by feeding it into the Big Data application and when using it in the context of evaluations or analyses, appropriate technical and organizational precautions must be taken to ensure that these requirements and/or restrictions on use are observed. In the absence of such measures, the right to use the data published as *Open Data* and the use in a Big Data application, which would in extreme cases otherwise belong to everyone, may lapse and the data provider may prohibit such use and even assess claims for punitive damages.

4. Data from publicly available sources

221 Mn. 71 *et seq.* of this guide above apply accordingly with regard to data from publicly accessible source (regardless of the content category).

F. DATA PROCESSING AND DATA CYCLE (LEVEL OF DATA PURPOSE)

I. Data processing

222 With the construction of a Big Data application containing personal data, every form of contact with personal data must be viewed as processing in the sense of Art. 4 (2) GDPR, which needs a lawful ground. This also applies, of course, to the use of personal data in a Big Data application if this data was initially collected and processed for other purposes (e.g. the performance of a contract) (cf. mn. 234 *et seq.*).

223 For the sake of simplicity, the term processing is also used below for the use of non-personal data. With regard to non-personal documents/data, various legal concepts can be considered for the use of non-personal data. For example, publishing, duplicating, copying, etc., may be considered.

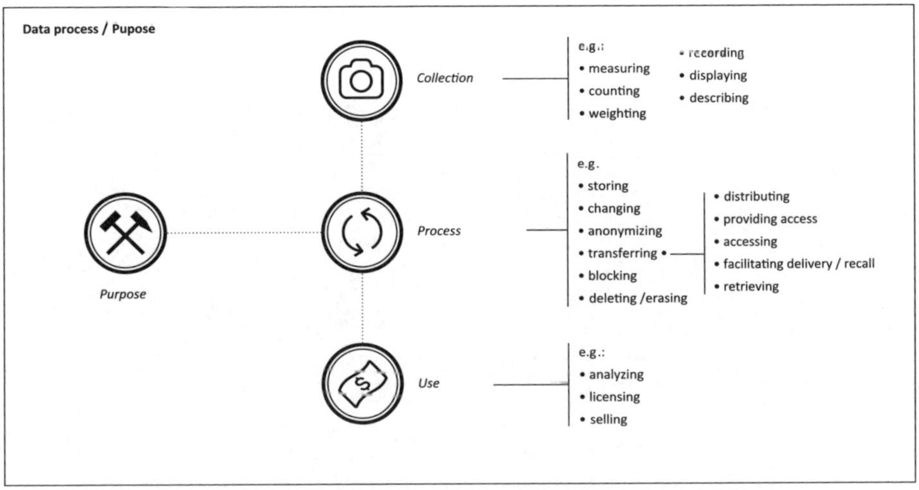

Figure 34: Data process/purpose

II. Life cycle of data

224 Data – regardless of whether it is person-related – is always subject to a life cycle ending in erasure. The length of its life cycle essentially depends on the purpose and the corresponding lawful ground for its initial collection and processing, but also for any subsequent processing, archiving or use in a Big Data application.

225 All data, each document and therefore each piece of information contained therein, whether personal or not, has an owner who is responsible for the life cycle of the data/document in question and the legal conditions to be complied with, or the subject of assignment for all rights and obligations associated with the data/document and its life cycle. The life cycle begins with the collection and proceeds with processing, modification, storage, transmission and analysis of the data and ends with its deletion.

226 As soon as the lawful ground no longer permits or even requires the processing of personal data or the period for which the data subject has consented to the processing of his data or the consent itself has expired, any further lawful ground to process these data no longer applies. They must therefore be erased.

227 In any case, the principle of data minimization as set out in Art. 5(1) (c) GDPR must be taken into account as a corrective measure when examining whether there are lawful grounds to continue to processing the personal data. According to the provision, the processing of personal data is limited to the data which are appropriate and relevant to their purpose and absolutely necessary for achieving the purpose of the processing. In addition, the second corrective measure is the principle of storage limitation laid down in Art. 5 (1) (e) GDPR, according to which personal data may not be stored for longer than is necessary for processing purposes. The third corrective measure is the prohibition of data retention: there is no lawful ground insofar as data are to be collected and stored for which there is no purpose at the time of collection *(data retention)*. The consideration that one does not need such data at the moment, but could possibly still need them in the future, would contradict the necessity principle, which is anchored in each aspect of Art. 6 (1) and in Art. 9 (2) GDPR, as well as the principle of the data minimization in Art. 5 (1) (c) GDPR. To persist in collecting and storing such retention data would be an administrative offence according to Art. 83 (5) (a) GDPR.

228 Even observing these principles is subject to a fine under consideration of the aforementioned corrective measures (cf. mn. 510 et seq.).

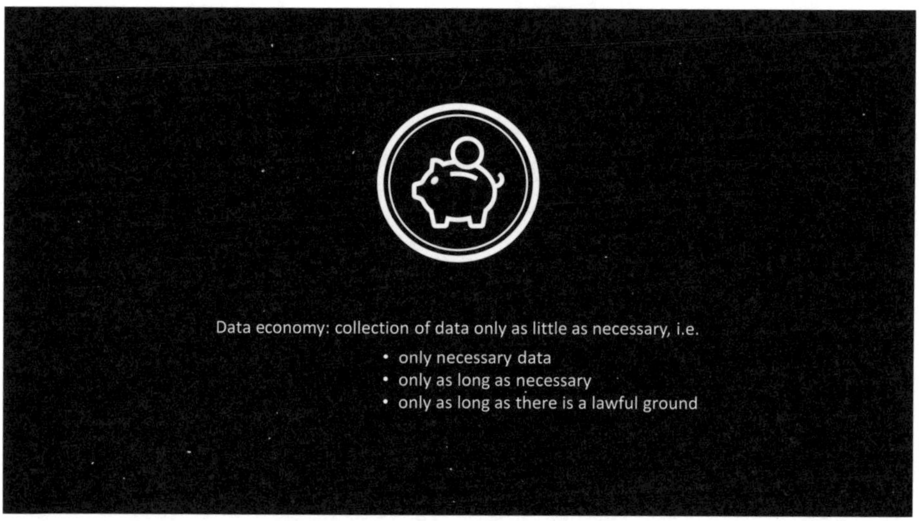

Figure 35: Principle of data economy

229 If non-personal data (purely factual data or anonymized data) are to be collected or processed which cannot be attributed to a natural person (for example because they were obtained from a M2M communication via an IP address or other connecting factors), no data protection restrictions apply to their use and subsequent archiving. However, this does not mean that such data may be used completely freely and stored without restrictions; rather, restrictions of use and limitations of service life must be observed from various other legal aspects (e.g. for reasons of observance of a virtual property right of admission, of licensing provisions for software or databases, also in the case of open

source or open data products), which in turn make it necessary to erase such data or even return it to the original supplier at the end of the permissible service life.

Guiding Principle:
Non-personal data (purely factual data or anonymized data) may not be used completely freely in Big Data applications; rather, any restrictions on use arising from other lawful grounds must be observed (third party licensing provisions, virtual householder rights, trade and business secrets, etc.).

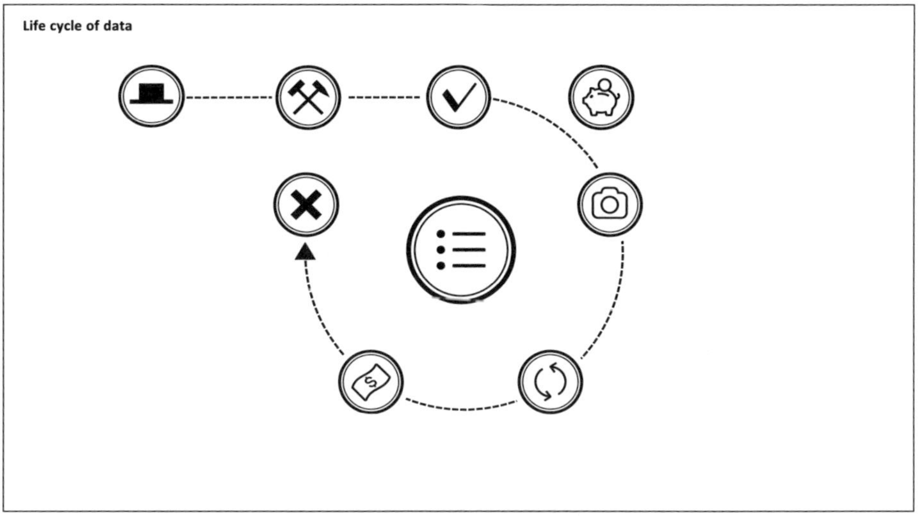

Figure 36: Life cycle of data

III. Collection of personal data for purposes other than their use in Big Data applications – a change of purpose

1. The purpose of data collection and processing

Both the contractual performance and the balancing of interests, but also all other legal requirements of data protection law, first presuppose a certain purpose for which the personal data are to be collected and processed. The purpose of the data collection and/or processing is at the same time the benchmark for the scope of the data collection and/or processing: the collection and processing of personal data is – no matter on which lawful ground it is based – only permissible to the extent that it is required by the legally-recognized and protected purpose of the intended data collection and/or processing. 230

The purpose is understood to be the objective pursued by the processing, whereby the collection and processing of personal data is always merely ancillary in nature, i.e. an aid to satisfy certain commercial, professional or industrial purposes of the controller when the pursuit of the controller's own purposes is important. Processing for other purposes is deemed to have taken place when the data are treated in the same way as goods which determine the purpose and object of the processing activity.[88] 231

[88] Simitis, in: Simitis, *Bundesdatenschutzgesetz*, 8th ed. 2014, § 28 mn. 22 et seq.

> **Guiding Principle:**
> All lawful grounds under data protection law, in particular contractual performance as well as balancing interests, presuppose a certain purpose for which the personal data are to be collected and processed.

232 In the case of consent (Art. 6 (1) (a) GDPR), specification of the purpose of the intended data collection and processing, for which consent is to be given, is also a required part of the declaration of consent and thus defines the limit of the data collection and processing authorized by the consent.

2. The "purpose" of contracts for the supply and use of data

233 In many cases, contractual rights to use data, for example from collective works, databases, open data projects or other data suppliers, are restricted to a specific purpose. This restriction on purpose follows from copyright contract law, which also applies to databases (§ 87b (1) UrhG); pursuant to § 31 (1) sentence 2 UrhG, the right of use to be granted by contract may be granted not only as a simple or exclusive right but also in terms of space, time or content. Content restriction of this sort concerning rights of use to databases, collective works or other data stocks of third parties, often state that the contractual data are only to be used for *own* or *own business* purposes. This is to prevent the recipient from distributing these data to third parties or within a group. Even if the data obtained through a data supplier were only passed on by a controller to another affiliate of the same group, this would be an inadmissible distribution to and/or use by third parties, depending of course on the rights granted to this data. In the area of contracts granting rights of use and exploitation of data, there is also no intra-group doctrine in the sense that the acquisition of data by a group company automatically and without special mention immediately covers their use by all other affiliates. Such a *group license* rather would have to be expressly agreed upon in the license agreement.

> **Guiding Principle:**
> The intended use of data for which industrial property rights exist within the framework of the Big Data application is, in turn, relevant to the scope of the licenses to be granted for this purpose.

3. The problem of dynamic purpose changes in Big Data applications

234 For Big Data applications, on the other hand, it is typical that data, often also personal data, are collected and first processed for a specific purpose that is lawful under data protection law, and only then, or parallel to this, are related to other data from other sources and processed for the purposes of Big Data analyses. The purpose of the Big Data analyses therefore differs from the purpose originally pursued by the initial collection and subsequent processing of these data. The processing of personal data and information for purposes other than those for which they were originally collected is lawful only within narrow limits.

> **Guiding Principle:**
> Especially in Big Data applications, processing of personal data for purposes other than those for which they were originally collected is standard, but only legally permissible within narrow restrictions under data protection law.

Further processing of personal data for a purpose other than that for which the original collection and (first) processing was authorized is initially possible with the consent of the data subject. Any consent with regard to a change of purpose must not be too vaguely described and must relate to the specific data processing processes. Consent may also relate to several purposes. The purpose in question must be as precise as possible at the time the data are collected and the controller must ensure that the data are not used for purposes that the data subject could not have expected. **235**

If no consent exists, an EU legal provision, such as performance of contract (Art. 6 (1) (b) GDPR), or a balance of interests or a Member State regulation can represent a lawful ground for a possible change in purpose. If consent is present, but ineffective for reasons of content or form, the data protection supervisory authorities are of the opinion that it is no longer possible to fall back on statutory grounds for permission because the controller requesting consent once created the impression that the decision of the data subject was the only important factor and that statutory grounds for permission were not independent of this. **236**

Guiding Principle:

If consent exists, but is ineffective due to content or formal reasons, it is no longer possible to fall back on statutory permissions.

If neither consent on the part of the data subject exists which relates specifically to the use of his personal data in the Big Data application, nor any statutory basis explicitly allowing the use of personal data in the Big Data application, is relevant, then another option is possible: it must be verified whether use by the data controller cannot be based on the purpose originally pursued and whether the subsequent processing in the Big Data application can be based on a change of purpose in accordance with Art. 6 (4) GDPR. This regulation thus renounces a strict limitation to purpose. Reference is made instead to the requirements of purpose definition and purpose compatibility. Survey purpose and any further processing purpose must therefore be compatible. Art. 6 (4) GDPR is thereby not a lawful ground on its own for subsequent further processing of personal data (argument from Art. 6 (1) GDPR, in which (4) is not mentioned), but an additional criterion whether previous and new processing purpose are compatible. **237**

With reference to this assessment, Art. 6 (4) GDPR contains a non-exhaustive catalogue of criteria for evaluating the compatibility of the collection and the further processing purpose, whereby the perspective of the data controller plays a decisive role: **238**

- the link between the original and the new purpose;
- the context of data collection;
- the types of personal data;
- the possible consequences of the intended further processing for the data subjects; and
- the existence of appropriate guarantees.

This set of criteria applies to a specific Big Data application and the data originally collected for other purposes that should now be evaluated in the Big Data application. **239**

Guiding Principle:

Where

- there is neither specific consent on the part of the data subject concerning the use of his personal data in the Big Data application
- nor is there a relevant statutory basis that specifically permits the use of personal data in the Big Data application,

the data controller can base his decision on the purpose originally pursued when the data was collected and make use of a change of purpose in accordance with Art. 6 (4) GDPR for subsequent processing in the Big Data application.

a) The link between the original and new purpose

240 From this perspective, any link between the purposes for which the personal data were originally collected and the purposes of the subsequent processing to be carried out must be taken into account in relation to the change of purpose. The more these purposes vary and the less they overlap, the more difficult it is to establish compatibility with regard to a change in purpose.

241 However, compatibility can be assumed if the original purpose for the data processing appears to justify further data processing where it represents the *logical next step*. If both processing purposes are linked in such a way that they must in theory build on or follow each other, the data subject must expect further processing and may be able to take this into account when making a decision regarding the lawfulness of the data processing.[89]

b) The context of data collection

242 This criterion must be assessed from the data subjects' perspective. The decisive element is the reasonable expectations of the data subjects with regard to the further use of their data.[90] According to recital 50 GDPR in view of *reasonable considerations*, the relationship between the data subject and the controller is to be taken into account.

243 The more surprising and unforeseen the further processing of personal data is for the data subject, the more likely it is that the further processing of the data will be incompatible with the original purpose. If it is suggested by the controller at the conclusion of the contract that no further processing will take place other than for the agreed purpose, the processing for another purpose can never satisfy the compatibility requirements of Art. 6 (4) GDPR.[91]

244 Lastly, reasonable considerations cover only lawful processing operations.[92]

c) The type of personal data

245 The type of personal data is also crucial. The more sensitive the data, the closer the new processing purpose must be to the original purpose. The Art. 29 data protection party lists in this context special categories of personal data of Art. 9 GDPR, as well as, for example, communication data, location-related data, or groups of persons particularly worthy of protection (e.g. children).[93]

d) Possible consequences of the intended subsequent processing for the data subjects

246 At this point, both negative and positive consequences of a change in purpose for the data subject must be compared to assess the compatibility of the change in purpose. An important factor here is whether the data is to be processed further by the person

---

[89] Cf. Buchner/Petri, in: Kühling/Buchner, *GDPR*, 2nd ed. 2018, Art. 6 mn. 187.

[90] Recital 50 GDPR.

[91] Cf. Buchner/Petri, in: Kühling/Buchner, *GDPR*, 2nd ed. 2018, Art. 6 mn. 187.

[92] Cf. ECJ, 19 October 2016, C-582/14 – *Breyer*.

[93] Gola, in: Gola/Schomerus, *BDSG*, 12th ed. 2015, § 4a mn. 2.

originally responsible or whether it is to be passed on to a third party. If a third party is to gain knowledge of the personal data, the consequences of this transfer are more difficult to assess for the data subjects with regard to further data processing. In principle, it should be noted that where the negativity of a compatibility assessment increases, the more difficult it will be for the data subjects to explicitly understand any further processing and to carry out an impact assessment, even if the further processing has predominantly negative consequences for the data subject.[94]

e) The existence of appropriate guarantees

This includes, inter alia, the encryption of personal data as well as pseudonymization **247**
or (even more so) anonymization. These protective mechanisms have to be taken into account with regard to compatibility. It is of particular importance for this matter whether the level of the protective mechanisms can be maintained in relation to the actual processing during any further processing or whether the purpose of the processing can also be achieved using pseudonymized or anonymized data.

---

[94] Cf. only Simitis, in: Simitis, *Bundesdatenschutzgesetz*, 8th ed. 2014, § 4a mn. 72 with numerous further references.

G. THIRD COUNTRY TRANSFER/APPLICABLE LAW (LEVEL OF APPLICABLE LAW)

The applicable law may change where the data are processed across national borders – whether by transfer or even by access from another country. 248

Figure 37: Principle of applicable law

A two-stage verification of transmission must be carried out where data are to leave the EU.[95] 249

The *first step* is to assess whether the transmission is permissible. This requires an examination of the elements listed in Art. 6 GDPR which justify a transfer of data (cf. above in mn. 184 *et seq.*); Art. 9 GDPR is to be considered if special categories of personal data are concerned. 250

The *second step* requires an examination of the specific requirements for transfers to third countries pursuant to Art. 44 *et seq.* GDPR. In short, the level of protection in the GDPR may not be *undermined* even in relation to a data receiver in a foreign country belonging to the EU (Art. 44 sentence 2 GDPR). The GDPR provides the following possibilities to ensure this purpose is achieved: 251

- *Adequacy decision of the EU Commission*, Art. 45 GDPR: The EU Commission can determine if the level of data protection of a third country (or at least of an area within it) is adequate by means of a decision. An example of this is the EU-US Privacy Shield;[96] companies in the USA can abide by these rules with the result that a transfer of data to this company is seen as a transfer within the EU.

---

[95] Wybitul/Ströbel/Rueß, *ZD* 2017, 503 (504).

[96] As of September 2019, the European Commission has recognized – in addition to the United States – twelve countries as providing adequate protection Art. 45 (9) GDPR: Andorra, Argentina, Canada (for commercial organizations), Faroe Islands, Guernsey, Israel, Isle of Man, New Zealand, Switzerland, and Uruguay.

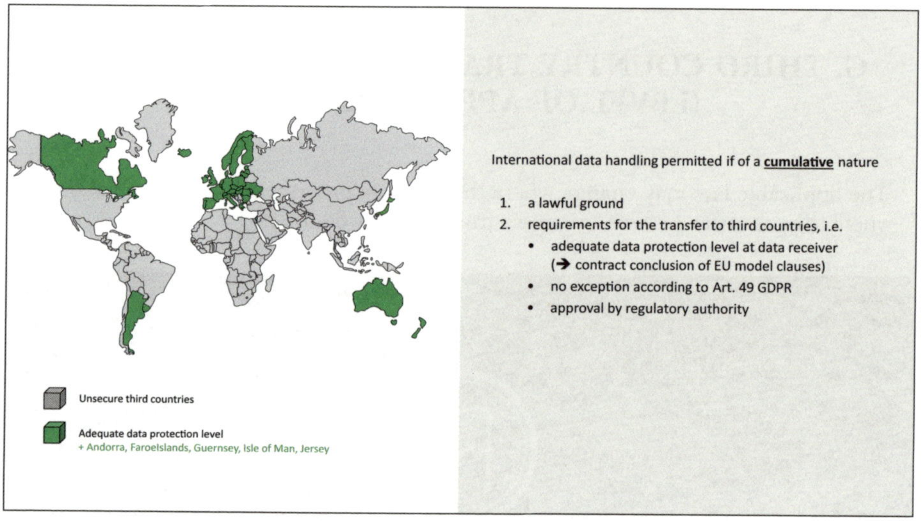

Figure 38: Countries with adequate levels of data protection

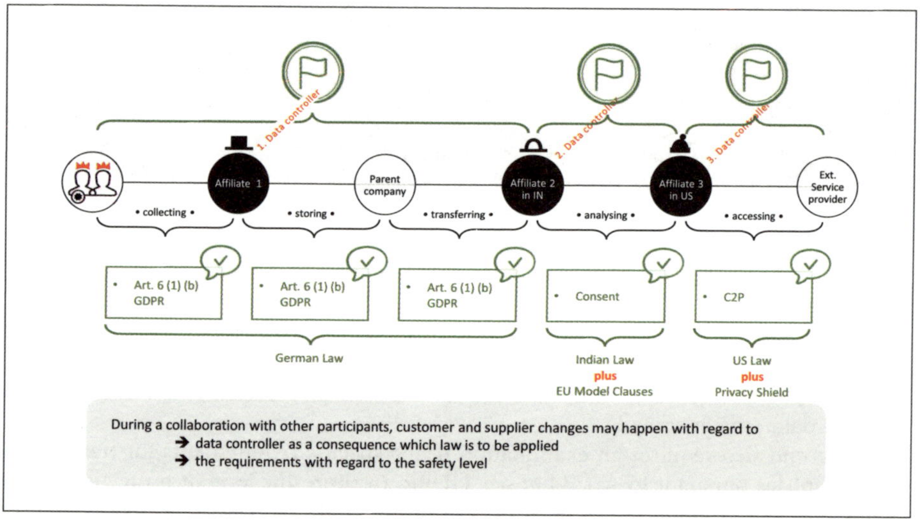

Figure 39: Change of applicable law in a sample processing chain

- *Standard data protection clauses* – Art. 46 (2) (c) GDPR. This legal instrument is also known as *EU standard contract terms* or *EU model clauses*. The EU Commission can decide on such term, which the recipient must then undertake to comply with in a contract with the responsible party and implement the rules described therein. As before, care must be taken to ensure that specification of the transfer is made as precisely and transparent as possible.[97]

[97] Commission decision C (2010) 593 for transmission to Processors, as well as Commission decision (2001) 497 – Set I and (2004) 915 – Set II each time for transmission between controllers.

- *Binding internal data protection regulations/binding Corporate Rules (BCR)* – Art. 46 (2) (b), 47 GDPR. If the data transfer is to take place within a company or a group of companies, corresponding internal data protection regulations can be concluded which satisfy the catalogue of requirements found in Art. 47 GDPR. These require an additional individual approval by the competent supervisory authority.
- *Code of Conduct (CoC)* – Art. 46 (2) (e), 40 GDPR. Associations and other bodies that represent the interests of certain responsible parties/contractors can develop corresponding codes of conduct, which must then be approved by a supervisory authority. A recipient in a third country can submit to such rules of conduct (e.g. by contract) and thus ensure a standard of protection.[98]
- *Certification* – Art. 46 (2) (f), 42 GDPR. Controllers and processors may submit to approved certification procedures by a supervisory authority or an accredited body. Together with legally binding and enforceable obligations to protect the rights of those affected, such certification can also ensure a standard of protection.
- *Consent* – Art. 49 (1) sentence 1 (a) GDPR. Insofar as the aforementioned conditions have not been met, explicit[99] consent given by the data subject can be considered, though rigorous requirements exist for the acceptance thereof (generally for this purpose cf. mn. 197 *et seq.*). In particular, the data subject must be informed of the risks associated with data being transferred to a third country without an appropriate level of protection and furthermore that this transfer is not ensured by other guarantees.
- *Other exceptions.* Art. 49 (1) GDPR lists further exceptions: (i) performance of a contract, (ii) important reasons of public interest, (iii) establishment, exercise or defence of legal claims, (iv) legitimate interests/public registers and (v) protection of the compelling vital interests of the person responsible. However, in the light of Big Data storage, these exceptions are likely to remain unusual.

Guiding Principle:

If a cloud platform located outside the EU is used, in addition to the conclusion of a processing agreement, measures must be taken in accordance with Art. 44 *et seq.* GDPR to ensure an adequate level of data protection exists where the data recipient is located.

---

[98] e.g. the European Union Data Protection Code of Conduct for Cloud Service Provider, https://ec.europa.eu/digital-single-market/en/news/data-protection-code-conduct-cloud-service-providers, as at 7/2018.

[99] This should again exclude "Opt-out"-solutions, cf. Wybitul/Ströbel/Rueß, *ZD* 2017, 503 (507).

H. DEVELOPMENT OF A BIG DATA APPLICATION

If data of any kind is to flow into a Big Data application, each individual stage of data processing must be examined in terms of data protection law: 252

- Has the (initial) collection or procurement of personal and non-personal data to be processed in the Big Data application already taken place lawfully in accordance with the relevant legal system where data is being collected?
- Is the transfer of data to group companies or external service providers legitimate and thus lawful?
- What happens if the Big Data application mixes data collected lawfully with data collected unlawfully?
- Combination with other data
- Evaluation and analysis of data
- Utilization and commercialization of data or evaluation/analysis results
- Anonymization and statistical evaluation.

The following must therefore be examined before setting up a Big Data application: 253

- which categories of data (or types of data) are to be collected, (added to) stored and (also through evaluations or analyses) processed by the controller, namely
  - data obtained from open sources,
  - personal data (cf. mn. 51–74),
  - purely factual data (cf. mn. 75 *et seq.*) or
  - anonymized data (cf. mn. 289 *et seq.*)

  (level of data content)
- and from which sources and thus possibly from which right holders these data originate, namely
  - from a survey of the data subjects,
  - from the owner of a device,
  - from a data supplier or from a database on the basis of an understanding concerning data use and/or license agreement from a data supplier or
  - from Open Data projects,

  (level of data retrieval) and
- whether these data have been lawfully acquired from the respective source/data provider itself, which must be assessed according to the location of the data source/data provider according to the law applicable at its location (level of data retrieval), (level of applicable law, cf. mn. 248 *et seq.*)
- whether the data controller has concluded any necessary contractual agreements for the data concerned or can rely on sufficient lawful grounds to legitimize the use of such data within the framework of a Big Data application (level of lawful grounds, cf. mn. 180 *et seq.*), as well as
- whether the data originally collected for operational purposes may also be processed for the purposes of the specifically intended evaluation/analysis in the Big Data application after the addition of further categories of data, as appropriate. (level of data purpose, cf. mn. 222 *et seq.*).

The body responsible for establishing a Big Data application may have to deal with quite different lawful grounds with regard to the same data – either at the level of the 254 data retrieval or at the level of content, i.e. whether the data contains personal content. For example, contracts must be concluded with the supplier of personal data from a database for the supply and use of this data in order to take into account the rights of use and exploitation (§§ 87a *et seq.* UrhG) to which this supplier is entitled in the database. The data obtained from this supplier may, however, be accessed by natural persons who have no contractual or other legal connection whatsoever with the data supplier (e.g. if the supplier has collected this data from public sources or collected it in any other way); the legality of obtaining such data from a data supplier must then be examined in accordance with data protection criteria. The conclusion of a contract for the supply and use of data with a data supplier does not necessarily imply statutory permissibility for the collection and acquisition of such data by the data supplier or the provision of such data by the data supplier to the relevant controller.

I. Collection of data

255 The same lawful grounds or the consent of the data subject may be used as the basis for lawful collection of personal data (cf. mn. 184 *et seq.*).

II. Obtaining and acquiring data from data service providers

1. Legality of the collecting data provided by a data supplier

256 If data is acquired from third parties who have collected and compiled this data as *commercial objects* (e.g. compliance data on natural persons and companies from a data service provider), it is initially important with regard to personal data to ascertain whether the data service provider selling this data was itself entitled to collect this personal data and store it for the purpose of further distribution. If such a data service provider cannot legally justify its own data collection and collection under data protection law, the further distribution of this data by such a data service provider is also inadmissible and the purchase and further use of this data in a Big Data application are in turn equally inadmissible.

257 It is irrelevant whether the operator of the Big Data application was informed or aware of the unlawful collection by the data service provider when purchasing such databases. The unlawfulness of its collection and further processing permanently taints the data sold; thus there is no *acquisition in good faith* in this sense.

258 If data collected unlawfully is combined by storage with lawfully collected and stored data, the unlawful nature of the unlawful data affects the entire database. This means that before data from other sources are added, the legality of their collection and acquisition and, if applicable, their acquisition from third parties must always be examined carefully. This is particularly true if the additional storage of such potentially infected data is irreversible, i.e. data which is subject to the illegality flaw cannot be erased again from the data records of a Big Data application.

> **Guiding Principle:**
>
> When acquiring personal data from data suppliers, it is always necessary to verify whether the data supplier itself was entitled to collect these personal data and to store them for the purpose of further distribution. If there is no such entitlement, the acquired data are unlawful; good faith acquisition does not change this.

2. Legitimacy of data acquisition from third parties

If data is acquired from third parties in order to then feed it into a Big Data application and combine it with other data, a distinction must also be made between the above-mentioned dimensions of *content of data*, on the one hand, and *source of data*, on the other. **259**

The processing of data with certain contents, e.g. personal data, may be permitted under data protection law without further steps. However, if this data comes from a third source, it is necessary to examine and consider whether this data in relation to the owner of this data source may be used lawfully at all for the purposes of the Big Data application, including the evaluations and analyses to be carried out therein, i.e. whether this data was obtained lawfully. As a rule, corresponding data usage or purchase agreements must be concluded with the authorized party for this purpose. **260**

The question of identifying the beneficiary in this sense is explained above under mn. 81–116. **261**

> **Guiding Principle:**
>
> In addition to the permissibility under data protection law of the acquisition of personal data, data usage contracts must also be concluded under civil law, in particular if the data to be acquired are protected by industrial property rights (copyright to collective works, database protection right, virtual property admission rights, trade secret, etc.).

3. Rectifying deficiencies

As has been noted, with respect to data content, unlawful collection and processing of personal data cannot be rectified by subsequent measures because the lawful ground under data protection law must already exist at the time of collection. Conversely, any further processing of personal data, at the level of data retrieval, can possibly be *cured* of deficiencies with regard to the permissibility of the processing of data obtained from third parties by the subsequent conclusion of retroactive license or similar acquisition agreements. This also applies to consent: although data protection law stipulates that the data subject's consent to the content of data relating to a natural person must already exist when his data are collected and processed and cannot be granted retroactively, license agreements or other data usage agreements concluded with retroactive effect are legally valid. **262**

However, at the level of data retrieval, deficiencies in data retrieval could be rectified by the subsequent conclusion of data usage contracts. Nonetheless, if at this level the data obtained are personal data and their collection or provision within the framework of data supply was inadmissible under data protection law, a possible solution at the level of data procurement does not at the same time cure a legal deficiency at the level of data content, i.e. on its lawfulness or unlawfulness under data protection law! **263**

> **Guiding Principle:**
>
> While the inadmissibility of data collection or data acquisition under data protection law cannot be rectified, the subsequent conclusion of user contracts with retroactive effect is legally possible through license agreements or other data usage contracts.

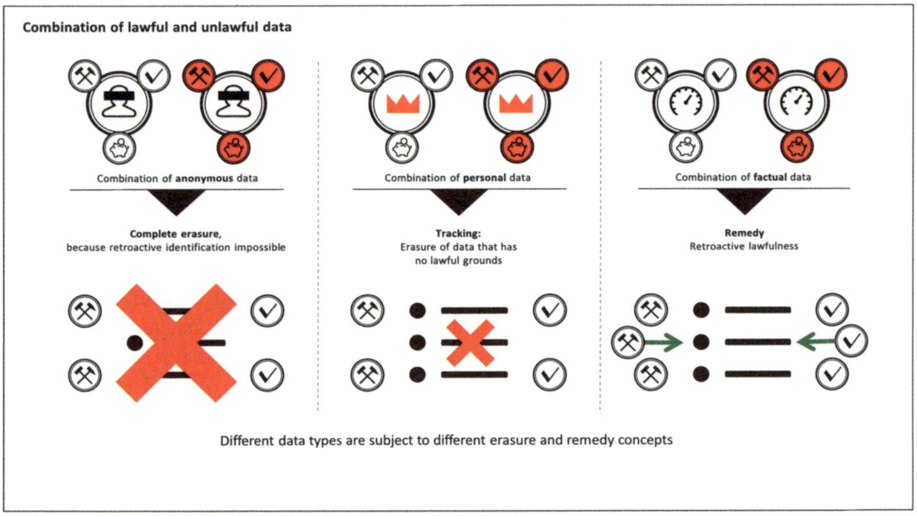

Figure 40: Combination of lawful and unlawful data

III. Combination of data

264 When mixing and combining different types of data – i.e. personal and non-personal data – various laws are applied cumulatively.

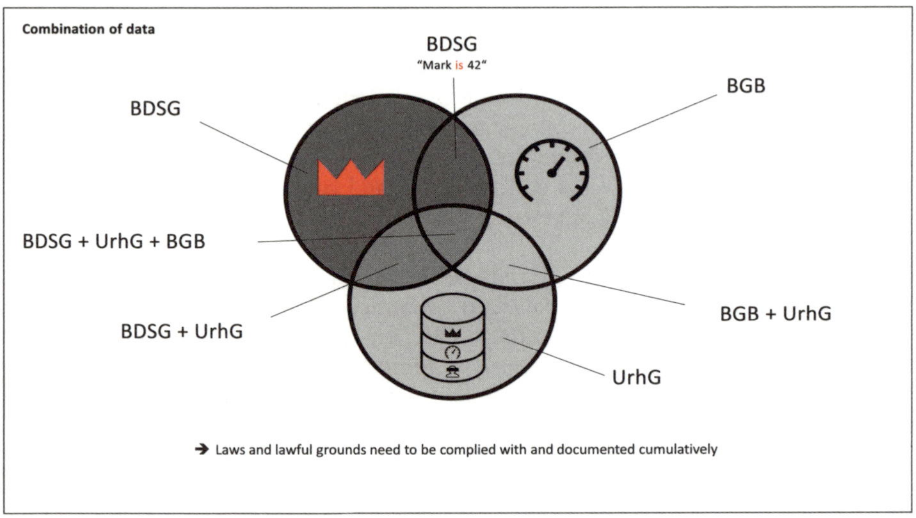

Figure 41: Combination of data and applicable laws

The example shown in Figure 42 illustrates this: if personal data (here Mark) is linked to factual data (here 42) by the word *is*, the application of the data protection legislation also extends to the factual data. **265**

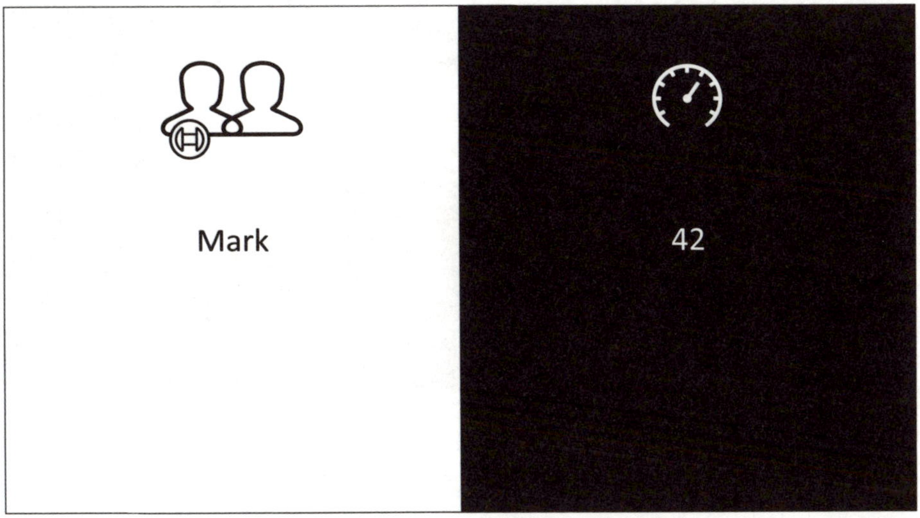

Figure 42: Exemplary personal and factual data

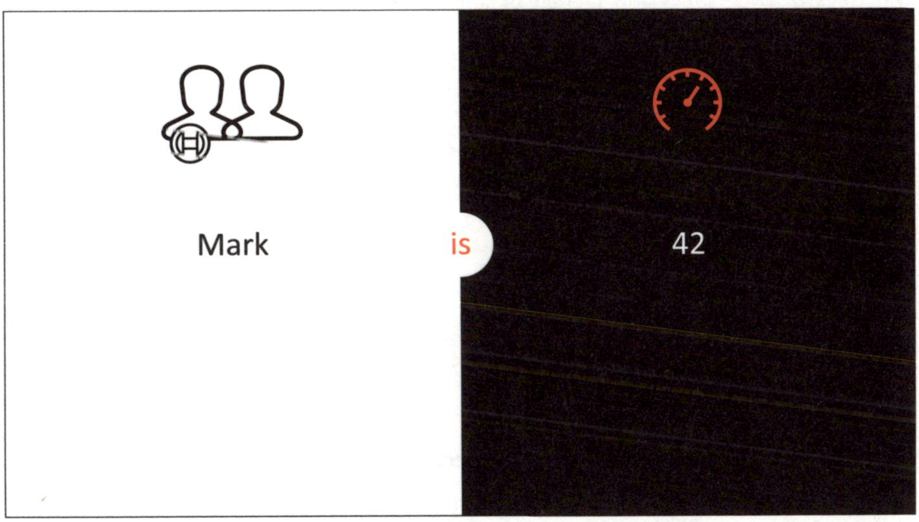

Figure 43: Combination of personal and factual data

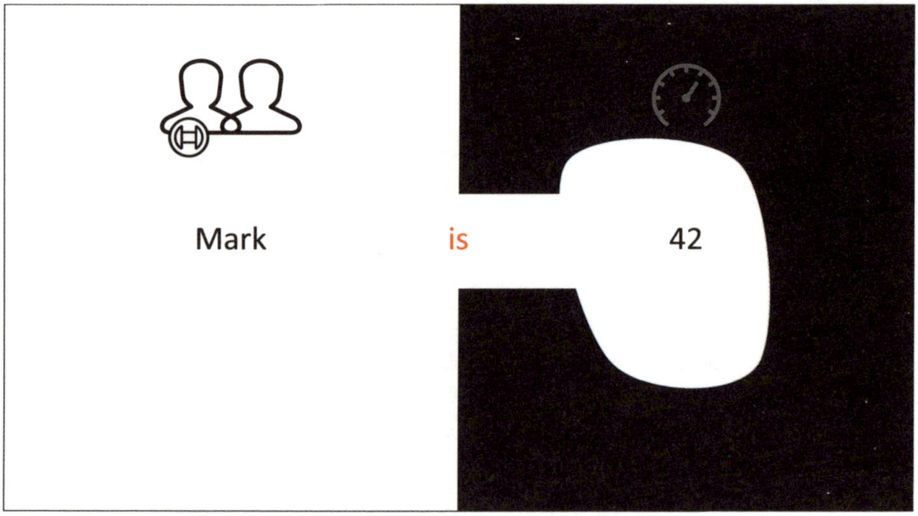

Figure 44: Application of data protection law to factual data

1. Lawfulness of combining different data categories at the level of data retrieval

266 At the level of data retrieval, contracts for the use of data, whether personal or not, must allow for a desired combination of personal data with other types of data, both with regard to personal and factual or anonymous data. If no such rights have been granted for the use of the related data by mixing and combining them with other data, this intended combination of different data categories in a Big Data application is already, on the part of the controller operating the Big Data application, an infringement of the rights of third parties (the data suppliers) with respect to the data. In order to avoid injunctive relief and/or claims for damages by these right holders, the permissibility of the intended combination of different data categories in relation to the suppliers/owners of sources of this data must therefore be clarified in advance.

Guiding Principle:

In order to avoid injunctive relief and/or claims for damages by holders of (copyright, database protection or other) rights to such data, the lawfulness of the intended combination of different data categories in relation to the suppliers/owners of sources of such data must be clarified in advance.

2. Combining personal data from different data sources

267 If personal data from one data source is combined with personal data from another data source, the subsequent processing, evaluation and/or analysis of this combined data requires that the personal data from each individual source be collected lawfully and transferred lawfully to the Big Data application based on a separate lawful ground. This transfer of data to the Big Data application often has a different purpose than applied for the original data collection; for personal data, therefore, there must be compliance with the requirements set out in mn. 234 *et seq*. If this basis under data protection law is missing even with regard to a single data category from a single data source, the total set

of personal data combined from several data sources will be tainted and thus its further storage in the Big Data application and its evaluation and/or analysis in the Big Data application will be inadmissible as a whole.

Guiding Principle:

When combining personal data from different data sources, any subsequent processing, analysis and/or analysis of this combined data requires that the personal data from each individual source have been lawfully collected and accordingly lawfully transferred to the Big Data application based on an independent lawful ground.

3. Combining personal data with factual data or anonymous data

In and of itself, combining personal data with other data – whether personal or not – **268**
is a legally-relevant processing operation for the personal data concerned, which requires a lawful ground either based on statutory permission or order, or through consent.

Guiding Principle:

The combination of personal data with other data – whether personal or not – is in turn a legally-relevant processing operation which requires a lawful ground either by statutory permission or order, or by consent. If this lawful ground under data protection law is missing, even with regard to a single data category, the entire set of personal data will be tainted and its further storage as well as evaluation and/or analysis in the Big Data application will be inadmissible as a whole.

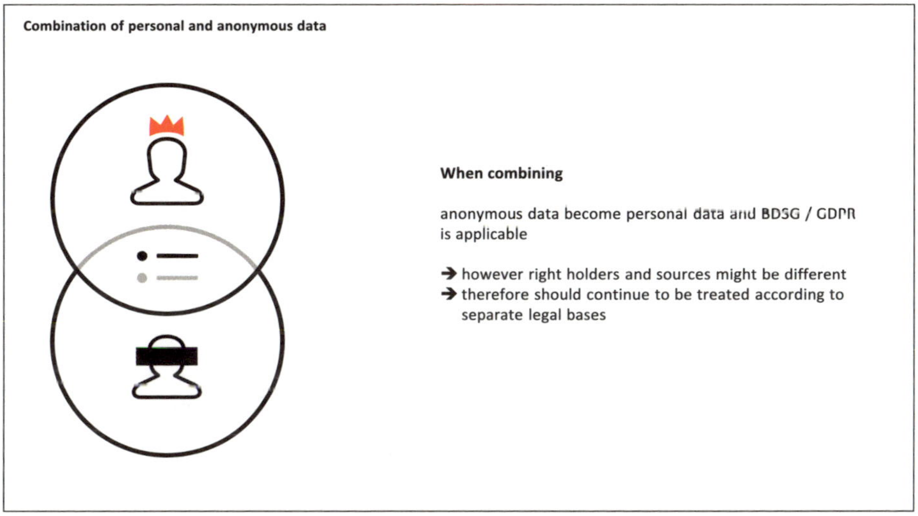

Figure 45: Combination of personal and anonymous data

4. Combination of personal data from different countries of origin

269 Where a Big Data application is intended for storage and processing of personal data which have been collected and contributed to by data controllers from different countries, it is necessary to ensure that each controller discloses the data to the data controller operating the Big Data application in accordance with its national data protection law (whether the data is transferred or *stored* directly in the Big Data application). As long as the personal data stored in a Big Data application originates from EU or EEA Member States, it can be assumed that the provisions of the GDPR will apply to this data in each case.

Guiding Principle:
Where a Big Data application is intended for storage and processing of personal data which have been collected and contributed to by data controllers from different countries, it is necessary to ensure that each controller discloses the data to the data controller operating the Big Data application in accordance with its national data protection law (whether the data is transferred or *stored* directly in the Big Data application).

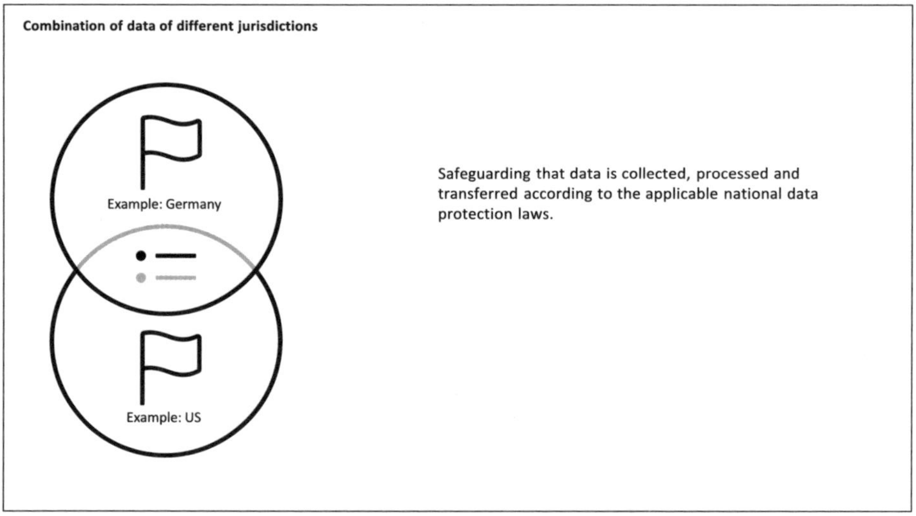

Figure 46: Combination of data of different jurisdictions

5. Combining different personal data collected for different purposes

270 Data is usually collected for different purposes. Thus, they are subject to different lawful grounds, different life cycles, and possibly different right holders. These variables must be taken into account when combining and mixing the data.

271 It is therefore advisable, as part of the technical and organizational measures, to initially process, save and store the data only in accordance with the respective purposes, unless combining different databases is permissible as such and also from the perspective of a change of purpose.

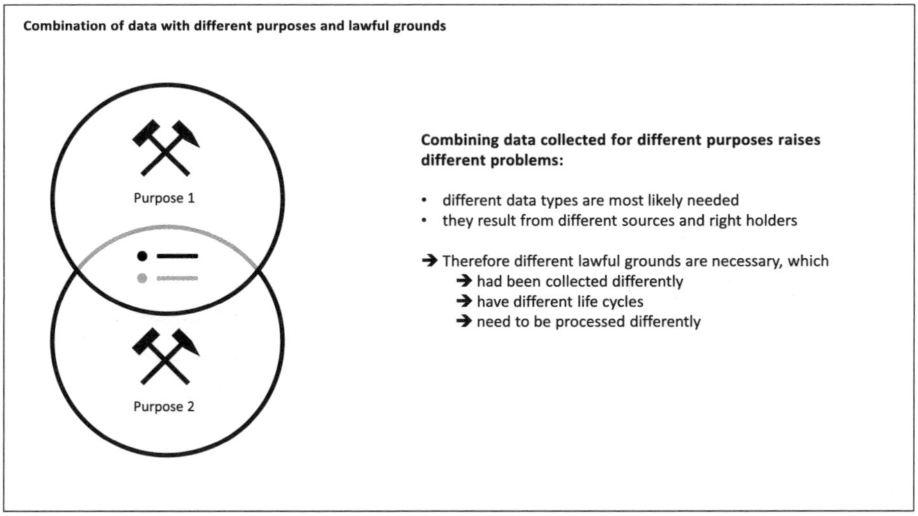

Figure 47: Combination of data with different purposes and lawful grounds

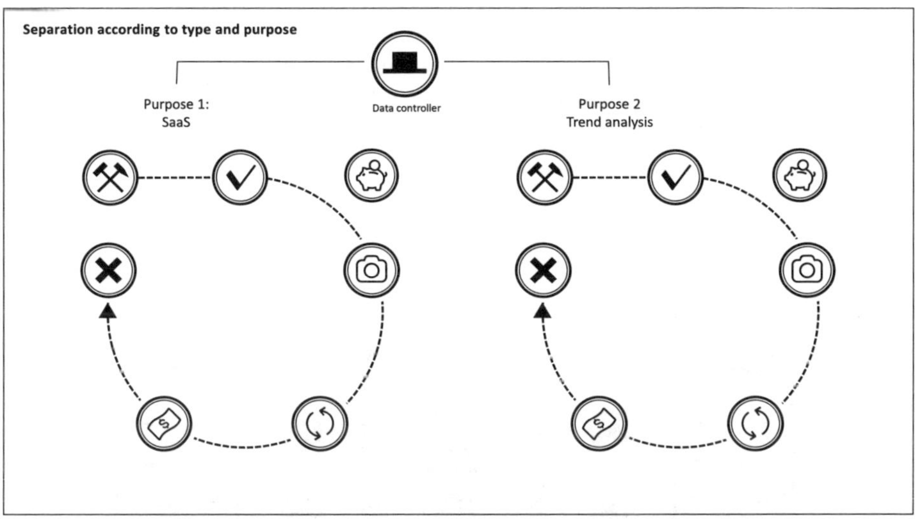

Figure 48: Separation according to data type and purpose

272 If, for example, customer data is to be transmitted to a parent company as part of contractual data processing so that it can be made available to the various other subsidiaries for the purpose of initiating further business opportunities (purpose of cross-selling), the parent company must also have appropriate technical and organizational measures in place to be able to legally manage the various data of various right holders, and perhaps various lawful grounds and life cycles.

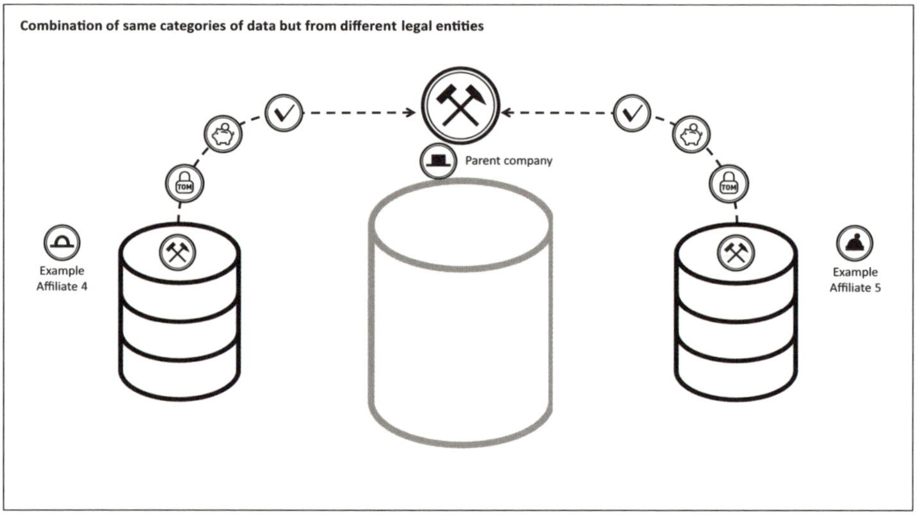

Figure 49: Combination of same categories of data but from different legal entities

273 In particular, the parent company must have rights and authorization management in place: if a customer of one of its subsidiaries withdraws its consent, the parent company must not only erase the data record in its own database, but must also ensure that the data it has passed on to other subsidiaries has also been erased.

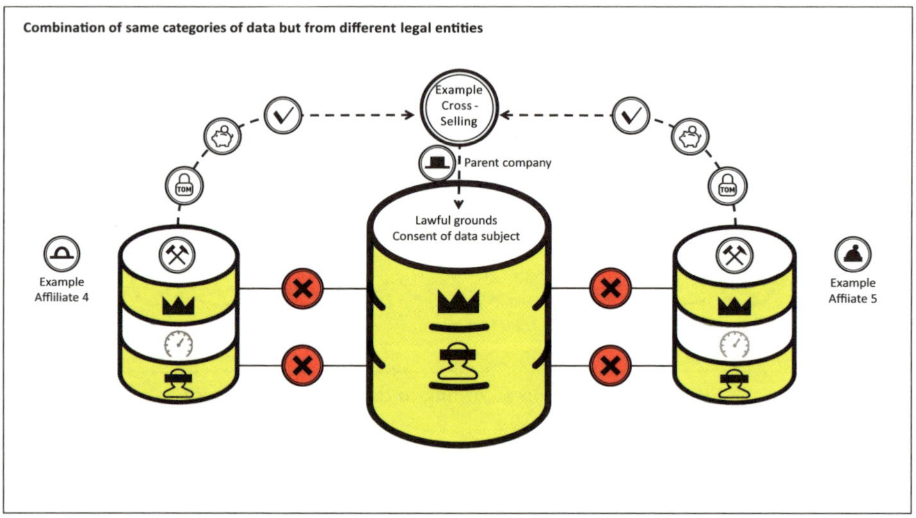

Figure 50: Combination of same categories of data but from different legal entities

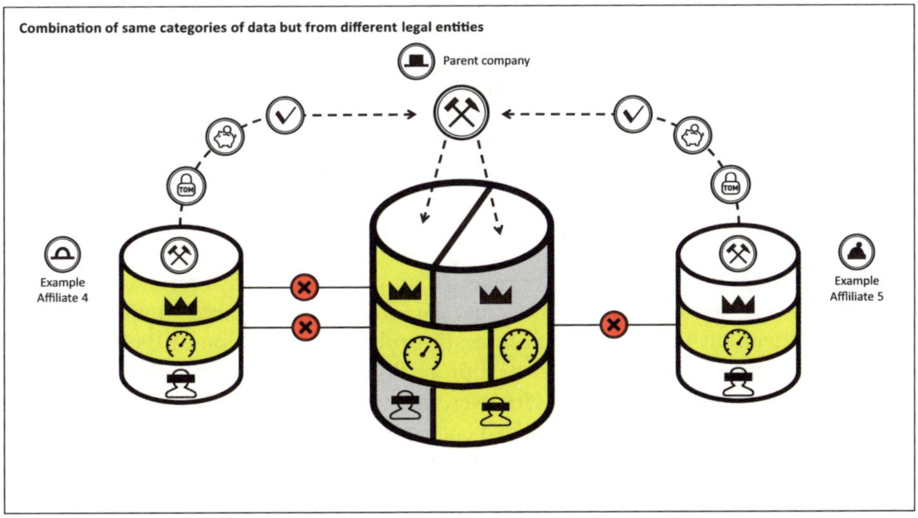

Figure 51: Combination of same categories of data but from different legal entities

> **Guiding Principle:**
> When combining data sets that were collected for different purposes, these different purposes and the resulting different life cycles, technical and organizational measures as well as usage restrictions from contracts with rights holders etc. must be taken into account in such a way that ultimately the strictest requirements apply to the entire combined data set.

6. Rectifying deficiencies

It is not possible to cure any unlawful processing of personal data in a Big Data application as lawful processing must be based on statutory permission or order, or by consent in each case at the moment of the data collection, further processing or transmission. This does not apply to purely factual data (e.g. data from databases without reference to a natural person) because only civil law rights of use granted by the entitled party are relevant; such rights may be granted with retroactive effect. 274

The combination or mixing of data with different content from different data sources does not change the individual data due to its content or the unlawful nature of its source. This particular defect of unlawfulness rather extends to the entire Big Data application once such unlawful data have been merged therein. The transfer of databases into a Big Data application therefore does not eliminate the need for lawful ground under data protection law or the lawful procurement from a specific database source; both levels of consideration instead remain relevant for the legal assessment of the operation of a Big Data application and the lawfulness of the evaluations and analyses carried therein. 275

Guiding Principle:
It is not possible to cure of the lack of lawful subsequent processing of personal data in a Big Data application because the lawful grounds must be given at the time of data collection, further processing or transmission. It is, however, possible to repair on the level of the admissibility of the data retrieval, in particular, of purely factual data, from a third data source. Nevertheless, the two levels must be considered separately, i.e. the subsequent conclusion of a data usage contract alone does not affect a permissible the use of this data under data protection law if it concerns personal data.

276 If personal data have been lawfully collected and evaluated in a Big Data application, and if these data are combined with factual data unlawfully acquired (under civil law), for example without the necessary licenses, the unlawful acquisition of the factual data does not affect the lawfulness (under data protection law) of the personal data to which these factual data have been added. However, this combined processing of personal data with additional, but unlawfully obtained, non-personal data must not take place for other reasons. The person entitled to these unlawfully acquired, non-personal data is entitled to an injunction against their use on the basis of his rights to these data, which of course also includes their use in combination with the stored personal data.

Guiding Principle:
While the unlawful acquisition of factual data does not affect the lawfulness of the processing of personal data to which those factual data have been added, the rightful owner of such unlawfully acquired non-personal data has a right to an injunction against their use on the basis of his rights with regard to those data.

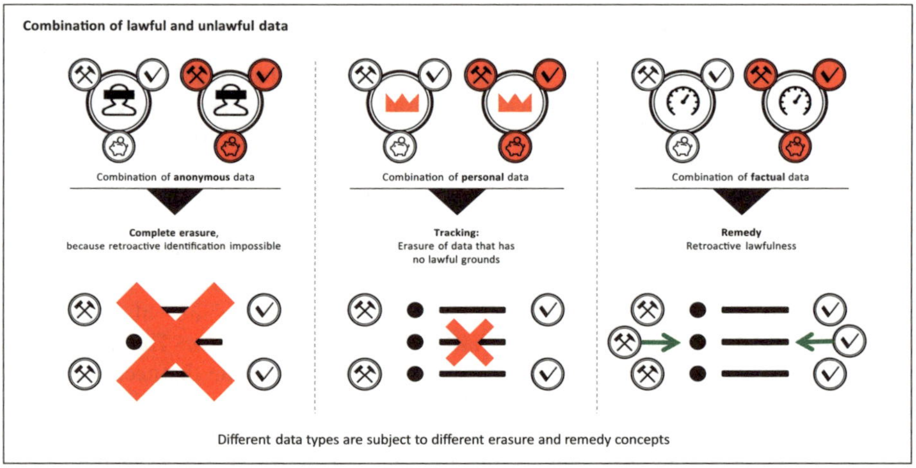

Figure 52: Combination of lawful and unlawful data

IV. Extending the range: anonymization/pseudonymization of data stored in a Big Data database

Anonymization or pseudonymization of personal data can be used in order to 277
comply with data protection requirements when processing personal data in a Big Data application. In view of the mass of data, however, it is questionable whether a personal reference can actually be removed in this way.[100] The additional storage of non-personal factual data or anonymized data changes the nature of the data to which such non-personal factual data or anonymized data are to be added (target data) as personal, pseudonymized or anonymized – on the contrary, the additional storage of such additional data can make the information profile of the data subject so specific that the data subject can still be (re-)identified. In the initial situation, pseudonymized or anonymized target data could thus become personal data once again, and thus data protection law would again have to be applied in full.

> **Guiding Principle:**
> The impact of the addition of data in a Big Data application on any possible re-identification of natural persons to whom pseudonymized or anonymized target data originally refer shall be assessed before any data is added.

1. Pseudonymization (Art. 4 No. 5 GDPR)

Pseudonymization is a procedure whereby the data subject receives an artificial 278
identifier (= pseudonym). As a result, further allocation data is necessary in order to enable direct conclusions to be drawn about persons identified with the pseudonym.

Example database with personal and factual data

ID	First name	Last name	Disease	Treatment
0001	Susi	Meyer	Breast cancer	Surgery

Figure 53: Example database with personal and factual data

Against this background, Art. 4 (5) GDPR defines pseudonymization as the processing 279
of personal data in such a manner that (i) the personal data can no longer be attributed to a specific data subject without the use of for additional information, (ii) provided that this additional information is kept separately, **and** (iii) is subject to technical and organizational measures ensuring that the personal data is not attributed to an identified or identifiable natural person. Since the technical process of pseudonymization is a processing operation within the meaning of Art. 4 (2) GDPR, a lawful ground is required. Often, the balance of interests in Art. 6 (1) (f) GDPR may be used as the basis.

[100] Referring to supposed anonymization in the past Katko/Babaei-Beigi, *MMR* 2014, 360 (361 et seq.); cf. also mn. 257*et seq*.

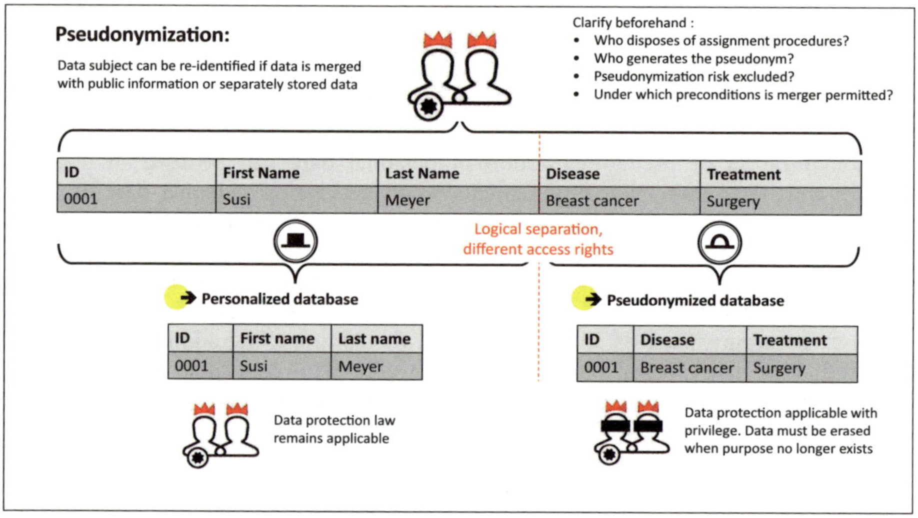

Figure 54: Pseudonymization

280 Three technical approaches can be used to achieve pseudonymization:[101]
- the data subject can choose the pseudonym himself;
- a trustworthy third party may assign the pseudonym and at the same time keep the allocation data ready (cf. mn. 303 *et seq.*); or
- the controller may assign the pseudonym.

281 It will depend on the individual circumstances whether pseudonymized data are still personal data if the person responsible does not have the allocation file. In the opinion of Art. 29 Data Protection Working Party,[102] pseudonymized data are to be regarded as indirectly determinable information about persons. If, despite the use of the pseudonym, it is possible to trace the person and reveal their identity – even if only under previously defined conditions – such pseudonymized data are also personal data in the sense of the GDPR; their collection and further processing are thus to be assessed according to the applicable legislative provisions. In view of the ECJ decision on the personal reference of dynamic IP addresses[103], which advocates a *"relative theory-expanding view"*[104], it could be argued that the controller cannot identify a person precisely if it has been contractually agreed with the owner of the allocation file that the person responsible may under no circumstances have access to the file; in that case, however, the use of pseudonymization is questionable.[105] Conversely, access to the association file may be blocked. If, however, with the help of additional data from other sources, the pseudonymized data record could be assigned to the natural person as the data subject again, a pseudonymization may exist which can be regarded as a protective instrument in favour of the rights of the data subject. However, it remains qualified as personal data.

282 As already outlined in mn. 279 above, pseudonymization means processing personal data in such a way that the personal data can no longer be attributed to a specific data

[101] Fundamentally Roßnagel/Scholz, *MMR* 2000, 721 (725).
[102] WP 136 Statement 4/2007 for the term "personenbezogene Daten" as of 20.6.2007, p. 21.
[103] ECJ, 19 October 2016, C-582/14 – *Breyer*.
[104] Mantz/Spittka, *NJW* 2016, 3582.
[105] In this direction Schreiber, in: Plath, *BDSG/DSGVO*, 3rd ed. 2018, Art. 4 GDPR mn. 20; generally rejecting this, Ernst, in: Paal/Pauly, *GDPR*, 2nd ed. 2018, Art. 4 mn. 40.

subject without additional information, provided that such additional information is kept separately and is subject to technical and organizational measures ensuring that the personal data are not attributed to an identified or identifiable natural person. In the case of pseudonymous data, in addition to the *intended* restoration of the personal reference, there is also the possibility of establishing a personal reference by breaching the assignment function. Strong pseudonymization thus requires the protection of this rule by the holder (e.g. a trustee or a trust office). Measures to protect against access by unauthorized persons may be of a technical and/or organizational nature, but may also include contractual agreements (such as a prohibition) or specify the conditions for disclosing the assignment function. If algorithmic allocation rules are used, a brute force attack on the allocation rule itself is also possible in order to reveal a pseudonym. Finally, linking data to the same pseudonym – especially if the pseudonym is used for a long period or in different roles and contexts – can lead to extensive databases which, due to numerous connecting factors, make it much easier to draw conclusions about a particular person. The more subtle the pseudonymization, i.e. the less likely it is to link data together, the higher the anonymity will be and thus the lower the probability of revelation. Influencing factors are, for example, the time of pseudonymization, the period of its validity, the resistance of the pseudonymization procedure to withdrawal, the number of pseudonymized identification features per data record, and the size of the population in which the data subject is concealed.[106]

The following must therefore be specified for pseudonymization: **283**

- the pseudonymization principle as such,
- the trust centre or trustee who keeps the pseudonymization principle and who must protect it from unauthorized access,
- the scope of the same pseudonymization principle being applied to different situations, which should be kept to a minimum, and
- the criteria under which the pseudonymization rule may be issued and used for re-identification.

Since pseudonymized data can be assigned to a natural person again at any time, the **284** principles of data protection law continue to apply unchanged to the personal data concerned, and even to pseudonymized data and any other personal and other additional data stored within the framework of the Big Data application. Their further processing through combination other data as well as their evaluation are therefore only permitted under the same conditions as for "open" personal data. Non-personal data will not be subject to data protection law only if it is neither stored nor otherwise linked to personal data.

Legal requirements for other legal reasons, for example the necessity of the legal **285** procurement of purely factual data, which from the outset have no personal reference, the licensing of databases required by copyright or other legal reasons, etc., of course remain unaffected.

Guiding Principle:

Pseudonymized data can be assigned to a natural person again at any time, so that their further processing by combining them with other data as well as their evaluating are only permissible under the same conditions as with "open" personal data.

---

[106] Cf. Scholz, in: Simitis, *Bundesdatenschutzgesetz*, 8th ed. 2014, § 3 mn. 217b with further references.

286 The process of pseudonymization is described as *"replacing the name and other identifiers with an artificial indicator"*. This indicator (e.g. discretionary numbers, hash value) replaces the identifying information as a pseudonym. Art. 4 (5) GDPR clarifies that it is not sufficient for pseudonymization to merely exchange the name of a natural person in a data set, but not to take into account other data intended for identification. Rather, all direct identification features (e.g. personal number or identifier), to which a reference function is attached to the named person must likewise be replaced and turned into a pseudonym.

287 If a method of pseudonymization is chosen, it is in the interest of data minimization (Art. 5 (1) (c) GDPR) that the relevant data is pseudonymized as quickly and as soon as possible during the data processing process, i.e. separated from the data elements (e.g. name, VIN, etc.) which enable assignment to a natural person.

288 Pseudonymization as well as the use of a data trustee for the organizational safeguarding of the pseudonymization should also be accompanied by regular privacy audits of the pseudonymization process and of the upstream data processing steps at the office responsible for the pseudonymization. The strict separation of the pseudonymized data from the pseudonyms and their assignment criteria must be examined in the course of these audits.

Guiding Principle:

With pseudonymization, the data subject is assigned an artificial indicator (= pseudonym), so that allocation data is necessary to enable direct conclusions to be drawn about the person identified with the pseudonym. In theory, however, pseudonymized data remain personal data, the use of which in Big Data applications is also subject to the general data protection requirements of permissible processing.

2. Anonymization

289 Anonymization is more than pseudonymization. In particular, anonymization excludes the application of data protection law because completion of the anonymization process removes the link to a person.[107] Although the GDPR does not contain a definition of the term anonymization as seen in § 3 (6) BDSG a. F, recital 26 GDPR, however, refers to this definition in its content. According to former version of the BDSG, anonymization was understood as changing personal data in such a way that single data about personal or factual circumstances can no longer be assigned to a certain person or such person can only be determined with a disproportionately large expenditure of time, costs, technology and labour (*de-anonymization*). At the same time, the literature currently assumes that this should not be associated with any content statement with regard to anonymization.[108] The following also applies to anonymization: changing the data embedded in it is a process involving personal data which requires a lawful ground according to data protection law, and which can be supported in many cases by the act of balancing interests in Art. 6 (1) (f) GDPR.

[107] Cf. Recital 26 sentence 6 GDPR; cf. also Art. 4(1) in conjunction with Art. 2 (1) GDPR.
[108] On behalf of the prevailing opinion Wójtowicz/Cebulla, *PinG* 2017, 186 (187).

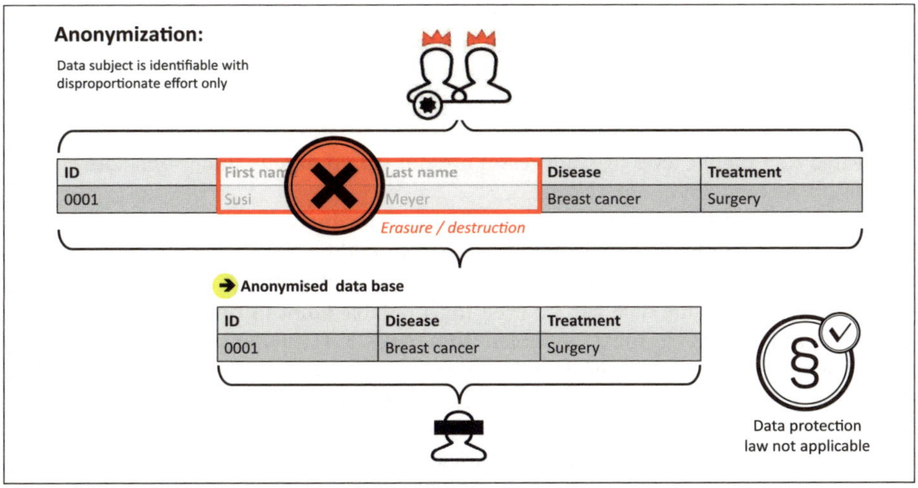

Figure 55: Anonymization

The availability of the knowledge required for de-anonymization is decisive. However, *availability* does not mean, either that an intention to de-anonymize exists or that the additional information is already or still available to the controller. Such additional knowledge or even the original personal data are available, of course, if the data are still on back-up copies, so that erasure of the data elements justifying the personal reference must be comprehensive, including all relevant storage media and forms. Absolute anonymization is only possible in the rarest of cases due to the possibilities offered by automated data processing anonymization. The legislator follows this approach by focusing on whether de-anonymization would require a disproportionately large expenditure of time, costs, technology and labour. The term *disproportionately* high effort makes it clear that this is always an individual decision to be taken from an objective perspective. In this respect, the possible interest of the storing party in de-anonymization of individual data and the resulting economic benefit, which may also justify high costs, will also be decisive; the data shall not be considered anonymous if the data controller is prepared to incur the disproportionately high expense.[109] **290**

After complete anonymization of originally personal data in the aforementioned sense, a personal reference has been fully removed and – if the definition applies in the individual case – can no longer be restored. Data protection law thus no longer applies; the exploitation of anonymized data is therefore unrestrictedly permissible under data protection law; legal requirements for other legal reasons, for example, the necessity of the lawful acquisition of purely factual data which from the outset have no personal reference, the licensing of databases which may be required under copyright law or for other legal reasons, etc., remain unaffected. **291**

Guiding Principle:

After anonymization of originally personal data, a personal reference is no longer necessary and may no longer be recoverable. Data protection law no longer applies and the exploitation of anonymous data is therefore irrelevant under data protection law; legal requirements on other lawful grounds remain unaffected by this. The question and possibility of re-identification with the aid of other data stored in the Big Data application must be examined closely.

[109] Gola, in: Gola/Schomerus, *BDSG*, 12th ed. 2015, § 3 mn. 44.

292 Anonymization methods can currently be subdivided into randomization and generalization methods.[110] Randomization is the process of distorting data in such a way that it can no longer be attributed to a single person (e.g. a few centimetres are subtracted from or added to the body size). Generalization means that reference data is elevated to a higher level (e.g. addresses are not stored exactly under one address, but only to an accuracy of about 10 km).

293 However, depending on the purpose of the Big Data analysis, anonymization may not be desired at all. Perhaps the personal reference should be restored at a certain point in time. Perhaps the data subject has an interest in this result. Often it will also not be clear from the outset how the data can be used for at a later point in time.

294 At the same time, it must be noted that Art. 25 (1) GDPR expressly mentions pseudonymization as a technical and organizational measure for implementing data protection principles within the framework of the *privacy by design* principle. Against this background it can be assumed that, instead of complete anonymization, a pseudonymization is often necessary, but also sufficient.

295 In addition, it must be examined at the data retrieval level whether the contracts concluded with the data suppliers or other owners of data sources (system operators, vehicle owners, etc.) permit the specific evaluation and analysis of the data to be included in such processing. If the data were obtained with the contractual purpose of being able to carry out any evaluations and analyses, the intended evaluation and analysis is also permissible in relation to the data suppliers or owners of the data sources. If the data use or license agreements concluded with this group of persons permit evaluations and analyses only for specific purposes, it must be examined beforehand whether the intended use still lies within the processing purposes for which the right to use the data concerned was granted in the relevant data use or license agreements. If the object of the evaluation and/or the purpose of the analysis exceeds the scope of the rights of use or license, the data supplier or owner of the data source shall be entitled to contractual injunctive relief and, as a consequence, claim for damages.

3. Encryption and secrecy

296 Encryption involves the use of an encryption system to convert plain text data into encoded text. The identification of the data in plain text is then only possible by the person in possession of the key. Although a third party can no longer read this encoded text, it still remains personal data, at least for those in possession of the key. Accordingly, the provisions of data protection law continue to apply.

297 Even if two contracting parties agree in a confidentiality obligation that they will only exchange personal data between themselves and thus not make it accessible to third parties, these parties are nevertheless bound by the provisions of data protection law, because – despite confidentiality – personal data is still involved.

Guiding Principle:

The encryption of personal data does not make it anonymous for all and thus does not exclude the application of data protection law. At least for those responsible who are still in possession of the key, such data remain personal data despite encryption.

---

[110] To this and to the following: Art. 29-Working Party, Opinion 5/2014 on Anonymization Techniques, p. 13 et seq.

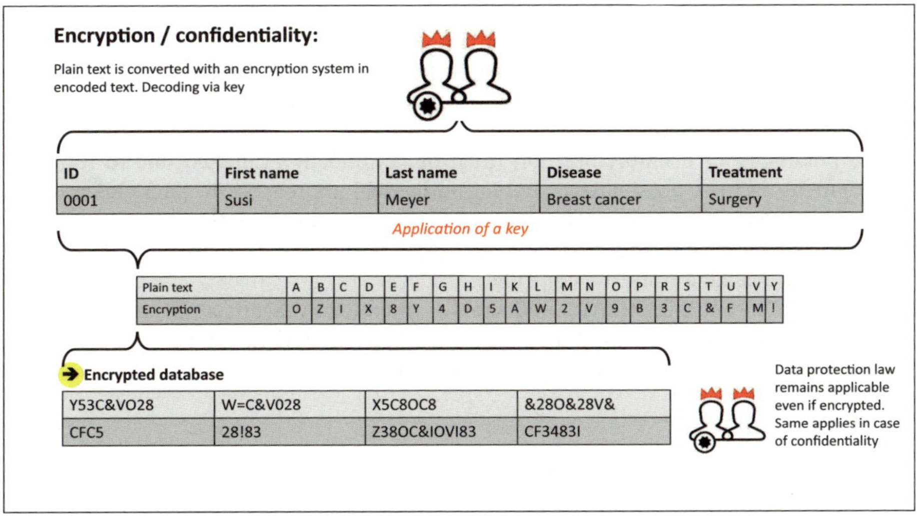

Figure 56: Encryption/confidentiality

4. De-anonymization for large amounts of data that allow re-identification

With Big Data applications and the increase in quality and quantity of the data processed therein, the risk increases that a personal reference is restored for data that was previously subjected to an (alleged) anonymization process. 298

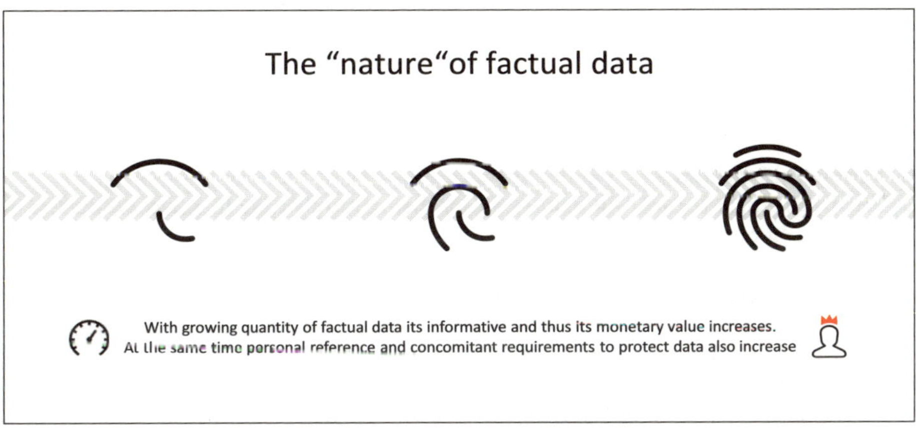

Figure 57: The *nature* of factual data

Against this background, absolute – i.e. irreversible – anonymization will often no longer be possible. Here it must be taken into account that anonymity can be lifted on the basis of certain additional knowledge and that the owner of this additional knowledge can still relate the data to a person. All such information to which the controller has access without disproportionately high expenditure must be included in any consideration of the process. The provision of raw data, i.e. data prior to anonymization, can be mentioned here as an example. However, the storage of certain information in a separate database 299 can also lead to de-anonymization without any undue effort (a common example is the combination of postal code, gender and age).

300 The requirements for protection from re-identification depend on each individual case and will have to be measured particularly in terms of the risks that could be associated with such a case: the greater the risk, the greater the requirements for the anonymization procedure.

301 The possibility of deanonymization must be continually evaluated due to technical development and the possibility of linking individual approaches to anonymization as well as to pseudonymization. For example, a reassessment of the situation can be indicated if new data is collected or – for instance through a company acquisition – new data are available from the controller.

302 The possibility of re-identification decreases when data is aggregated, i.e. when many individual data records are combined into one higher-level data record. This technique should often be considered with regard to Big Data applications.

5. Data Trustee

303 It is conceivable that a data trustee will carry out pseudonymization and manage the allocation data. The trustee agreement must then regulate the following:

- if the data trustee first receives the raw data in order to perform pseudonymization, it must completely erase the raw data after pseudonymization,
- if the data trustee is an affiliated company that provides pseudonymized data for the Big Data application with the operator of the Big Data application or with a company providing the pseudonymized data for the Big Data application, these companies may waive any instruction or voting rights to which they are legally entitled on the basis of their shareholding in the data trustee's company in order to avoid that disclosure of the allocation data be forced outside the data trustee agreement,
- and in which details the technical and organizational conditions at the data trustee are regularly audited by an independent third party (*Privacy Audit*),
- whether and under what conditions a (re)merger may take place and who may undertake it,[111]
- whether and under what cases the obligations of the data trustee are guaranteed by contractual penalties.

304 Usually, the data trustee will neither be another controller due to a lack of interest in the processing nor a processor due to a lack of instruction.[112]

305 Where appropriate, the function of the data trustee may also be divided between two different legal entities in such a way that technically both must always cooperate in order to make the allocation file available to the trustor or a beneficiary. Consequently, the two trustees mutually control each other and thus at least reduce the risk of a collusive interaction of only one trustee with one of the participants. Due to his particular professional obligations, one of the two trustees may also be a notary or a lawyer not mandated by any of the other parties, in which case the distribution of technical tasks between the two trustees should be divided in such a way that each of the two trustees fulfils the requirements of his specific role for professional technical and organizational measures (qualified data storage in appropriately secured and fail-safe computer centres and/or data storage facilities) (which may not always be the case in a business operation regularly geared to other needs).

---

[111] Ernst, in: Paal/Pauly, *GDPR*, 2nd ed. 2018, Art. 4 mn 42.

[112] Dierks, in: *Telematikplattform für Medizinische Forschungsnetze*, Rechtsgutachten zur elektronischen Datentreuhänderschaft, p. 63.

Guiding Principle:

The necessary separation between profile data and allocation data or real name data for pseudonymization can be achieved by involving a data trustee.

The strict separation of the pseudonymized data from the pseudonyms and their allocation criteria is especially to be examined when auditing a data trustee. 306

a) Requirements for a data trustee

In order to achieve a clear separation between the data trustee and the person responsible, the data trustee should be an independent person who is legally, physically and personally separated from the other parties involved; in some cases, such person must have the right to refuse to give evidence and can invoke a prohibition of seizure, as would be the case with notaries or lawyers.[113] Against the background of the required separation, a data trustee should always be selected outside the group in question in order to rule out any rights to issue instructions under company law. The data trustee should have sufficient knowledge about data protection law; in this case both requirements for the data protection officer (cf. Art. 37 (5) GDPR) and for processors (cf. Art. 28 GDPR) can be invoked. 307

For reasons of data minimization (Art. 5 (1) (c) GDPR), an agreement must be reached with the data trustee that raw data will be erased by the data trustee after pseudonymization.[114] In order to avoid any conflict of interest that might arise should the data trustee have his own interest in the data, it may even be appropriate to select someone from a different industry.[115] 308

b) Contractual penalty for breach of duties or for overcoming joint management controls

In agreements with the *data trustee*, it generally makes sense to include contractual penalties for breach of trustee duties. An appropriate and effective contractual penalty has the fundamental advantage that it underlines the seriousness of the data trustee's abstention duty and, in particular, in the event of breach, a claim for liquidated damages against the data trustee can thus enforced more easily because there would be no need to prove loss resulting from the breach. 309

V. Transmission of data from several controllers to a central Big Data application

If a Big Data application is to evaluate not only personal data collected in another context by the body operating the Big Data application, but if personal data from different controllers are to be combined in a Big Data application and combined with each other and/or with factual data and/or data collected from publicly accessible sources and evaluated and/or analysed, the sole transfer of the personal data from a body which originally collected this data to this common Big Data application shall constitute a legally-relevant transfer of personal data to the body which operates the common Big Data application and is thus responsible for the evaluation and/or analysis of the data (cf. also mn. 267 *et seq.*). 310

---

[113] Schild et al, in: *Praxis der Kommunalverwaltung*, from: 11/2015, § 33 HDSG mn. 20.

[114] Metschke/Wellenbrock, in: Berliner Beauftragter für den Datenschutz und Informationsfreiheit/Hessischer Datenschutzbeauftragter, *Datenschutz für Wissenschaft und Forschung*, p. 35.

[115] Metschke/Wellenbrock, in: Berliner Beauftragter für den Datenschutz und Informationsfreiheit/Hessischer Datenschutzbeauftragter, *Datenschutz für Wissenschaft und Forschung*, p. 35.

311 Neither the BDSG a. F. nor the GDPR contain an exception for a group of companies, meaning in this case that personal data can freely be transferred between companies of a group. Therefore, the transfer of personal data or their provision in a Big Data application to another company belonging to the same group is a transfer of personal data relevant under data protection law and thus in need of a lawful ground, i.e. for this transfer there would either have to be statutory permission or order, or consent from the data subject (cf. mn. 184 *et seq.* above).

Guiding Principle:

The pooling of a Big Data application, in particular within a corporate group, and the provision of personal data for this Big Data application by several other companies belonging to a corporate group is a transfer of personal data to the central company operating the pooled Big Data application which requires separate authorization under data protection law.

312 Such separate authorization for the transfer of personal data to another controller (e.g. within a group) operating the Big Data application is not necessary, however, if the entity operating the Big Data application continues to keep the data stocks made available to it by individual entities separate from one another either physically or by means of authorization concepts and the further processing and evaluation of these analyses per entity is carried out separately on their behalf and in accordance with their instructions (cf. mn. 133 *et seq.*). In this case, only processing would need to have the requirements applied that are set out in mn. 129 *et seq.* (for the use of cloud platforms, cf. mn. 159 *et seq.*).

313 A transmission of such data relevant to data protection law – thus requiring independent lawful ground under data protection law – only arises if a controller passed on personal data collected by it to another controller so that the latter could independently evaluate such data for its own purposes and in accordance with its own ideas and concepts (for possible conditions of the lawful ground in this case cf. mn. 181 *et seq.*).

Guiding Principle:

Personal data cannot be freely transferred between companies of a group. Therefore, transferring or providing personal data in a Big Data application to another company belonging to the group is a transfer of personal data that is relevant under data protection law and therefore in need of a lawful ground. In this case, there must either be statutory permission or order, or the data subject must have given his consent.

314 If employees of the *data-maintaining* units are delegated to the centrally operating unit of a Big Data application for its establishment or ongoing support and/or further development of that application or are otherwise transferred to that unit, the remarks under mn. 152 *et seq.* shall apply. The provision of non-personal data may be subject to restrictions arising from the license agreements or other data procurement agreements concluded in this case.

VI. Evaluation and analysis of data

1. Lawful grounds for the evaluation and analysis of personal data

315 The same lawful grounds or the consent of the data subject, which have already been described in the context of the collection of personal data, can be considered as lawful grounds for the evaluation and analysis of personal data (cf. mn. 184 *et seq.*).

However, it should be noted at this point that the substantive and formal requirements for consent already dealt with in mn. 197 *et seq.* show that consent is very rigid, i. e. that the collection and processing of personal data based on consent may only ever take place within the limits of the consent given. If these limits are exceeded, for example because it was only in the course of using a Big Data application that further analysis purposes and/or types of evaluation arose which were not taken into account in the declaration of consent, it would not be permissible to process personal data beyond the limits of the consent given. Since the processing of personal data beyond the limits of the consent given cannot be based again on a lawful ground, the consenting party would therefore have to obtain an extended consent (for example, if the evaluations/analyses to be carried out were to be expanded according to criteria or in connection with newly stored data that had not previously been mentioned in the declaration), which of course would make the entire process cumbersome and would entail the risk that no renewed consent is given. Especially in the case of Big Data applications, it is typical that the controller does not know conclusively from the outset which evaluations are to be created and with which further data from other sources these data of the data subject are to be combined and evaluated. Such evaluation and analysis tools typically continue to develop dynamically over time. In a Big Data application based on the consent of the data subjects, either the content of the consent declarations would have to be so extensive and therefore generally indefinite that they no longer meet the requirements of specificity and transparency required for their effectiveness, or the data subjects would regularly have to be asked for supplementary declarations, which would obviously be impracticable. 316

Guiding Principle:

The processing of personal data is lawful if the data subject has freely given his unambiguous consent on the basis of full and transparent information on the categories of data concerned, their use and any recipients of the data and the purposes for which they are processed, concerning the processing of his personal data as described, for one or more specific purposes.

Data protection law does not play a role in the evaluation of non-personal data. However, depending on the circumstances of the individual case, such evaluation or analysis may lead to the (unauthorized) disclosure of trade or business secrets of the data supplier or of the persons/companies concerned, so that possible risks of civil liability for damages (§ 10 GeschGehG) and criminal liability under § 23 GeschGehG should be examined in advance. 317

2. Big Data applications for the analysis of data with reference to employees or applicants

a) Applicant analysis

Personnel decisions (*People Analytics*) may be supported by data analyses, which connect personnel data, company data as well as other data with each other, and which generate prediction models. Such Big Data applications are particularly conceivable in the selection of candidates with the highest possible performance (for applications relating to existing employees, cf. mn. 352 *et seq.* below). 318

319 According to data protection law, the examination of such people analytics applications concerns two aspects:

- On the one hand, as a basis for the algorithms of people analytics applications, data of the successful employees in the company could be analysed in order to incorporate their characteristics into an algorithm for checking applications.
- On the other hand, the people analytics applications developed in this way are applied to applicant data, which in turn is processing of personal applicant data and thus relevant under data protection law.

320 Candidate analysis is not relevant for data protection law if only non-personal data, factual data and/or anonymized data are included in the algorithm for creating a benchmark for the analysis of candidate data. However, at the data retrieval level, any restrictions from agreements concluded with the suppliers of these data must of course be observed (cf. mn. 217 *et seq.*).

321 **aa) Collection and Processing of Employee Data in Developing Algorithms for People Analytics Applications.** For development of *role models* as a basis for developing algorithms in people analytics applications, information about the training, profession, skills, performance or work behaviour of successful employees can be considered personal data under data protection law in the sense of Art. 4(1) GDPR. Even special types of personal data in the sense of Art. 9 (1) GDPR can be considered for the development of such role models, for example data on the health of successful employees in the company, their union membership or even – if available – their genetic data.

322 It may be considered to develop such role models using only data from key employees who have already reached a certain status in the company. However, the anonymization of this data for the purpose of avoiding the application of data protection regulations is unlikely to be suitable as to the small number would unlikely completely rule out re-identification of the individual employees. For this reason, the collection and analysis of employee data for the purpose of developing *role models* already constitutes processing of relevance under data protection law, which accordingly requires a lawful ground.

323 **(1) Specific justification for employee data:** A justification of this data collection and processing from Art. 88 (1) GDPR in conjunction with § 26 (1) sentence 1 BDSG must already be untenable solely because the collection and analysis of such data is not necessary for the execution of the employer-employee relationship with the employees selected as *role models*. Since the data of applicants are not required for this phase of the development of people analytics applications, a lawful ground from establishing an employment relationship in the sense of § 26 (1) sentence 1 BDSG is equally irrelevant.

324 **(2) Justification through a balance of interests:** The only justification remaining for the collection and evaluation of data of successful employees for the development of role models for people analytics applications is therefore based on the condition of overriding general interests in Art. 6 (1) (f) GDPR, which is applicable, according to prevailing opinion beyond the special legal situation for the processing of employee data in § 26 BDSG.

325 The safeguarding of the legitimate interests of the entity responsible for a people analytics application is obvious, as that entity is entitled to recruit only those candidates who are particularly likely to have a successful career in the company.

326 The answer to the question as to whether the protected interests of the employees prevail essentially depends on the categories of data with reference to these *role models* to be included in the algorithm. In the case of data relating to the training and/or qualification of such employees, the overriding interest in not processing this data to

develop role models in people analytics applications is not readily apparent. However, there are clear overriding interests of these employees in the case of health data, genetic data or sexual orientation data. These examples represent two ends of a spectrum which of course contains other scenarios that are not so clear cut.

(3) Consent. Legal uncertainties can be avoided by obtaining the consent of those employees whose data would be used to develop algorithms for a people analytics application. 327

As already explained in mn. 197 *et seq.* above, consent – in addition to fulfilling all other formal and substantive requirements – is only effective when given voluntarily. Whether such free will can exist in an employment relationship has often been disputed. In the opinion of the German Federal Labour Court, a general invalidity of the consent of employees cannot be assumed only because there was no free decision within the framework of an employment relationship.[116] Recital 155 GDPR shows that this must also be possible under the GDPR and the German regulations issued on its basis in § 26 BDSG. This possibility is thus already made evident in § 26 (2) BDSG that *"for the evaluation of the voluntariness of the consent in particular the dependence of the employee existing in the employment relationship as well as the circumstances under which the consent was given are to be considered"*. Voluntary choice could therefore exist, in particular, if a legal or economic advantage exists for the employee or if the employer and the employee pursue similar interests. 328

On the basis of these examples mentioned in § 26 (2) sentence 2 BDSG, one could argue at best that the department responsible for a people analytics application and the key employees of this department who are used for the development of role models pursue similar interests insofar as they are both interested in the selection of suitable applicants and the most successful career path possible in the company for these applicants. However, this argument probably only applies to key employees whose personal data are to be used to select applicants in their own field. 329

In addition, however, the assessment of the voluntary nature of the consent given may of course be based on the fact that, in connection with the request for such consent, the voluntary nature of the consent is emphasized and, at the same time, that refusal of consent is neither documented nor leads to any disadvantages for the employee concerned. 330

In each case the consent should be obtained in writing (§ 26 (2) sentence 3 BDSG), thus as embodied declaration of intent with handwritten signature of the employee concerned (§ 126 BGB), not least in order to abide at all times by the requirement of the justification and the proof of the legitimacy of the data processing according to Art. 5 (2) GDPR. 331

As always, if data collection and further processing is based solely on consent, the employee concerned may revoke his consent at any time in accordance with the principle of good faith. 332

bb) Analysis of applicant data in people analytics applications. It is permissible to people analytics applications on applicant data resulting from employment application documents or from an interview (§ 26 (1) sentence 1 BDSG). This requires that the comparison of such data with features of particularly successful key employees of the employer is necessary to establish an employment relationship. 333

As long as the people analytics application does not contain any discriminatory elements and does not contain criteria which are not covered by the employer's right to 334

[116] BAG, *NZA* 2015, 604.

ask questions in the application procedure, the criterion *"to establish of an employment relationship"* should be validated since an employer may legitimately base his recruitment decision on objective criteria which lead to the expectation of a successful career in the company.

335 A people analytics application could be used to analyse personality traits of the applicants such as, for example, a graphological assessment of the handwritten CV or an analysis of written work of the applicant for personality traits. However, such a people analytics analysis would probably only be permissible with the prior consent of the applicant due to the associated impact of the personality right protected by Art. 1 (1) and Art. 2 (1) GG. Due to the special situation of employment applications, there are also considerable doubts about the voluntariness of such consent, which could lead to the inadmissibility of such a people analytics application.

336 However, if the potential employer analyses written samples of the applicant's work, such as essays or dissertations, with the aid of plagiarism recognition software, this should in turn be permissible under § 26 (1) sentence 1 BDSG because the employer can probably cite a legitimate interest in not wanting to employ a plagiarist, which would fall under the criterion *"establish of an employment relationship"*.[117]

Guiding Principle:

The use of people analytics applications for applicant analysis has a double dimension in terms of data protection law, on the one hand, with regard to the key employees whose data is used to develop the algorithm and, on the other hand, with regard to the applicants. Evaluations of employment application documents or the results of job interviews may only be used in association with an employer's right to ask questions in job interviews.

b) Employee analysis

337 People analytics applications in use in existing employment relationships include, in particular, analyses for the purpose of employee retention or language analyses as well as analysing data relating to the progress of a project.

338 **aa) Analyses for the purpose of employee retention.** Employee retention analyses rely in particular on data from social networks or publicly available data that an employer can obtain and collect through the use of search engines.

339 **bb) People analytics application with reference to data from social networks.** Where analyses for the purpose of employee retention are concerned, it is recognized in theory that an employer may view and process data of his employees which they post to occupation-related social networks since, through such act, the employees generally release this data for occupation-related purposes.[118]

340 Data in other social networks may be collected by the employer and processed in the context of analyses for the purpose of employee retention at least if these data have been released by the data subject to the public and not only to a limited circle of users.[119]

341 **cc) People analytics application with reference to other publicly accessible data.** The same applies to publicly accessible data relating to employees which the employer can generally find and process by using internet search engines.

---

[117] Cf. Dzida, *NZA* 2017, 541 (544).

[118] Dzida, *NZA* 2017, 541 (544); Faust, *NZA* 2010, 427 (431).

[119] Just as Dzida, *NZA* 2017, 541 (545).

dd) Limit of people analytics applications. Although *personality screening* constitutes a limit to people analytics applications and their use for existing employees, the borderline to inadmissible personality screening is unclear.[120] The boundary to inadmissible personality screening will probably only be crossed when the collected data are close to the core of a personality right and are processed into a prognosis that is also close to the core of personality rights. A people analytics application which, for example, aims to determine whether employees are generally prone to criminal offences, is therefore likely to be problematic.[121] However it might also be possible to differentiate here whether the employee in question is working in a particularly sensitive position and whether the analysis in question refers only to relevant criminal offences (e.g. in the case of armoured car drivers with regard to property offences). 342

Guiding Principle:

For the purpose of employee retention, the employer may access and analyse employee data from social networks and publicly accessible data insofar as it can obtain and collect this data through the use of search engines. The same applies to employee data in professional social networks. People analytics applications, on the other hand, which cross the already blurred lines of an inadmissible personality screening, are not permitted.

c) Stress and mood analyses

Finally, stress and mood analyses are technically possible based on speech files from telephone conversations or other recordings and which focus on the use of certain words, pitch, speaking speed and breathing rhythm.[122] Apart from the fact that, under German law, the criminal law barriers in § 201 German Criminal Code (*Strafgesetzbuch*, StGB) must be observed when monitoring and recording telephone conversations, stress and mood analyses of conversations and telephone conversations of an employee or job applicant may only be permitted with their prior consent;[123] mn. 197 *et seq.* apply accordingly. 343

Guiding Principle:

People analytics analysis for the purpose of identifying retention measures using social media data may be performed if the social media is either job-related or accessible to everyone without any access restrictions. The limit of people analytics applications is reached when it is used for personality screening, which is the case, for example, regarding stress and mood analyses from employee language files.

d) Databases for project analysis

Data from or relating to projects carried out within a company could subsequently be evaluated and analysed in a permissible manner with regard to conclusions and consequences that can be drawn from the completed course of a project (*lessons learned*), even if personal data are used and evaluated. An employer cannot be denied the right to evaluate the data reflecting the project work of individual employees under objective criteria in order to gain objective insights from this analysis for the structure and organization of future projects. Even if this did not yet come close to personality screening, one should bear in mind in any case that such data can be suitable for 344

[120] Däubler, *Gläserne Belegschaften*, 7th ed. 2017, mn. 120.
[121] So the opinion of von Dzida, *NZA* 2017, 541 (545).
[122] Cf. Gola/Pötters/Wronka, *Handbuch Arbeitnehmerdatenschutz*, 7th ed. 2016, mn. 1315.
[123] Zoebisch, *DuD* 2011, 394 (397); Dzida, *NZA* 2017, 541 (545).

performance monitoring and control. Even if the employer should not, in fact, use these data for such latter purposes, the mere suitability of the data and the system collecting these data are sufficient to trigger a co-determination right of the employee representatives responsible (works council, in Germany § 87 (1) No. 6 Works Constitution Act – BetrVG).

345 If the relevant employee representative group were ignored or if a corresponding Big Data analysis were carried out contrary to the vote of the employee representation in question, the relevant employee representation could not only seek an injunction, but could also enforce it on a short-term basis by obtaining a temporary injunction without the employer having been heard. As soon as a corresponding interim injunction would have been served, it would have to be complied with by the employer; since an objection to an interim injunction or an appeal against a court order does not have a suspensive effect, the introduction of such a Big Data project analysis system would not be able to take place until a legally binding decision has been reached on any appeal lodged by the employer.

> **Guiding Principle:**
>
> Data from or relating to projects within the company can be analysed retrospectively for conclusions and consequences from the course of the project; any rights of co-determination of the responsible employee representative must be taken into account.

e) Prohibition of completely automatically generated individual decisions

346 Finally, Art. 22 (1) GDPR must be considered with regard to the use of people analytics applications. According to this provision, the data subject (i.e. an applicant or employee) has the right not to be subjected to a decision based solely on automated processing (including profiling) which produces legal effects concerning him or similarly significantly affects him. This does not apply if the decision is based on the applicant's or employee's explicit consent (Art. 22 (2) (c) GDPR; the other exceptional circumstances mentioned in Art. 22 (2) GDPR are not relevant here).

> **Guiding Principle:**
>
> Art. 22 GDPR is to be observed for any use of people analytics applications. According to this provision, the data subject concerned has a claim to a final decision made by a person, taking into account his individual objections.

3. Collective agreements

347 According to § 26 (4) sentence 1 BDSG (which is based on Art 88 GDPR), the processing of personal data of employees, including even special categories of personal data in the sense of Art. 9 (1) GDPR, for purposes of an employment relationship but also on the basis of collective agreements made by companies located in Germany, can be permissible. The contracting parties of a collective agreement (works council and employer's management) must, however, observe the limits and conditions in Art. 88 (2) GDPR, i.e. appropriate and special measures must be taken in such collective agreements in order to safeguard human dignity, the legitimate interests and the fundamental rights of the employees affected, in particular with regard to the transparency of processing, the transfer of personal data within a group of companies or a group of companies exercising a joint economic activity, and any monitoring systems installed at the workplace. Whether and to what extent the same also applies to employee

representatives for companies located outside Germany is governed by the applicable national provisions of the BetrVG.

Thus, it is not yet clear whether a collective agreement can effectively include any data processing procedures, which are relevant with regard to data protection law, if such procedures which would not be lawful according to Art. 6 (1) (b)–(f) GDPR and § 26 (1) BDSG, but which could only be rendered lawful by means of consent from the data subject in the sense of Art. 6 (1) (a) GDPR. Consent is, however, a highly personal manner whereby only the data subject himself on the divulgence of his own personal data. It is therefore clear that consent cannot be delegated to another and thus a works council cannot be entitled on the basis its mandate to conclude collective agreements to also make decisions for employees regarding the revelation of their own personal data, which moves outside of the legal permission as described in § 26 (1) BDSG.[124] **348**

Under works councils' legislation, this limitation results from the authority to conclude collective agreements, which is part of the mandate of a works council, as in § 75 (2) BetrVG, according to which the employer and works council must protect and promote the free development of the personality of the employees of the company in question. Since the right to informational self-determination exists from the fundamental right to the free development of personality, it follows from this mandate of the works council under the applicable legislation that the works council cannot conclude any collective agreements which would lead to the disclosure of personal data of the employees beyond the limits of the statutory grounds for permission. Thus, if the processing of employee-related data in people analytics applications is to be based on a collective agreement, the collective agreement must be legally permissible and thus valid. This is always the case if the processing of employee-related data in people analytics applications permitted in the collective agreement takes place within the limits of the legally-permitted circumstances and the collective agreement is therefore only a variation thereof in relation to the specific people analytics application. **349**

Guiding Principle:

Collective agreements are only suitable as a legal ground for data protection for people analytics applications if and to the extent that they justify measures which could also be justified on the basis of statutory conditions of permission.

A collective agreement cannot replace consent that would be required in the absence of a collective agreement.

4. Rights of the works council to participate (in Germany § 87 (1) No. 6 BetrVG)

Pursuant to § 87 (1) No. 6 BetrVG, the works council has a right of co-determination in the introduction, development and ongoing operation of a people analytics application if the people analytics application in question is a *"technical facility designed to monitor the conduct or performance of employees"*. The *designation* of such an application for performance monitoring is already accepted if the people analytics application only makes it technically possible to generate corresponding performance measurement and monitor data, regardless of whether the employer actually uses such data for this purpose. As the employment purposes of people analytics applications have shown (cf. mn. 339 *et seq.* above), people analytics applications are not only theoretically suitable for this purpose but are even designed to generate performance measurement and monitor data. Therefore, the introduction of people analytics applications is always subject to co-determination. **350**

[124] Cf. Ernst, *ZD* 2017, 110 (111).

351 If the introduction of a people analytics application has not already been approved by the works council or if a people analytics application has been introduced despite refusal by the relevant employee representative body, a temporary injunction may be sought to prohibit the introduction of the people analytics application.

Guiding Principle:
If performance measurement or monitoring is even possible through people analytics applications, the introduction and use of a people analytics application is subject to co-determination, i.e. with the approval of the works council.

5. Special cases

a) Scoring

352 According to the provision in § 28b BDSG a.F., in force before 25 May 2018, a probability value for certain future behaviour of the data subject may be collected or used (scoring) for the purpose of deciding on the establishment, execution or termination of a contractual relationship with the data subject (e.g. the granting of a cash or trade credit) where:
- the data used to calculate the probability value based on a scientifically-recognized mathematical-statistical method can be demonstrated to be relevant to calculating the probability of the behaviour in question,
- in the case of the calculating the probability value by a credit agency, the prerequisites for the transmission of the data used in accordance with § 29 BDSG a.F. have been met and, in all other cases, (i.e. the calculation of the probability value not by a credit agency but, for example, by the lender himself) the prerequisites for the permissible use of the data used to calculate the probability value in accordance with Art. 6 (1) GDPR are met,
- more than address data are used for the calculation of the probability value, and
- in the case of the use of address data, the data subject has been informed of the intended use of such data prior to the calculation of the probability value. The information shall be documented.

353 The GDPR no longer contains specific regulations for scoring; however, the prerequisites described above from § 28b BDSG a.F. have been adopted in § 31 BDSG.

354 The use of a probable value determined by credit agencies (e.g. Creditreform, SCHUFA or Arvato-Infoscore) about the willingness of a natural person to pay and his ability to pay is only permissible in the case of the inclusion of information about claims if the requirements under to § 31 (1) 1 BDSG have been met and only such claims about services still outstanding and in default have been taken into account. In addition, the following claims can be lawfully included:
- such claims have been established by a final or provisionally enforceable judgment for which a debt instrument pursuant to § 794 ZPO exists,
- such claims have been established in accordance with § 178 German Insolvency Code (InsO) that have not been disputed by the debtor at the verification meeting,
- such claims have expressly been acknowledged by the debtor,
- in cases where the debtor has been reminded in writing at least twice after the due date of the claim, the first reminder of which is at least four weeks old. Moreover, the debtor has been informed beforehand, but at the earliest at the first reminder, of a possible verification or inclusion in the rating by a credit agency and the debtor has not contested the claim, or

- whose underlying contractual relationship can be terminated without notice due to payment arrears and in respect of which the debtor has previously been informed of possible consideration by a credit agency.

In accordance with the principle laid down in Art. 5 (2) GDPR, according to which the controller must be able to prove the lawfulness of his processing of personal data at any time, the aforementioned requirements for scoring must be examined before undertaking corresponding scoring activities. Furthermore, the results of the verification and the underlying business processes must be documented in such a way that the existence of each individual admissibility requirement can be explained and proven. **355**

Guiding Principle:

Scoring using Big Data applications is only permitted in accordance with the provisions of § 28b BDSG a.F. or from 25 May 2018 in accordance with Art. 6 (1) (f) GDPR in conjunction with § 31 BDSG.

b) User profile

Until 24 May 2018, the creation of user profiles in Germany was still permitted under the conditions laid down in § 15 (3) TMG (though it was disputed whether this sufficiently transposed Art. (3) ePrivacy-Directive) and has already been discussed in mn. 66 above. From 25 May 2018, the criteria developed to § 15 (3) TMG are to be considered at most in the context of an overriding interest situation as in Art. 6 (1) (f) GDPR (cf. mn. 192 *et seq.*). In its paper of 26 April 2018, "On the applicability of the TMG for non-public places starting from 25 May 2018", the conference of the Independent Data Protection Authorities of the German Federation and States hold the opinion that, due to the primacy of the GDPR, the statutory data protection regulations of the TMG are no longer to be used. For profiling under the GDPR in all other respects, the same regulations are to be considered as with the introduction of systems for automated decision-making, as regulated in Art. 22 GDPR. **356**

VII. Continuation of personal reference even after evaluation and analysis of data

1. Analysis of personal data records insofar as personal references still exist or can be restored

Data records stored in a Big Data application with the complete address or other additional information suitable for re-identification personal data because, in principle, they can be traced back by the controller to the actual individuals. This means that they are to be treated as personal data until they are erased. **357**

Insofar as intended analyses of personal data records are aimed at individual characteristics of the natural persons concerned, the preparation of these analyses must also be checked for their legitimacy under data protection law. As is also the case for all previous steps regarding the structure and maintenance of a Big Data application, the evaluation of these personal data records for producing analyses must be examined if such processing can be supported on the basis of contract performance, as in Art. 6 (1) (b) GDPR. If this is not relevant, the evaluation of these personal data records could also be supported for the production of analyses on the basis of overriding interests as in Art. 6 (1) (f) GDPR. In this case, a protected interest of the controller can usually be recognized in all rules regulating the production of such analyses. However, the general **358** interest of the data subject in avoiding the processing of personal data which he has not initiated or which does not benefit him are often an obstacle to processing the personal data. In such a case, evaluating personal data records for the production of analyses cannot be based on a case of a balance of interests, as in Art. 6 (1) (f) GDPR.

359 The only remaining option for a lawful ground would therefore be the interested party's consent to a later evaluation of his data records by the controller responsible for the Big Data application in order create the analyses. However, the risks and disadvantages associated with obtaining and managing consent (cf. mn. 197 *et seq.*) would be avoided if evaluations of the relevant data sets on a pseudonymized basis were sufficient for the analyses.

> **Guiding Principle:**
> The processing of personal evaluations or analyses by supply to third parties is a transfer of personal data which requires separate lawful basis under data protection law.

2. Evaluation of pseudonymized data records

360 Under German law, the evaluation of pseudonymized data records in user profiles can no longer be based on the legal ground of permission in § 15 (3) TMG since application of the GDPR has priority. In other European countries, of course, the evaluation of pseudonymized data records in user profiles will be governed by the GDPR only. The basic rule outlined in mn. 357 *et seq.* above therefore remains unchanged.

3. Evaluation of non-personal data, factual data or anonymized data

361 If solely non-personal data, factual data or anonymized data stored in a Big Data application are evaluated, and if this evaluation does not result in a new personal reference owing to a combination of data occurring in the evaluation, such evaluation is not relevant under data protection law and therefore generally permissible without restriction insofar as there are no other restrictions resulting from the agreements on the provision and use of this source data obtained from third parties.

362 If, in the course of such an evaluation, a new personal reference arises precisely due to the combination of different categories of data, the restrictions on the processing of personal data apply again, as already explained in mn. 357 *et seq.* above.

VIII. Use of personal data or person-related evaluation/analysis results

363 If the evaluation and analysis results from Big Data applications are utilized, for example by making them available to third parties, while maintaining a personal reference, this use constitutes further processing and, in case of doubt, also transmission. This renewed use and/or transmission process requires a lawful ground either by statutory permission or by consent, as outlined in Art. 6 (1) GDPR. The lawful grounds relevant for this have already been explained under mn. 357 *et seq.* above; they are valid for the further use and transmission of the relevant evaluation and/or analysis results to third parties.

Guiding Principle:

If evaluation and analysis results from Big Data applications are used commercially, for example by making them available to third parties, while maintaining a personal reference, this use constitutes further processing and, in case of doubt, also transmission, which require a lawful ground either by a statutory permission or order, or by consent. Otherwise, any usage restrictions arising from the data usage agreements with third parties must be observed.

In addition to limitations under data protection law, restrictions on the use of non- **364**
personal data may also result, for example, from licenses or other data procurement agreements concluded on the basis of the underlying raw data or from the fact that the use of such evaluation/analysis results ultimately meant the disclosure of trade or business secrets in violation of §§ 6, 10 and 23 GeschGehG.

Guiding Principle:

The evaluation and analysis of personal data with other data – whether personal or not – is itself a processing activity, which requires a lawful ground either by statutory permission or order, or by consent. In addition, for each planned evaluation or analysis, it must be examined whether the planned evaluations and analyses are still within the contractual limitations of the granted rights of use or license.

I. ERASURE OBLIGATIONS

All data, documents and any information contained therein, whether personal or not, are owned by someone who is responsible for the life cycle of the data/document in question and for compliance with the legal conditions. In other words, the assignee of all rights and obligations associated with the date/document and its life cycle. The life cycle begins with the collection, processing, modification, storage, transmission and analysis of data and ends with its erasure. 365

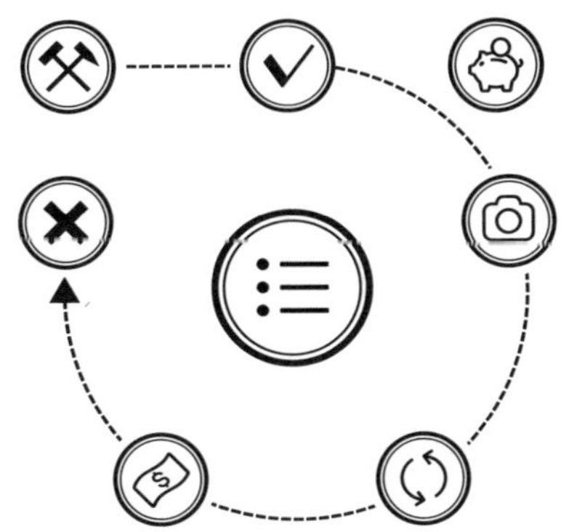

Figure 58: Example: Fulfilment of purpose

- Legally, there are retention obligations and periods for many, but not all document types. A *retention period* is a period prescribed by law, the articles of association or purpose for the mandatory retention of documents and/or data. The affected documents and/or data may not be erased or removed before the expiry of a retention period. Upon expiry of such period, the respective documents and/or data may be erased with regard to the purpose connected to such period. If these documents and/or data contain personal data, they must be erased, unless there is a legal situation allowing for further storage beyond the retention period or agreement from the data subject. Retention periods can have different starting points, which are not necessarily identical with the time of their first collection by the data controller. The end of the respective retention periods also depends on this as well as on the duration of the retention period per data category.
- A *erasure period* is a period which each business division defines itself by applying legal requirements to the data and/or document types occurring in the division. An erasure period is adapted to the specific processing, in particular, the purpose and legal basis of the processing. An erasure period for documents and/or data containing personal data describes the earliest point in time at which the lawfulness of the respective processing no longer exists in accordance with Art. 6 (1) GDPR. Upon expiry of such period, the documents and/or data covered therein must be erased. An erasure period can be at least as long as a simultaneously applicable retention period.

- In the case of physical files, *retention* means storing them in such a way that the stored files can also be accessed, and the individual file can be retrieved. With electronically available data (including scanned documents), *retention* ultimately means the saving and archiving of the databases in such a way that the individual data record can be retrieved.

366 At the end of the retention periods, obligations to erase such data and documents correspond to some of the stored/archived data: the provisions of data protection law must be observed whenever such data records and documents contain personal data. According to Art. 4(2) GDPR, every single process of collection, processing, transmission, but also every form of storage (under data protection law, storage is also regarded as a form of data processing, so that all processing requirements explained below also apply to every form of storage of personal data) of personal data in automated files is fundamentally inadmissible, unless the following is true of every single processing process:

- a legal situation allowing for data retention,
- a legal situation expressly requiring storage,
  or
- the data subject had consented to storage for an unlimited period of time.

367 As soon as the legal circumstances no longer permit or even order the storage of personal data or the period of consent to storage or the consent itself has expired, any further authorization to retain this data no longer exists. They must therefore be erased.

Guiding Principle:

All data and each document with the information contained therein is subject to a retention period with different start and end points for each data category. When a retention period ends, be it for legal, corporate or other prescribed reasons, the personal data in question must be erased. This is because the end of the retention period is linked to the end of the legal circumstances which had permitted or even expressly prescribed storage. Once the period has lapsed, a lawful ground for further retention only exists in exceptional cases, often on the basis a balance of interests pursuant to Art. 6 (1) (f) GDPR.

368 It cannot be ruled out that several statutory provisions, which permit or even require the retention of personal data, may complement each other. For example, the period for which the retention of personal data was even expressly ordered (e.g. commercial and fiscal retention obligations), may under some circumstances be followed by another period going beyond that in which the further storage of personal data is no longer required by law, but which may still be maintained by the controller on legal grounds of permission (for example (i) on the basis of an obligation of the manufacturer of products, during the entire period in which product liability claims can be asserted, to be able to react effectively to them with the help of documentation from the design, production and/or distribution process, or (ii) on the basis of a manufacturer's warranty covering many years or even the entire life cycle of a product). Legal retention obligations can, but do not have to, automatically end the life cycle of the document in question with their expiration.

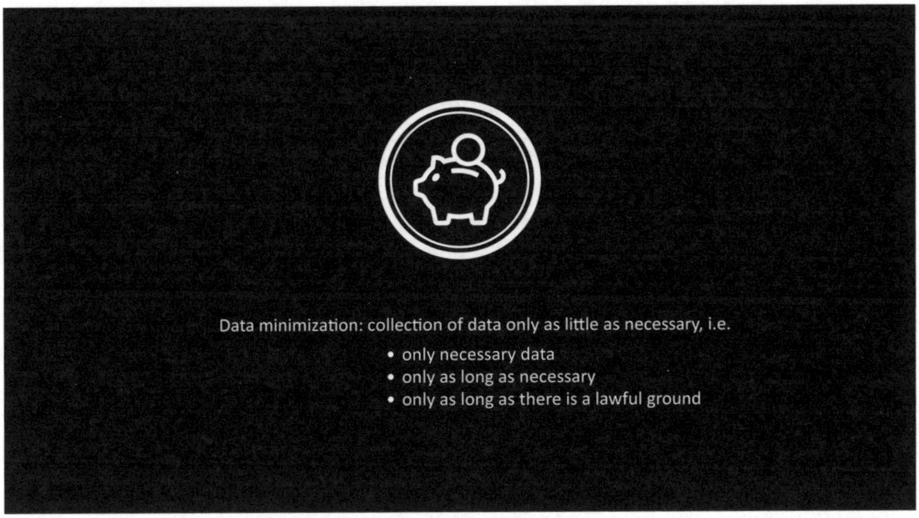

Figure 59: Principle of data minimization

In any case, the principle of data minimization as defined in Art. 5 (1) (c) GDPR must be taken into account as a corrective mechanism when examining whether there are legal circumstances which permit the continued storage of personal data. According to this principle, the processing of personal data is limited to data which are appropriate and relevant to their purpose and absolutely necessary for achieving the purpose of the processing. In addition, the second corrective mechanism is the principle of storage limitation laid down in Art. 5 (1) (e) GDPR: personal data may be stored no longer than is necessary for processing purposes. 369

If non-personal data (purely factual data or anonymized data) are to be collected or processed, no data protection restrictions apply to their use and subsequent archiving when the data cannot be assigned to a natural person via an IP address or other points of contact, for example because they were obtained from M2M communication,. This does not mean, however, that such data may be used completely freely; rather, restrictions on use and duration of use must be observed from various legal perspectives (e.g. for reasons of observance of virtual householder's rights, of licensing provisions for software or databases, even for open source or open data products), which, in turn, make it necessary to erase such data or even return it to the original supplier once the permitted duration of use has expired. 370

Guiding Principle:
Non-personal data may also be subject to obligations under license agreements or other protective rights in favour of third parties to erase the data stored in a Big Data application.

I. Development of an erasure concept

Each part of the data stock of a Big Data application that is used for the same technical purpose in the company forms a *data type*. The content of the information of the data in the data type is further distinguished: data with similar information content form a *data category* (e.g. surname, first name, address, religious affiliation). Whether 371 such data is archived in physical documents in files, whether it is electronically available data, or in which systems this data is stored does not matter; erasure rules for this data are to be equally applied to specific applications as to data generated and processed in business activities based on typical office communication applications (Word, Excel or Access). The same applies to file databases, which must also be structured in such a way that individual files can be found again.

372 Rules for erasing data from a Big Data application can result from the following:

- legal regulations which prescribe the retention of data and documents for a certain period of time (archiving obligations), upon the expiry of which there is no right to further retention and therefore erasure is mandatory;
- company or group internal guidelines and (central) instructions;
- statutory provisions on limitation or preclusion periods for claims whose establishment or defence requires or at least helps to obtain certain data and documents. Here the purpose for which data and documents can be used and the legal framework set for this purpose plays a critical role;
- with regard to employee data, collective agreements such as collective bargaining agreements and works agreements may also provide for limitation or preclusion periods in individual cases for the assertion of claims for which data or documents are necessary to substantiate or defend them;
- contracts in which obligations concerning the return, retention and erasure of the data in question have been bilaterally agreed upon (e.g. license agreements);
- any works agreements concluded with local works councils;
- finally, there will be many types of data for which only the intended use will determine the duration of the retention period.

373 In order to develop an erasure concept for a Big Data application, it is therefore essential to first identify each unique type of data used in the Big Data application and, at the same time, to determine the technical purpose for these data or documents that may extend beyond the Big Data application. An erasure rule can be defined for each data type and the concomitant data categories using the criteria listed above. Each erasure rule consists of both an erasure period and a start time from which this period is counted.

Guiding Principle:

For each Big Data application, an erasure concept must be developed in which an erasure rule consisting of an erasure and a start time, from which this erasure period begins, is defined for each type of data and the data categories used in the Big Data application.

II. Implementation of a data erasure concept

374 Once the erasure rule has been clearly defined, its implementation by the controller can then be determined. This can either be done automatically by implementing erasure routines, or by organizational measures in which manual erasure or, in the case of actual records, their destruction in accordance with their data and information protection type, is carried out at the time determined by the erasure rules.

375 How erasure rules are implemented for electronically-stored data thus depends on the technical possibilities that the application can offer in the specific system environment of the responsible department. The lack of automated erasure procedures in individual applications or document destruction procedures therefore does not release the user from compliance with erasure rules, let alone from the obligation to develop an

erasure concept. The continued storage of personal data beyond the legally permissible maximum duration is therefore also an administrative offence, which can be punished with fines and other consequences, if the systems in which the data are stored do not allow for automated erasure procedures.

III. Necessary elements of a data erasure concept?

1. Description of retention and erasure obligations

Personal data may only be retained as long as this is expressly required by a statutory provision, as long as retention is permitted by law or with the consent of the data subject. If none of these conditions exists (any longer), the relevant personal data is to be erased due to the legal prohibition of retaining personal data where there is no valid lawful ground for doing so. **376**

For non-personal data, the (license) contractual return or erasure obligations are to be observed first and foremost. Even if such obligations have not been expressly agreed in a contract, the right to use the data ends upon expiry of the right of use. Erasing the object of the license ensures that– even only accidental – continued uses, which would otherwise infringe an industrial property right, do not occur and the company is thus not exposed to claims due to industrial property right infringements. **377**

2. What is the relevant law for determining retention and erasure obligations?

Both with regard to commercial and fiscal retention obligations as well as concerning data protection law, the law of the country where the controller (= business) has its seat is decisive. This also applies if this business uses IT infrastructure services of a service provider located in another state (the servers used are located elsewhere)! Collective agreements apply only to the business for which they were concluded by the parties of that business. **378**

The situation is different for group and central instructions therein. Of course, these apply equally to all affiliates worldwide, no matter where they are based, but they must comply with the applicable national laws at the headquarters of each affiliate. **379**

3. Legal retention obligations

Under German law, the most prominent examples of a mandatory statutory obligation to retain and archive personal data are under commercial law (§§ 238, 239, 257, 261 German Commercial Code – HGB) and tax law (§§ 147 German Tax Code – AO), which provide for retention periods of six years and ten years, respectively. **380**

German law also features comparable statutory provisions that permit the retention of certain categories of data for certain periods of time, however do not make it mandatory. An example of this is the legal right under § 97 (3) sentence 2 TKG to retain traffic data from telecommunications connections that are required to calculate a charge for up to six months after sending an invoice. If individual data categories are required for this purpose, they may be retained, and the company must decide whether and to what extent it wishes to make use of this right of retention. The data must be erased if the company decides against retention or if the data is not necessary to achieve the purpose in question. **381**

4. Erasure periods for archiving data on the basis of consent

382 If personal data are stored and kept by the person responsible on the basis of consent given by the data subject, the subject matter of the consent determines the permitted duration of retention. The right to the continued retention of the relevant personal data expires at the end of a retention period resulting from the content of the consent or a consent limited in advance. Unless there is another lawful ground for continued retention for the period thereafter, the relevant personal data must be erased from the Big Data application.

383 The same applies if the data subject withdraws his consent in accordance with Art. 7 (3) GDPR. Retention of the pertinent data remains permissible until the withdrawal takes effect upon receipt of the withdrawal declaration by the controller: the retention of personal data in a Big Data application based on this consent must be terminated immediately.

384 If the controller has transferred personal data to a third party on the basis of consent, such consent will regularly also constitute authority for the third party to further process and store the personal data transferred to him. If the data subject withdraws such consent, the recipient's right to further process the personal data also ends. Although the GDPR does not expressly include any obligation to inform the third party of a withdraw consent received only by him, a corresponding obligation will, however, exist for person responsible for transmitting personal data to a third party. This obligation will at least consist in the application of the legal right expressed in Art. 17 (2) GDPR (right to be forgotten) and include a corresponding duty to inform on the part of the recipient of a withdrawal declaration to also inform those relevant third parties of the existence of a withdrawal declaration.

5. Determining erasure periods from the purpose of use, the applicable statutory provisions and the business process reference of the processed data

385 Even if legal storage obligations and periods do not exist, unlimited storage of personal data in Big Data applications is inadmissible for the reasons mentioned above. In this case, erasure periods must be derived from the specific purpose for which the data types are used, whereby the purpose is in turn determined by the purpose of the Big Data application for which the data categories are used. Thus, it cannot be ruled out that individual data categories may be used in several business processes and may therefore be subject to different erasure periods. For example, the data category *address data of customers* is legally required for the archiving of commercial letters mailed out by the controller, in particular invoices, for a period of ten years from the end of the year in which the commercial letter was sent. However, if the customer relationship has already ended, for example, five years after the relevant invoice was issued, the customer data must be erased in the CRM system of the responsible office but must still be stored in their administrative systems in order to fulfil the archiving obligation.

386 However, return and erasure periods can also result from contractual obligations. License agreements in particular regularly contain provisions according to which the licensed material must be returned to the licensor and/or completely erased from the licensee's systems at the end of the license agreement. Such specific erased obligations, however, can hardly be integrated into a generally valid erased concept aimed at regular erasure processes for ensuring GDPR compliance.

6. Types of data for which the intended use provides the basis for determining the retention period

a) Determining a purpose and associated lawful ground for personal data

When personal data are collected, it is first necessary to determine the purpose for which the relevant data categories are required and therefore why they are to be collected. In many cases – for example in the use of data in Big Data applications – the data initially collected for a specific purpose and then later processed for other purposes. This *change of purpose* is only permissible under certain conditions (cf. mn. 234 *et seq.*). **387**

b) Purpose and retention of non-personal data

In general, non-personal data can be retained indefinitely if there are no contractual obligations to return, erase or destroy the data. Of course, this presupposes that such non-personal data have been lawfully acquired and/or collected by the data controller. If a necessary examination of all databases of a responsible company reveals that a database, even with non-personal data, has not been collected or otherwise obtained in a legally permissible manner, such databases shall also be erased regardless of whether a purpose still exists. **388**

However, there is no legal obligation to erase or destroy non-personal data if they have been lawfully obtained or collected. Here it is at best a question of economic viability why such data remain stored even if they are no longer used by the authority or otherwise: the further retention of such data only uses resources and thus costs money without any corresponding added value. **389**

> **Guiding Principle:**
> It is first necessary to establish the applicable national law in order to develop the necessary subject matter of an erasure concept. Each national legal system then imposes retention and related erasure obligations by law, based on the consent of the data subject, the legal provisions applicable to specific purposes, the business process of the processed data and the purpose of use.

IV. Start times of retention and erasure obligations

The relevant national law usually also regulates the starting point of legal retention obligations or rights. **390**

- The creation of the personal data represents the logical time for retention obligations or rights to begin. An invoice, for example, is created when it is issued, but the traffic data relevant to bill for telecommunications connections are created much earlier, namely at the time of the establishment, existence and termination of the respective connection. The charges are then determined from these raw data and billed at regular intervals. Under German law, the raw data and the data of the fee calculation can then be retained for the legally specified period of six months from the time of the preparation of the fee calculation (§ 97 (3) sentence 2 TKG).
- The statutory retention obligations under commercial or tax law always being at the end of the year in which the corresponding document subject to retention obligations was created; this allows synchronization with the calendar year change. For example, all invoices issued within one year must be kept for the duration of the year of issue

plus a further ten years. Assuming that the first invoice of a year was issued on 2 January, it must be kept until 31 December of the year of issue plus a further ten years, i.e. for a total of almost eleven years. If, in addition, a certain period is still necessary for the technical implementation of the erasure and if the need for such a supplementary period is plausible, there are also no objections to a slight extension of the retention period beyond the period of the statutory storage obligation.

- The same applies to the standard limitation period in § 195 BGB, which can often be used to justify retention periods in the absence of a statutory retention obligation. In addition, these limitation periods commence only at the end of the year in which the respective requirement arose (§ 199 (1) BGB).

391 Accordingly, the starting times shall be determined in accordance with the relevant national law. In many cases, however, the start times for the beginning of erasure periods are also dynamically linked, for example, to the end of a contractual relationship. This applies in particular to erasure periods for data types that have been collected, processed and stored in connection with continuing obligations such as rental agreements, service agreements or employment relationships.

Guiding Principle:

When drawing up an erasure concept the start times of the data categories must also be determined in addition to determining the retention periods for each data category. These do not necessarily have to be identical with the time when the data was first collected by the person responsible.

V. Assignment of data types to erasure classes

392 As soon as the data types and their associated retention periods and start times have been determined, erasure classes can be formed from combinations of erasure period and start time. All data types that have a relevant combination of erasure period and start time are then assigned to these erasure classes. This provides a complete overview of the erasure times to be adhered to by a company and the data types to be erased at each of these times.

393 This procedure corresponds to the guideline for developing a deletion concept by deriving deletion periods for personal data presented as DIN standard 66398 (as of May 2016) and has already proven to be used effectively in numerous companies. A procedure making use of this DIN standard for creating an erasure concept for Big Data applications and the resulting erasure concept also enable the data controller for the Big Data application to prove that personal data has been handled lawfully in terms of compliance (*accountability*), as in Art. 5 (2) GDPR.

VI. Resolution of conflicts when using one data type in different databases

394 The different business process references for individual data categories mean that, depending on the relevant business process, the same data type found in corresponding data categories must be erased at different times. Since erasure requires that the data no longer exist physically or are unrecognisable and can no longer be used, the first question to be asked whenever the same category of data has to be erased at different times depending on the business process reference is the following: can the company's

data-holding systems access the same data source or can the same data categories in the company be found in several places within the systems supporting the relevant business process? While in the latter case the erasure of the data categories concerned only has to take place in the respective system, the erasure of a data category used several times from a uniform data source can of course only take place when the longest archiving and erasure period has expired. For systems and business processes that have a shorter erasure period, access to these data categories is only to be restricted in such a way (in the sense of Art. 18 GDPR; e.g. by blocking this data), so that they can no longer be used in the respective business process reference. For the other business processes that allow a longer erasure period, however, they must remain available.

Guiding Principle:

When developing erasure concepts, it must also be taken into account that data of data categories being used differently may also be subject to different retention and erasure periods. The longest retention period is of course decisive for the final erasure; before that period has expired, the data may have to be blocked for specific uses for which they would have had to be deleted at an earlier point in time if viewed in isolation.

VII. What does "erasure" of data mean in contrast to its "blocking", "masking", "pseudonymization" or "anonymization"?

Complete erasure of personal data means that the data no longer exists or is unrecognisable after the erasure process has been completed and can no longer be used, even in a separate Big Data application. Erasure has been successfully undertaken, for example, by physically overwriting data objects several times or by destroying the data carriers on which they are stored. Of course, this requirement for an erasure process also means that the erasure must not only take place on the respective production systems, but also on all backup systems and backup copies, since these are not only suitable, but are even intended to enable the use of the copied data again. 395

In contrast, blocking personal data is a "*limitation of processing*", as defined in Art. 4 (3) GDPR, i.e. the marking of stored personal data with the aim of restricting their future processing. By locking/restricting the processing as such, conflicts can be solved concerning the use of a data type in different databases (cf. above mn. 394 *et seq.*). However, personal data are also to be blocked if they are to remain stored only for archiving purposes – their use in a Big Data application is no longer necessary. According to § 147 (5) and (6) AO, however, a data controller must grant a tax auditor reading access to the archived data stocks and the respective application in order to make these data stocks readable for this purpose. The colleagues of the finance and controlling departments as well as internal audit departments are likewise to be granted reading access. The processing of the data stored only for archiving purposes is to be restricted, however, in all other respects so that access to these data from productive systems or a Big Data application is no longer possible or not possible for all users entitled to this system. Such a blocking is thus not only a possibility, with regard to access to personal data, but even a necessity in terms of data stored for archiving purposes only in order to satisfy the principle of data minimization in Art. 5 (1) (c) GDPR; it is also true of personal data stored in a Big Data application. A violation of the principle of data minimization is again an infringement punishable with a fine (Art. 83 (5) (a) GDPR). In addition, due to the commercial nature of the use of personal data in companies, there is a risk of criminal 396 liability for the respective management in accordance with § 42 (2) BDSG, where the penalty ranges from a fine to a prison sentence of up to two years.

397 Pseudonymization or anonymization of personal data should not be confused with or equated to deleting or erasing personal data:

- In the case of pseudonymization (sometimes also called masking), personal data are processed in such a way that they can no longer be assigned to specific data subjects without additional information, whereby this additional information is to be kept separately and is subject to technical and organizational measures that ensure that personal data are not assigned to an identified or identifiable natural person (according to the legal definition in Art. 4 (5) GDPR). Since, however, the additional information, which can be used for allocating data to an identified or identifiable natural person, is still available from the responsible place, pseudonymized data are still personal data, even if owing to the procedure of pseudonymization the data are especially protected from misuse. For pseudonymized data the regulations and restrictions of the GDPR thus apply without reservation. From this it follows that even with bare pseudonymization in Big Data applications, the necessity to erase data cannot be sufficiently fulfilled.

> **Guiding Principle:**
> Complete erasure of personal data means that they no longer exist or are unrecognisable after completion of the erasure process and can no longer be used. This definition means that blocking personal data as described in Art. 4 (3) GDPR as well as their pseudonymization as per Art. 4 (5) GDPR are not sufficient.

- The anonymization of personal data is no longer regulated in the GDPR. This process is merely referred to in recital 26 GDPR whereby anonymized information is no longer subject to data protection regulations, and that anonymized information is only such information which no longer indicates any relation to identified or identifiable natural persons and this relation is also later – in particular by consulting further information – no longer or only with a completely disproportionate expenditure recoverable (thus the legal definition in § 3 (6) BDSG a.F. still stands). The anonymization of personal data, which occasionally goes hand-in-hand with the transfer of such data to Big Data applications, thus does not mean that these data are erased in terms of data protection law; rather, by removing the personal reference, the respective date is changed in such a way that it can no longer qualify as personal data and is therefore no longer subject to the statutory provisions. Complete anonymization ends the qualification of the relevant data as person-related. This is equivalent to erasure as long as it is no longer other possible to refer back to the original data subject, e.g. data mining or Big Data comparisons do not completely anonymize data and thus the data still remain personal. What remains important is that anonymization is itself a type of processing that requires a lawful ground. As a rule, the balance of interests approach in Art. 6 (1) (f) GDPR should legally allow for anonymization:

398 The following has therefore been made clear:

- the pseudonymization of personal data does not meet the requirements for the erasure of personal data,
- blocking personal data is not equivalent to erasure, since the personal data is still available and only accessible to a limited group of users in the event of blocking.

If and to the extent that a necessary erasure of personal data were only replaced by pseudonymization or blocking, the continued storage of such a type of pseudonymized or blocked data (even if it were *only* in a Big Data application) beyond the legally-required erasure periods remains inadmissible retention in terms of data protection law and thus processing of personal data, which according to Art. 83 (5) (a) GDPR is as an administrative offence which can be punished with a fine. Here, too, the threat of punishment pursuant to § 42 (2) BDSG (fine or imprisonment for up to two years) also applies. **399**

VIII. Obligation to erase personal data regarding a data subject

1. Reasons

a) Personal data

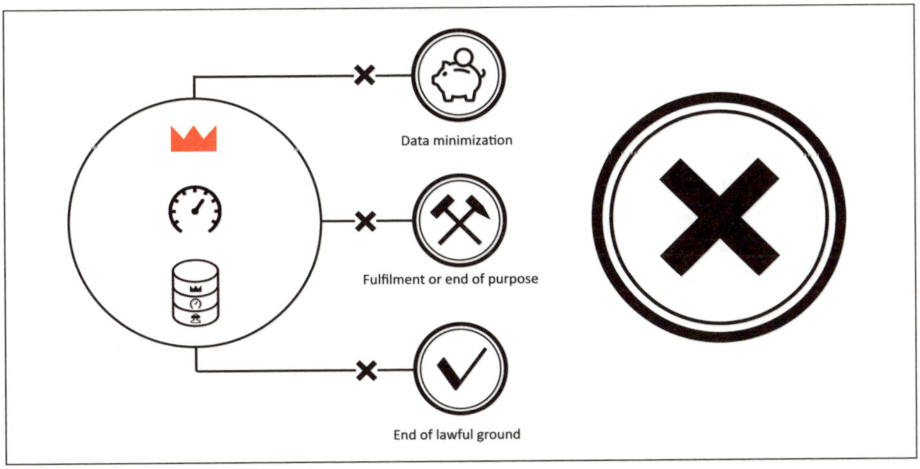

Figure 60: Reasons for data erasure

According to Art. 17 (1) sentence 1 GDPR the data subject has an individual right to obtain erasure of personal data concerning him where one of the following applies: **400**

- the personal data are no longer necessary for the purposes for which they were collected or otherwise processed – if necessary, after a change of purpose permitted in accordance with Art. 6 (4) GDPR;
- the data subject withdraws consent on which the processing is based in accordance with Art. 6 (1) (a) or in the case of special categories of personal data in accordance with Art. 9 (2) (a) GDPR and there is no other legal ground for processing in the Big Data application, e.g. on the basis of a statutory lawful basis;
- the data subject has lodged an objection in accordance with Art. 21 (1) GDPR to the collection and processing of personal data based on the balancing of interests (cf. mn. 192 *et seq.*) and there are no overriding legitimate grounds at the controller for the processing, particularly in the Big Data application,
- the data subject objects to the processing of his personal data on the basis of Art. 21 (2) GDPR, processing which has taken place on the grounds of the overriding interests of the processor (cf. mn. 192 *et seq.* above) for direct marketing purposes in a Big Data application or

- the data subject has lodged an objection in accordance with Art. 21 (1) GDPR to the collection and processing of personal data based on the balancing of interests (cf. mn. 192 *et seq.*) and there are no overriding legitimate reasons at the data controller for processing in the Big Data application,
- if the personal data have been collected in relation to or through websites with the consent of minors and subsequently stored in a Big Data application, but who have reached the age of 16 and have withdrawn such consent or requested the erasure of the data collected and processed under such consent.

401 Of course, this also applies to personal data in a Big Data application.

402 If the data subject's request for erasure is directed at the operational processing procedures in which the personal data were first collected and processed and from which they were then retained in a Big Data application, both the data still retained as personal data in the Big Data application and the data retained in the operational processing procedure in which they were originally collected (e.g. in the context of a web shop for the purpose of selling products or services) must be erased.

b) Non-personal data

403 Reasons for the erasure of non-personal data and documents may arise from an underlying contract, i.e. in particular from license agreements for software or databases or other know-how which the controller may only use for a limited period of time.

404 Even if such erasure or destruction obligations have not been expressly agreed upon, the termination of a license agreement means that the right of use and thus also the right to retain such data also end, so that the licensed object is to be erased.

405 Moreover, it is a matter of economic common sense to erase even non-personal data when they are no longer needed for their original purpose of use or for a later newly discovered purpose of use.

> **Guiding Principle:**
>
> Beside the general obligation of the controller to erase data upon expiration of the relevant retention periods, the individual erasure claim of the data subject also comes into effect, according to Art. 17 GDPR.

2. Date

406 As soon as and insofar as one of the above-mentioned reasons for erasure exists, the data concerned shall be erased *without delay*, i.e. without culpable delay (§ 121 (1) BGB). The criterion shall in principle be determined on a case-by-case basis. It is therefore necessary to consider the circumstances under which the data controller has to carry out a legally complex and thus time-consuming examination both of the grounds for erasure and the grounds for exclusion in Art. 17 (3) GDPR. A one-month waiting period before initiating the erasure process is not permissible: Art. 12 (4) GDPR prescribes that the erasure must be already have been carried out *at the latest* one month after receipt of a corresponding erasure request. Assessing and undertaking the request are to begin without delay in each case and the entire erasure process must also be undertaken without delay and, at the latest, completed within the one-month period in accordance with Art. 12 (4) GDPR. The opinion has been expressed that an action is to be qualified as *without delay* when it has been carried out within two weeks.[125] However, taking two weeks as a benchmark would conflict with the wording of the provision where earlier erasure would have been possible for the controller. The

[125] Cf. Paal, in: Paal/Pauly, *GDPR*, 2nd ed. 2018, Art. 17 mn. 31.

authorities responsible for the processing procedure in which the data were originally collected and processed, as well as those responsible for the Big Data application, must each define appropriate business processes for this purpose and, if necessary, technically provide for and implement automated erasure procedures,[126] whereby automated deletion is not part of the controller's obligations. A legal obligation only exists with regard to the outcome (i.e. the erasure), not to the mechanism of erasure. The controller may therefore choose how to perform the erasure obligation. Making erasure technically possible is already to be provided for in the structure of the Big Data application (privacy by design, Art. 25 GDPR).

3. Reasons for exclusion

Art. 17 (3) GDPR as well as § 35 BDSG list various reasons to justify why a claim for erasure of personal data does not have to be followed in exceptional cases even though there is a reason for erasure (cf. above, mn. 376 *et seq.*). However, these reasons for exclusion are at most tailored to the erasure of data in the operative processing in which and for the purposes of which the personal data were originally collected and processed. The exclusions for the erasure obligations foreseen in Art. 17 (3) GDPR should not, in general, be relevant for personal data stored in Big Data applications. It must be considered in each case that the reasons for exclusion found in Art. 17 GDPR as well as § 35 BDSG protect the controller only from the performance of individual erasure claims, but do not give him thereby at the same time legal justification for unlimited storage. **407**

At first glance, this reasoning may not seem to apply to a reason for exclusion of *statistical purposes* in Art. 17 (3) (d) GDPR; however, *statistical purposes* in this context refer only to those in the public interest and not statistical evaluations for the purposes of a non-public body. **408**

> **Guiding Principle:**
> Even if the majority of exclusion cases listed in Art. 17 (3) GDPR for individual erasure claims of the data subject do not have practical relevance for Big Data applications, it is, however, particularly important to consider that these exclusion reasons do not provide the controller with any legal justification for unlimited storage.

4. Right *to be forgotten*

If the controller responsible for a Big Data application has previously made the personal data affected by a withdrawal available to an unlimited number of third parties, and if the data must now be erased due to a withdrawal of consent, the controller responsible for the Big Data application must inform these third parties that the data subject has requested the erasure of all links to his personal data or of copies or replications of this personal data (Art. 17 (2) GDPR, right *to be forgotten*). However, the obligation of the controller responsible for the Big Data application is limited to this duty to provide information; Art. 17 (2) GDPR does not create any obligation to guarantee the actual erasure of links, copies or replications of the personal data affected by a withdrawal by these third party data recipients or to take responsibility in any other way. **409**

Accordingly, the authority carrying out the initial collection of personal data is not obliged to check that the third-party data recipients have implemented an effective data erasure concept. This applies regardless of whether the data is to be used in a Big Data application of the data collector or in another entity operating the Big Data application. **410**

[126] Cf. Wybitul/Rauer, *ZD* 2012, 160 (162).

5. Right to limitation of processing

411 Pursuant to Art. 18 GDPR, a data subject may request that the data controller restrict the processing in accordance with a blocking provision, where:

- the accuracy of the personal data is contested by the data subject for a period of time which enables the controller to verify the accuracy of the raw data held by it
- the processing of personal data is unlawful and the data subject opposes the erasure of the personal data and instead requests that use of the personal data be restricted
- the controller no longer needs the personal data for the purposes of the processing in the sense of the GDPR (for instance because the data subject is no longer active), as might be the case with Big Data applications, but the data subject requires the data to establish, exercise or defend legal claims, or
- the data subject has objected to processing of his personal data, particularly processing in a Big Data application by the controller, according to Art. 21 (1) GDPR, as long as it is not yet certain whether the legitimate grounds of the controller override those of the data subject.

IX. Erasure obligations towards licensors, data suppliers etc. independent of the data content

412 Irrespective of the obligation to erase personal data which exist in relation to a data subject, all types of data which have been acquired from a third party on the basis of data use or other license agreement[127] shall be erased or returned by the authority responsible for the Big Data application to the data supplier when the relevant right of use in relation to the right holder has expired. This is, in particular the case when the following are true:

- a time-limited data usage or other license agreement has expired,
- a data usage agreement or other license agreement has been terminated by the data provider or other licensor in an ordinary or extraordinary manner, or the parties have terminated such a data usage agreement or other license agreement by mutual consent,
- the data supplier or other licensor was not in any way entitled to grant the contractually owed rights of use to the data/databases since, in this case, the authority responsible for the Big Data application had no right whatsoever to *own* these data; this applies all the more if the actual right holder even expressly demands erasure of the data concerned,
- the data concerned – whether personal or not – have been obtained without authorization, i.e. without a corresponding data usage or other license agreement, and have been stored and processed in a Big Data application, or
- the data in question were obtained as Open Data, but the requirements or other conditions attached to the use of such data sets are not (any longer) satisfied in the Big Data application in question.

[127] In particular, data from databases or database extracts, data from collective works or other data which are the subject of industrial property rights or ancillary copyrights.

X. Uniform erasure period for all documents and data

Determining a uniform retention period of any document and data type which would be valid for all document and data types, beyond the legal retention periods and, even in case of doubt indefinitely, is inadmissible in data protection law. Such uniform retention cannot replace a differentiated archiving and erasure concept, in which a different definition has been used for retention and erasure periods according to individual document types and/or data categories beyond the legal retention periods. **413**

The mere retention of personal data, without any other processing operations taking place, is already a processing operation subject to the principle of legality in Art. 5 (2) GDPR, with the consequence that the retention of personal data by a controller is only then and insofar lawful as this can be justified by a lawful ground found in Art. 6 (for all categories of personal data with the exception of the special categories) or Art. 9 GDPR (specific to special categories of personal data). **414**

In addition, a special criterion comes into play in connection with the archiving of documents and the concomitant data types: If one considers the life cycle of personal data held by a controller, then this is usually characterized by multiple changes of the processing purpose. **415**

A primary objective is to be fulfilled when the controller first collects and processes personal data i.e. the purpose for which the personal data were originally collected. In many cases, this primary purpose is the performance of a contract with the data subject, for which, for example, name, address, contact data, order data, invoice data and payment transaction data are collected and processed. The principle of legality in Art. 5 (1) (a) GDPR requires that this primary purpose of collection and processing of personal data has already been authorized by law. **416**

After this primary collection and processing purpose has been fulfilled, a longer time limit typically follows during which the data originally collected and processed for the performance of the primary contract purpose are retained by the controller, and are thus stored in a legally-relevant manner (in the sense of Art. 4 (2) GDPR), are processed, although they are typically no longer *accessed* or changed in any way. This processing also needs a lawful ground, though usually of a different type because the personal data is not stored for the original purpose of its collection and initial processing. Rather, this original purpose of collection and processing are replaced by the purpose of satisfying legal storage obligations or at least legal storage rights. **417**

If, in addition, the respective personal data are also to be used in a Big Data application, this constitutes a renewed change of purpose, which must pass a compatibility test in accordance with Art. 6 (4) GDPR (cf. mn. 234 *et seq.* above) in addition to the existence of a lawful ground for use in the Big Data application. **418**

The combination of these three stages of processing personal data shows that the retention period is different for each data category and therefore has to be defined for each data category. Retention which disregards consideration of these categories inevitably leads to retention periods which can no longer be lawful from the individual data category and which must inevitably be unlawful. **419**

Guiding Principle:

Determining the general storage of any document and data types, which would be valid for all document and data types, beyond the legal retention periods, and even in case of doubt indefinitely, is inadmissible under data protection law. Such a general retention cannot replace a differentiated archiving and erasure concept, in which a different definition has been used for retention and erasure periods according to individual document types and/or data categories beyond the legal retention periods

XI. Erasure obligations for cross-border data processing

420 Each controller responsible for a Big Data application shall be responsible for compliance with the national law in force in its country of residence and the retention and erasure obligations laid down therein (cf. mn. 378 *et seq.*). This shall also apply if it uses a service provider to operate its IT infrastructure, which might be located in another country. In such a situation, the controller must ensure that the IT infrastructure service provider it uses, for example, for the operation of its Big Data application, is also in a position to technically implement the retention and erasure obligations applicable to the controller under the relevant law. On the part of the IT infrastructure service provider, which acts as a multi-client service provider, this means that its systems must be able to technically implement various retention and erasure obligations, depending on the client.

421 Where a controller transmits data or documents to another entity responsible for the Big Data application without the receiving entity being the processor of the transmitting entity, both the transmitting and receiving entities shall be responsible for their respective compliance with their national retention and erasure obligations. The sending entity need not check whether the receiving entity is in a position to do so – the sending entity only has to ensure that the receiving entity also complies with a level of data protection which matches European standards where personal data are transferred to a responsible entity established outside the EU Member States. This can be done through various legal instruments, including the following:

- the agreement of EU standard contract terms with the receiving entity,
- the inclusion of such receiving entities, which are group companies, in so-called Binding Corporate Rules, which may exist throughout the group, or
- the self-certification of US-based recipients according to the principles of the EU-US Privacy Shield.

422 However, even in these cases, the transmitting entity does not have to actually examine, in terms of prior verification, whether the receiving entity, with its technical infrastructures and processes, actually performs all the obligations assumed by it.

Guiding Principle:

In the case of cross-border processing of data in a Big Data application, the retention and erasure obligations applicable in the controller's country of establishment shall apply. If the Big Data application is only operated on behalf of several controllers, the processor must ensure that it is able to implement the retention and erasure periods applicable in the countries in which its clients are domiciled in the Big Data application, independently of one another.

XII. Storage locations and erasure obligations

All retention and erasure obligations are based exclusively on the respective data categories. These retention and erasure obligations apply, therefore, regardless of the format in which the data has been stored so that these obligations must be observed irrespective of whether the data has been stored in a standard Office format or, for example, only in a read-only format (such as PDF). **423**

The retention and erasure obligations also apply irrespective of where the data to be deleted are actually stored. Erasure processes are therefore to be carried out in relation to data and documents regardless of whether they are stored in productive systems, archive systems, on backup storage media or on central or local distributed servers or on end-user devices (PCs, laptops, portable hard drives, DVDs, hard disks, etc.). In particular, the common practice of individual users creating their own storage locations on local drives and/or hard disks installed in their devices or in their email system for Big Data applications set up and operated by them alone makes company-wide compliance with erasure obligations virtually impossible. This is because central access to and enforcement of such local user interaction devices in order to erase data sets independently of the will of the individual device user is not possible, or only possible with disproportionate technical effort. For this reason, it makes sense to ensure compliance with legal and/or contractual existing erasure and destruction obligations by at least obliging the users by corresponding further central instructions to only store data sets in Big Data applications (for which legal or contractual erasure or destruction obligations exist) on data processing and storage media that are subject to central access. The storage of personal data on one's own local device and drive is therefore prohibited. **424**

Guiding Principle:
Retention and erasure obligations apply regardless of Big Data Application's technical storage location, i.e. also for archive and backup storage media, centrally or locally distributed servers or end devices as well as all other storage media.

XIII. Four-eyes principle and documentation

The erasure or destruction of data sets can, even without corresponding erasure or destruction obligations also cause considerable damage to the business. As such, for the purposes of ensuring organizational security that only the *correct* data stocks can be erased, it is recommended that manual erasure processes for larger data sets on central storage units are only possible in accordance with a *four-eyes principle*: larger data sets can only be erased when two authorized persons act together (not individually) and by using their individual registration data at the system. Especially with Big Data applications, this serves to maintain their functionality and a maximum level of quantity and quality of the data available for evaluation. **425**

The erasure activities carried out must in turn be documented so that, with regard to both personal and non-personal data, the data controller is in a position to provide evidence that he has complied with existing legal and/or contractual erasure or destruction obligations in its Big Data application. Of course, the data to be erased or destroyed must not be copied again and stored for the purpose of documenting their **426** erasure (Art. 11 (1) GDPR); rather, the erased data must be described abstractly so that proof of erasure is successful.

427 The erasure and/or destruction of personal data is, moreover, to be made transparent in the data subject information on the Big Data application pursuant to Art. 13 (2) (a) or 14 (2) (a) GDPR. The data subjects are also to be made aware of the length of time the data will be stored, if this should not be possible, the criteria for determining their duration. Therefore, in accordance with Art. 30 (1) (f) GDPR, the erasure and destruction periods for personal data determined by the controller and laid down in the erasure concept are to be documented in the processing directory which the controller has to maintain for the Big Data application. If this information is missing from the processing directory or from the data subject information, this would also be an administrative offence, which could be punished with a fine. With regard to the other consequences under criminal law, cf. mn. 510 *et seq.* above.

428 The erasure of personal data is – as the provision on a processing directory in Art. 30 (1) (f) GDPR shows – part of the processing procedure, for which, on the one hand, the justification principle in Art. 5 (2) GDPR is to be observed, and for which, on the other hand, technical and organizational measures must be defined for the protection of this data. The controller for the Big Data application must thus be able to prove by appropriate documentation in the processing directory that it uses a procedure which leads technically in actual fact to a complete erasure of the data in such a way that they are no longer readable and physically no longer present.

Guiding Principle:

The erasure activities performed are to be documented as general procedural regulations in the context of a processing list (Art. 30 (1) (f) GDPR) as well as in each case after executing an erasure procedure for the observance of the justification principle in Art. 5 (2) GDPR. The storage and erasure periods are, in all other respects, to be made transparent in accordance with Art. 13 (2) (a) and/or Art. 14 (2) (a) GDPR with regard to the data subjects in the data subject information.

J. RELEVANT RIGHTS OF DATA SUBJECTS IN BIG DATA APPLICATIONS ACCORDING TO THE GDPR

I. Information obligations according to Art. 13, 14 GDPR

The following table lists the information obligations which are to be fulfilled in accordance with Art. 13 and 14 GDPR towards the data subject. The extent of their resemblance to the former version of the BDSG is also readily apparent. 429

Privacy policy according to § 4 (3) BDSG a.F/§ 13 (1) TMG	Duty to provide information in accordance with Art. 13 (collection from the data subject) and 14 (collection from other sources) GDPR
The identity of the controller (§ 4 (3) sentence 1 No. 1)	Identity and contact details of the controller and, in the case of entities not established in the EU or contract processors, the name and contact details of their representatives within the EU (Art. 13 (1) (a), 14 (1) (a) GDPR)
	Contact details of the data protection officer, where applicable (Art. 13 (1) (b), 14 (1) (b) GDPR)
The purposes of the collection, processing or use (§ 4 (3) sentence 1 No. 2).	Purposes for which the personal data are processed and the legal basis for the processing (Art. 13 (1) (c), 14 (1) (c) GDPR)
	In the case of processing pursuant to Art. 6 (1) (f) GDPR (weighing of interests), the primary legitimate interest of the controller for the Big Data application or of third parties as potential recipients of the communication must be imparted as justification, including information on the right to object pursuant to Art. 21 (4) GDPR (Art. 13 (1) (d), 14 (2) (b) GDPR).
The categories of recipients only to the extent that the data subject does not have to expect transmission to them under the circumstances of an individual case (§ 4 (3) sentence 1 No. 3)	Recipients or categories of recipients of personal data (Art. 13 (1) (e), 14 (1) (e) GDPR).
	Transfer to authorities in a third country and the existence or absence of a decision on adequacy or reference to guarantees and their availability (Art. 13 (1) (f), 14 (1) (f) GDPR).
	Storage period or criteria for determining such period (Art. 13 (2) (a), 14 (2) (a) GDPR)

Privacy policy according to § 4 (3) BDSG a.F/§ 13 (1) TMG	**Duty to provide information in accordance with Art. 13 (collection from the data subject) and 14 (collection from other sources) GDPR**
	Notification about data subject rights (information, rectification, erasure, restriction, objection, data portability; Art. 13 (2) (b), 14 (2) (c) GDPR)
	Existence of a right to lodge a complaint with a supervisory authority (Art. 13 (2) (d), 14 (2) (e) GDPR)
If personal data is collected from the data subject on the basis of a legal provision which obliges the data subject to provide information, or if the provision of such information is a prerequisite for the granting of legal benefits, the data subject must be made aware of this or of the voluntary nature of the data provided. If necessary, according to the circumstances of the individual case or on request, the data subject must be informed about this legal provision and the consequences of the refusal to provide information (§ 4 (3) sentences 2 and 3).	Information as to whether the provision of personal data is a statutory or contractual requirement or a requirement necessary to enter into a contract, whether there is an obligation to provide such data and possible consequences of failure to provide such data (Art. 13 (2) (e) GDPR)
	Information about the existence of automated decision-making including profiling, referred to in Art. 22 (1) and (4) GDPR, and – at least in these cases – meaningful information about the logic involved as well as the significance and the envisaged consequences of such processing for the data subject (Art. 13 (2) (f), 14 (2) (g) GDPR)
Information about: – Type, scope and purpose of the collection and use of personal data as well as – concerning the processing of its data in countries outside the scope of Directive 95/46/EC in a generally intelligible form (§ 13 (1) TMG)	Information about: – Categories of personal data that are processed only if personal data have not been collected from the data subject (Art. 14 (1) (d) GDPR) – Transfer to an entity in a third country and existence or absence of a decision on adequacy or reference to guarantees and their availability (Art. 13 (1) (f), 14 (1) (f) GDPR)
	In addition, if personal data are not collected from the data subject (Art. 14 (1) and (2) GDPR): – the categories of personal data processed (Art. 14 (1) (d) GDPR) – Information on the source from which the personal data originate and, if applicable, whether they originate from publicly accessible sources (Art. 14 (2) (f) GDPR).

Figure 61: Information obligations

The non-performance of the information obligations in accordance with Art. 13 or 14 GDPR may result in sanctions, cf. to mn. 510 *et seq*. **430**

Guiding Principle:
For a Big Data application in which personal data are retained and processed, a privacy policy must be drawn up in which the data subjects receive the information listed in Art. 13 and 14 GDPR.

II. Rights of data subjects pursuant to Art. 15 *et seq*. GDPR

According to Art. 12 and 15–21 GDPR, the data subject whose personal data is processed as such in a Big Data application (*Big Data subject*) has various rights which he can assert with regard to the entity responsible for the Big Data application as the controller in each case. The Big Data subject may contact the (Group) data protection officer for the purpose of asserting his rights. In this case, appropriate processes for timely treatment must be set up within one-month (Art. 12 (3) sentence 1 GDPR); if the rights concerned are not satisfied within this period, the entity responsible for the Big Data application must inform the Big Data subject of the reasons for this. In this case, the respective data subject affected by a Big Data application could complain to the responsible supervisory authority in accordance with Art. 12 (4) GDPR, Art. 77 (1) GDPR; the Big Data subject is to be instructed about this right of complaint in each case in conjunction with a notification about reasons for delay. **431**

The entity responsible for the Big Data application may require the Big Data subject to identify himself. Non-satisfaction of the data subject's rights may in turn result in the legal consequences described in mn. 510 *et seq*. of this guide. **432**

1. Right to access

In accordance with Art. 15 GDPR, the Big Data subject has the right to be access information about his personal data, as well as the following information: **433**
a) the processing purposes;
b) the categories of personal data to be processed; and
c) the recipients or categories of recipients to whom the personal data have been or will be disclosed, in particular recipients in third countries or international organizations;
d) the envisaged period for which the personal data will be stored as such in the Big Data application (if possible) or, if this is not possible, the criteria for determining such period;
e) if the personal data are not collected from the data subject, all available information on the origin of the data; and
f) the other rights of data subjects explained below.

2. Right to rectification

According to Art. 16 GDPR, incorrect or incomplete personal data must be corrected by the controller responsible for the Big Data application at the request of the data subject. **434**

3. Right to erasure and *to be forgotten*

435 According to Art. 17 (1) GDPR, the Big Data subject has the right to the erasure of his personal data, if the conditions listed in Art. 17 (1) GDPR are given and there is no reason for exclusion mentioned in Art. 17 (3) GDPR.

436 The Big Data subject has the right to be forgotten in the cases listed in Art. 17 (2) GDPR (cf. mn. 409 et seq. above) if the controller responsible for the Big Data application had previously made public the personal data of a Big Data subject, but is obliged to erase it in accordance with Art. 17 (1) GDPR. Whether a case of *making public* in the sense of the GDPR, i.e. accessibility to an indefinite circle of persons, is given in each situation, must be examined on a case by case basis, in particular for each Big Data application in a company; if such a case is present, processes are to be established in such a (functional and technical) manner which gives effect to the right to be forgotten.

4. Right to restriction of processing

437 The Big Data subject may request that the controller responsible for the Big Data application restrict processing in accordance with a blocking if the following are present:

- the accuracy of the personal data is contested by the Big Data subject for a period of time which allows the controller responsible for the Big Data application to verify the accuracy thereof;
- processing of the personal data is unlawful, and the data subject affected by the Big Data opposes the erasure of the personal data and instead requests the restriction of their use;
- the controller responsible for the Big Data application no longer needs the personal data for the purposes of processing in the Big Data application and these are personal data in the sense of the GDPR (e.g. because the Big Data subject is no longer active), but because the data subject needs it for to establish, exercise or defend legal claims, or
- the Big Data subject has objected to the processing of his personal data in the Big Data application by the controller in accordance with Art. 21(1) GDPR, pending the verification whether the legitimate grounds of the controller override those of the data subject.

5. Right to data portability

438 According to Art. 20 (1) GDPR, the Big Data subject has the right to receive his personal data concerning him from the Big Data application in a structured, commonly used and machine-readable format. The Big Data subject also has the right to transfer this data to another controller without hindrance from the authority responsible for the Big Data application, provided that:

- the processing is based on a consent pursuant to Art. 6 (1) (a) GDPR or Art. 9 (2) (a) GDPR or on a contract with the Big Data subject pursuant to Art. 6 (1) (b) GDPR and
- the processing in the Big Data application is carried out using automated means.

439 When exercising his right to data portability in accordance with Art. 20 (1) GDPR, the Big Data subject has the right, in accordance with Art. 20 (2) GDPR, that the personal data be transferred directly from the controller responsible for the Big Data application to another controller to be named by the Big Data subject, insofar as this is technically feasible. The controller responsible for the Big Data application therefore has

not only to establish a corresponding process for this but has also to create the technical prerequisites for such an export of the data of the Big Data application while still treating them as personal data, or to take into account the existence of such possibilities when setting up a Big Data application (privacy by design, Art. 25 GDPR).

6. Right to lodge a complaint

According to Art. 77 GDPR, Big Data subjects also have a right to lodge a complaint **440** with the data protection supervisory authority responsible for the Big Data application if the Big Data subject is of the opinion that the processing of his personal data in the Big Data application is unlawful. In accordance with Art. 13 (2) (d) GDPR, the Big Data subject must be informed of this by the controller responsible for the Big Data application within the framework of the data protection declaration.

> **Guiding Principle:**
> If personal data are stored and processed in a Big Data application, the data subjects have the rights according to Art. 15–21 GDPR. Therefore, the processes and technical conditions necessary for the satisfaction of these respective rights are to be created.

III. Records of processing activities according to Art. 30 GDPR

The following table lists the requirements for the procedure directory/records of **441** processing activities for a Big Data application.

Procedure directory (§ 4e sentence 1 BDSG a. F.)	**Records of processing activities (Art. 30 (1) GDPR)**
Name or company name of the responsible entity for the Big Data application as the controller (No. 1). Owners, directors, managing directors or other managers appointed by law or under the company's constitution and persons in charge of data processing (No. 2) Address of responsible entity (No. 3)	Name and contact details of the controller and, if applicable, of the joint controller, of the representative of the controller and of a possible data protection officer (a)
Purposes of data collection, processing or use (No. 4)	Purposes of processing (b)
Description of the groups of persons concerned (Big Data subjects) and the related data or data categories (No. 5)	Description of categories of data subjects and categories of personal data (c)
Recipients or categories of recipients to whom the data may be communicated (No. 6)	Categories of recipients to whom the personal data have been or will be disclosed in or from the Big Data application, including recipients in third countries or international organizations (d).

Procedure directory (§ 4e sentence 1 BDSG a. F.)	**Records of processing activities (Art. 30 (1) GDPR)**
Planned transfer of data to third countries (No. 8)	If applicable, transfers of personal data to a third country or to an international organization, including the indication of the third country or the international organization concerned, as well as the documentation of appropriate guarantees for the data transfers referred to in Art. 49 (1) GDPR (e).
Standard periods for erasure of data and analysis results related to specific Big Data subjects by the controller responsible for the Big Data application (No. 7)	If possible, the time limits foreseen for the erasure of the different categories of data (f).
General description enabling a preliminary assessment to be made as to whether the measures pursuant to § 9 BDSG a. F. to ensure the security of the processing are appropriate (No. 9); pursuant to § 4g (2) sentence 2 BDSG previous version only for the internal directory.	If possible, a general description of the technical and organizational security measures referred to in Art. 32 (1) GDPR (g)

Figure 62: Record of processing activities

442 Violations of the obligation to draw up and maintain records of processing activities in accordance with Art. 30 GDPR may result in the legal consequences described in mn. 510 *et seq*. below.

443 If third party services are used to operate the Big Data application as processor, the processor shall also maintain a processing directory of this type.

> **Guiding Principle:**
>
> For each Big Data application in which personal data are stored and processed, records of processing activities in accordance with Art. 30 GDPR shall be kept both by the controller responsible for the Big Data application and, where applicable, by the processor.

444 In addition, comparable documentation obligations may also arise for non-personal data, for example if the number and type of use of such data by the data provider is relevant to remuneration.

IV. Implementation of technical and organizational measures to protect personal data from unauthorized access

445 According to § 9 BDSG a. F., the controller responsible for the Big Data application had to adopt the technical and organizational measures listed in the Annex to the BDSG a. F. only in accordance with its protective aims and to examine these regularly to see whether they still met the risk potential to which the raw data, the data records generated in the Big Data application and the analysis results relating to specific Big Data subjects had been exposed.

446 Art. 32 (1) GDPR formulates this requirement much more generally. Accordingly, the controller responsible for the Big Data application has to take appropriate technical and organizational measures, taking into account the state of the art, the implementation

costs and the type, scope, circumstances and purposes of the processing as well as the different probability of occurrence and severity of the risk for the rights and freedoms of natural persons, in order to guarantee a level of protection appropriate to the risk. As examples of such measures, some measures are then listed, namely:
- the encryption of personal data,
- the ability to ensure the ongoing confidentiality, integrity, availability and resilience of the systems and services associated with the processing,
- the ability to restore the availability and access to personal data in a timely manner in the event of a physical or technical incident, and
- a process for the regular testing, assessment and evaluation of the effectiveness of the technical and organizational measures taken to ensure the security of processing.

The wording of the regulation differs in many ways from the BDSG a. F.; nevertheless, **447**
the principles and considerations developed in § 9 BDSG a. F. and its annex will have to be consulted if one is to envisage the meaning and purpose of Art. 32 GDPR.[128] This results in the following protective goals and the measures listed as examples. Whether and which of these measures are to be taken must then be assessed in each individual case, taking into account the specific technical and structural conditions at the controller responsible for the Big Data application.

1. Access control

Unauthorized physical access is to be prevented, whereby the term is to be under- **448**
stood spatially. Measures for entry control, in particular also for the lawful authority of authorized persons include the following:
- designation of authorized persons (internal and external)
- access control system
- access control system such as badge reader, magnetic card or chip card
- register of key holders
- requirements for external persons (visitors, cleaning staff or other external companies)
- attendance records
- visitor badges
- alarm system, factory security or other protective measures outside business hours
- establishment of security zones with access restrictions
- secured supplier entry and exit
- door security (e.g. electric door openers, card readers, TV monitors, security personnel)
- installation of airlocks
- closed data centre operation
- mutual monitoring
- suitable measures for building security (e.g. special glazing, intruder alarm, floor checks, sealing off outlet pipes)

2. (Virtual) Access control

Unauthorized access to Big Data applications must be prevented. Measures regarding **449**
user identification and authentication must be taken, such as:
- lock function at work stations
- identification of a terminal or user to the Big Data application
- password procedure (e.g. special characters, minimum length, regular password change)
- function-based assignment of individual terminals and identifiers

[128] Cf. Paulus, in: Wolff/Brink, *BeckOK DatenSR*, 25th ed., as at 1.8.2018, Art. 32 GDPR mn. 6.

- functional and/or temporal restrictions on the use of terminals and identifiers
- control of user access rights
- obligation to comply with data secrecy according to § 5 BDSG a. F./Art. 5 (1) (f) GDPR
- use of user codes for files and programs
- use of encryption programs for files and data carriers
- differentiated admission requirements
- guidelines for file organization
- acquisition and analysis of data usage
- specific control over the use of utility programs, where they are likely to circumvent security measures
- controlled destruction of data media
- work instructions and procedures for data acquisition
- control, permission and monitoring systems
- program checks and release processes

3. Admission control

450 Unauthorized activities with or in the Big Data application beyond the granted authorizations must be prevented. Measures for a needs-based design of the authorization concept and access rights as well as their monitoring and logging include in particular:
- work stations with function-bound access keys
- differentiated authorizations (profiles, roles, transactions and objects) including documented authorization concept
- automatic control of access rights, e.g. through identification keys
- keeping access logs
- analysis of access logs
- card reader at the terminal
- time limit for access
- allocation of limited access rights only to certain data or functions
- regular examination whether authorizations granted are still required, cancellation of authorizations for employees who have left the company

4. Data medium control

451 Unauthorized reading, copying, modification or deletion of data media must be prevented. Possible measures for this could be:
- encryption of data media
- locked storage of data media
- tracking the delivery of data media to employees and their return to a locked storage facility

5. Access and user control

452 It must be ensured that those authorized to use the Big Data Application can only access such content, including their evaluations and analysis results, for which they are authorized and that personal data cannot be copied, changed or erased without authorization during processing and use and after storage in the Big Data Application and any previous systems for processing this data. Measures of access and user control may include, among others:
- authorization concept
- user ID with password
- secure interfaces

- data media management
- certificate-based access authorization
- system internal authorization administration
- authorization management by the responsible system administrator

6. Control of disclosure, transmission and transport

The following aspects of the disclosure of personal data relating to Big Data subjects **453** shall be regulated: electronic transmission, data transport, transmission control, measures taken during transport, transfer and transmission or storage on data carriers (manual or electronic) and subsequent verification. Such measures may include in particular:

- designation of authorized persons and control of authorization during data transfer by presentation of suitable proofs of authorization
- mutual monitoring
- secured supplier entry and exit
- use of encryption during transmission or tunnel connections (e.g. VPN)
- electronic signature
- inventory checks
- separate, secure storage of data media with confidential content
- access authorization to archived data media
- prohibition on carrying bags or other luggage in restricted areas
- monitoring the destruction of data media and waste materials (e.g. misprints)
- control over the making of data copies
- documentation of data acquisition and transmission programs and data transmission
- documentation of transmission locations and routes
- regulations for packaging and transport of data media (e.g. security containers, personal collection, courier service or accompanied transport)
- encoding
- plausibility and completeness checks
- deletion of residual data before switching data carriers
- remote maintenance concept including access restricting regulations
- tracking of remote maintenance accesses

7. Input and storage control

The traceability and documentation of the administration and maintenance of the **454** raw data, the data prepared in the Big Data application and the analysis results related to specific Big Data subjects in the Big Data application must be guaranteed. Measures for subsequent verification as to whether and by whom data have been entered or removed (deleted; erased) can include, in particular:

- documentation of organizational responsibilities for data entry
- obligation to comply with data secrecy
- keeping a protocol of data entries
- maintenance of file usage protocol
- work instructions, process descriptions.

8. Contract control

If necessary, C2P, which is to take place only as directed, shall be guaranteed if the **455** controller responsible for the Big Data application uses third parties to operate a Big Data application and/or to maintain it and/or the underlying database management

system – in particular remotely. Measures (technical/organizational) to distinguish the areas of responsibility between the controller and the processor may be in particular:
- clear contract terms
- formalized order placement (order form)
- criteria for the selection of the contractor
- checking the performance of the contract and the contractual performance results
- regular performance of data protection and/or IT security audits by internal or external auditors

9. Availability control

456 The data in the Big Data application must be protected from accidental destruction or loss. Measures for data backup (physical/logical) can include the following, in particular:
- backup procedure
- mirroring of hard disks (e.g. RAID process)
- uninterrupted power supply (UPS)
- early fire detection/smoke detection systems
- protection from smoke in data centres
- protection from water ingress, other water or moisture damage
- redundancy in air conditioning and power supply (including emergency power system and sufficient fuel supply)
- virus protection/firewall
- separate storage
- measures concerning the ageing of data media
- measures relating to archive copies when introducing new releases of the relevant application with which the archived data was created.
- data carrier administration and regular data carrier inventory
- emergency plan

10. Separation control

457 Accordingly, data which were acquired for different purposes are to be generally processed separately, unless an independent lawful basis and the conditions for a change of purpose in Art. 6 (4) GDPR (cf. mn. 230 *et seq.*) exist for their additional storage with other data in the Big Data application in individual cases. Measures for the separate processing (storage, change, erasure, transmission) of data with different purposes can be:
- *internal multi-client capability*/designated purpose
- separation of functions (production/testing/development)

11. Recoverability

458 Measures must be in place which allow systems used for the establishment and operation of Big Data applications can be restored in the event of a disruption. Such measures can be, for example:
- definition of disaster recovery measures depending on the findings of protection requirements
- regular updating of the defined disaster recovery measures
- training of the defined measures with the employees concerned
- regular practice of disaster recovery
- documentation of the results of the disaster recovery exercises and their analysis to effect improvement

12. Reliability

All functions of the Big Data application are to be available and any malfunctions that occur are to be reported. Measures for this could be, for example: 459
- automatic monitoring of the system, depending on possible protection requirement findings
- implementation of a SIEM system and definitions of actions/reactions to security incidents
- automated reports for compliance, IT security, and senior management

13. Data integrity

Personal data stored in the Big Data application must not be able to be damaged by system malfunctions. Measures for this can be, for example: 460
- transmission of checksums that indicate whether data has been changed
- Message Authentication Codes to detect both transmission errors and manipulations
- measures, such as acknowledgement messages or sequence numbers, to detect and prevent total loss of messages, unwanted duplication or changes in the sequence of several messages

14. Sanction for non-existent or inadequate technical and organizational measures

Whereas the non-application or inadequate application of technical and/or organizational measures for the protection of personal data within the scope of the BDSG a.F. was not yet punishable as an administrative offence with fines until 24 May 2018, the non-application or inadequate application of technical and organizational measures for the protection of personal data from 25 May 2018 onwards is not permitted. Pursuant to Art. 83 (4) (a) GDPR, a breach of Art. 32 GDPR is an administrative offence that can be punished with fines of up to EUR 10 million or, in the case of a company, of up to 2 % of the total annual turnover generated worldwide in the previous financial year, whichever is greater. 461

However, there is no risk of criminal liability; the non-application or application of insufficient technical and organizational measures for the protection of personal data is neither a criminal offence within the meaning of § 44 BDSG a.F. nor within the meaning of § 42 BDSG applicable from 25 May 2018. 462

Guiding Principle:

For a Big Data application, in which personal data are stored and processed, technical and organizational measures according to Art. 32 GDPR are to be carried out and documented.

V. General principles for the processing of personal data in Art. 5 GDPR

1. General principles for the processing of personal data

According to Art. 5 (1) GDPR, personal data must be 463
- processed lawfully, fairly and in a transparent manner in relation to the data subject (*lawfulness, fairness and transparency*);
- collected for specified, explicit and legitimate purposes and not further processed in a manner incompatible with those purposes; […] (*purpose limitation*);

- adequate and relevant to the purpose and limited to what is necessary for the purposes for which they are processed (*minimization of data*);
- accurate and, where necessary, kept up to date; every reasonable step must be taken to ensure that personal data that are inaccurate, having regard to the purposes for which they are processed, are erased or rectified without delay (*accuracy*);
- kept in a form which permits identification of data subjects for no longer than is necessary for the purposes for which the personal data are processed; personal data may be stored for longer periods insofar as the personal data will be processed solely for archiving purposes in the public interest, scientific or historical research purposes or statistical purposes in accordance with Article 89(1) subject to implementation of the appropriate technical and organizational measures required by this Regulation in order to safeguard the rights and freedoms of the data subject (*retention limitation*);
- processed in a manner that ensures appropriate security of the personal data, including protection against unauthorized or unlawful processing and against accidental loss, destruction or damage, using appropriate technical or organizational measures (*integrity and confidentiality*);

464 Compliance with all these principles, even in the case of Big Data applications, shall be ensured by the controller responsible for processing personal data in the Big Data application (which shall be determined in accordance with the principles set out in mn. 122 *et seq.*). The essential general principles listed in Art. 5 (1) GDPR for the processing of personal data in Big Data applications have already been addressed in one form or another in this guideline, as far as they are relevant in the situation mentioned here.

2. Principle of accountability (Art. 5 (2) GDPR)

465 In view of the large number of data processing operations and their lawful grounds it is important for the principle of accountability laid down in Art. 5 (2) GDPR that the authority be valid via one of the following: declarations of consent (if necessary) pursuant to Art. 6 (1) (a) GDPR, by the balancing of interests (Art. 6 (1) (f) GDPR) or by contracts to be concluded with the Big Data subject (Art. 6 (1) (b) GDPR). According to this Art. 5 (2) GDPR, the controller responsible for the Big Data application is obliged to ensure compliance with the principles in Art. 5 (1) GDPR and must, above all, be able to prove compliance.

3. Sanctioning a breach of these principles

466 A breach of one of the principles of processing of personal data in Art. 5 (1) GDPR, or missing proof for the observance of these principles to be documented pursuant to Art. 5 (2) GDPR, constitute an administrative offence which can be punished by fines; on possible legal consequences, cf. the explanations under mn. 510 et seq. A breach of the accountability principle in Art. 5 (2) GDPR represents a penalty which can involve fines even where the data processing was permissible but only insufficiently documented.

K. DATA PROTECTION IMPACT ASSESSMENT

Pursuant to Art. 35 (1) GDPR, the controller carries out an assessment of the impact of the envisaged processing operations on the protection of personal data. This is true for Big Data applications which have been newly implemented or which have not yet operated after having been evaluated (even on a test basis). This obligation exists, in particular, if the processing is likely to entail a high risk for the rights and freedoms of natural persons. **467**

According to Art. 35 (4) GDPR, the data protection supervisory authorities are obliged to draw up and publish a list of the processing operations for which, in their opinion, a data protection impact assessment must be carried out. The Art. 29 Data Protection Working Party has fulfilled this obligation by publishing Working Paper 248 "Guidelines on Data Protection Impact Assessment" (DPIA) and determining whether processing is *"likely to result in a high risk for the purposes of Regulation 2016/679"* of 4 April 2017 (hereinafter *WP 248*). Immediately after the GDPR became applicable, various German state data protection supervisory authorities published their own, somewhat differing, catalogues, The controller responsible for a Big Data application should therefore check whether the supervisory authority locally responsible at its headquarters has published such a catalogue and whether the criteria listed therein are relevant, if at all possible, before using the Big Data application for the first time and before any new evaluation of its content. **468**

In its WP 248, the Art. 29 Data Protection Working Party sets out, on the basis of explanations and diagrams, when in its opinion a data protection impact assessment must be carried out without exception. The Group identifies ten criteria that indicate a high risk to the rights and freedoms of a natural person: **469**

- scoring/profiling,
- automatic decisions leading to legal consequences for the data subjects,
- systematic monitoring,
- sensitive data (special categories of personal data set out in Art. 9 GDPR),
- data that are processed on a large scale (criteria: number of data subjects, amount of data, etc.),
- merging/combining data obtained through different processes,
- data of incapacitated data subjects or those of limited incapacity,
- use of new technologies or biometric procedures,
- data transfer to countries outside the EU/EEA, or
- data processing which prevents data subjects from exercising their rights.

The more criteria are met, the higher the Art. 29 Data Protection Working Group estimates the risk for the data subjects and therefore considers a data protection impact assessment to be necessary. If less than two of the above criteria are met, a data protection impact assessment is not always required. On the other hand, a data protection impact assessment is not required if, inter alia, there is no high risk for the data subjects, or if there is a legal basis for the processing and this expressly does not specify a data protection impact assessment as a prerequisite. WP 248 also mentions examples for which a data protection impact assessment must be carried out. With regard to Big Data applications in general, the criteria listed below could be considered. For this reason, the controller responsible for a Big Data application should conduct a **470** data protection impact assessment for the development and ongoing operation of the Big Data application when the following are present:

- data that are processed on a large scale (criteria: number of data subjects, amount of data, etc.),
- merging/combining data obtained through different processes,
- use of new technologies, and
- scoring/profiling or also the inclusion of special personal data from Art. 9 GDPR in the relevant Big Data application;

471 This means that a total of three, but possibly even more, of the criteria listed in Art. 29 Working Party can be relevant in each case. In addition, the Art. 29 Data Protection Working Party makes it clear in WP 248 that, in cases of doubt, i.e. if it is difficult to distinguish between the above criteria, a data protection impact assessment should always be carried out. It is precisely on the basis of this rule of doubt that the controller responsible for a Big Data application should carry out a data protection impact assessment and document it and the reasons why it assumed (or possibly did not consider it necessary) that a data protection impact assessment had to be carried out.

472 For the sake of completeness, it should therefore be mentioned that violations of the obligation to carry out a data protection impact assessment are also classified as an administrative offence, which may entail the legal consequences explained in mn. 510 *et seq*. of this guide.

473 If a data protection impact assessment is necessary, it should be repeated after three years at the latest. Failure to comply with this obligation to repeat is also subject to fines.

Guiding Principle:

As a rule, a data protection impact assessment must be carried out for each Big Data application and repeated after three years at the latest.

L. SYSTEM DATA PROTECTION WHEN OPERATING BIG DATA APPLICATIONS

Large data sets containing personal data can typically pose high risks to the fundamental rights of data subjects. Depending on the resulting categories of data in a Big Data application, the security requirements for such Big Data applications can vary. Of course, this also applies if the data is stored by an external cloud storage provider. There are other requirements associated with this, too. **474**

System data protection refers to the requirements involved in the technical and organizational design of a data processing system.[129] In the scope of applying the GDPR, one can assume that aspects of system data protection will now be determined by data protection by technology design – *privacy by design*.[130] This principle permeates the entire design of information technology systems – from hardware to software[131] – and of course includes the storage of the data. System protection is intended to prevent danger to the fundamental rights of those affected as far as possible by means of technical and organizational measures. **475**

I. System data protection for personal data

The manifold possibilities of Big Data applications lead to the expectation that authorities and courts will place high demands on system data protection. Whether these requirements are also sufficient in the case of the Big Data application in question must be determined on the basis of the potentially endangered rights and freedoms of the data subject. **476**

In general, data protection law is based on the following rights developed by the German Federal Constitutional Court: **477**

- general right of personality (Art. 2 (1) in conjunction with Art. 1 (1) GG), from which the court successively evolved
- the fundamental right to informational self-determination and, in addition,
- a fundamental right to ensure the confidentiality and integrity of information technology systems.

Nothing else arises at the European level from Art. 7 (respect for private and family life) and Art. 8 (protection of personal data) of the EU Charter of Fundamental Rights and Art. 16 TFEU (fundamental right to data protection). **478**

1. Fundamental right to informational self-determination

Under German law, the fundamental right to informational self-determination results from the right to the free development of personality in Art. 2 (1) GG in conjunction **479**

---

[129] Cf. Polenz, in: Kilian/Heussen, *Computerrechts-Handbuch*, 34. EL, as at May 2018, 1st section, Part 13 mn. 1; Hackenberg, in: Hoeren/Sieber/Holznagel, *Multimedia-Recht*, 46th update, January 2018, part 16.7 mn. 43.

[130] Just as Schneider, in: Wolff/Brinck, *BeckOK DatenSR*, 25th ed., as at 1.8.2018, Völker- und unionsrechtliche Grundlagen, mn. 105 et seq.

[131] Cf. also Buttarelli, *Opinion S7/2015 – Bewältigung der Herausforderungen in Verbindung mit Big Data*, p. 17.

with the principle of human dignity in Art. 1 (1) GG.[132] It is intended to take into account the dangers and violations of personality which arise from information-related measures under the conditions of modern data processing. The fundamental right to informational self-determination guarantees an individual the right to decide for himself about the disclosure and use of his personal data.[133]

480 The fundamental right to informational self-determination consists of a double protective function. It is, on the one hand, an expression of the right to self-preservation and, on the other hand, an expression of the right to self-portrayal. For the former, an individual is guaranteed a spatially and thematically defined area which should basically remain free of unwanted inspection. For the latter, it is the individual who is solely responsible for determining the disclosure and use of personal data. The necessary technical and organizational measures for the protection of personal data stored in a Big Data application must be incorporated in the area of system data protection against the background of this fundamental right to informational self-determination.

2. The fundamental right to ensure the integrity and confidentiality of information technology systems

481 When developing the fundamental right to guarantee the confidentiality and integrity of information technology systems, the German Federal Constitutional Court assumed that a *"potentially extremely large and meaningful database"*[134] could be available on information technology systems and that access to it could pose a risk to personal rights. These dangers go beyond those associated with access to personal data and from which the individual would already be protected by the right to informational self-determination.[135]

482 As is clear from the name of the fundamental right developed in this way and against this background, the German Federal Constitutional Court presupposes that the integrity and confidentiality of the systems must be guaranteed. The resulting protective content of this fundamental right will still have to be clarified.

3. Indirect effect of fundamental rights between private individuals; Interpretation of guidelines

483 When developing and deriving these specific fundamental rights from general fundamental rights, the German Federal Constitutional Court had to decide on state action by means of an infiltration of information technology systems. It should, therefore, first be noted that fundamental rights initially only have a binding effect between the state and its citizens. However, they also have an indirect third-party effect in the relationship between private individuals. From this it follows, in particular, that fundamental rights – such as here the fundamental right to guarantee the integrity and confidentiality of information technology systems – must be taken into account in the interpretation of guidelines.

484 The design of information technology systems that are to be made usable for Big Data applications will have to be measured in a special way against this fundamental right. This applies to both the hardware and software components of such systems. This

[132] BVerfG, BVerfGE 65, 1/42.

[133] Gersdorf, in: Gersdorf/Paal, *BeckOK Informations- und Medienrecht*, 21st ed., as at 1.5 2017, Art. 2 GG mn. 17.

[134] BVerfG, 27.2.2008 – 1 BvR 370/07 = MMR 2008, 315 (318).

[135] Gersdorf, in Gersdorf/Paal, *BeckOK Informations- und Medienrecht*, 21st ed., as at 1.5.2017, Art. 2 GG mn. 21.

assumption is necessary against the background of the large amount of data, the resulting conclusions about individual decisions, and the associated danger for the right to self-preservation as part of the general right of personality. Big Data allows both past and future-related conclusions to be drawn about the behaviour of individuals, about whom the individuals themselves are often unlikely even to be aware. This hitherto unattained possibility of using data far surpasses the possibilities that the German Federal Constitutional Court had in mind when making its decision. When evaluating state interventions in or accesses to Big Data applications, particular restraint on the part of state authorities is required, particularly due to the large amounts of personal data in such applications, especially since a particularly high number of persons affected by such interventions or accesses must always be assumed.

Guiding Principle:

The fundamental rights of the data subject to informational self-determination as well as the integrity and confidentiality of IT systems and their impairment by the Big Data application must be examined closely when designing the technical and organizational measures for the protection of personal data in a Big Data application. The greater the possible impairment or threat to these rights, the higher the level of security to be achieved.

4. Ensuring confidentiality through technical and organizational measures

It is thus already necessary as part of the fundamental rights of data subjects to **485** protect the confidentiality and integrity of the data processing system with Big Data applications. This is referred to in particular in Art. 5 (1) (f) GDPR, which declares these terms a principle of the processing of personal data. This principle is expanded on, inter alia, in Art. 32 (1) (b) GDPR.[136] In order to ensure the ongoing confidentiality, integrity, availability and resilience of the systems and services, appropriate technical and/or organizational measures must be implemented – under consideration of a risk-based approach.

The term *measure* has to be understood very broadly. It covers all actions taken to **486** comply with data protection requirements.[137] Even if it will not always be possible – but also not absolutely necessary – to draw a clear dividing line, it will be possible to relate technical measures more to the process of processing while organizational measures can be linked to external framework conditions for the design of technical processing.[138]

Art. 32 (1) GDPR lists the following points of reference of a risk-based approach that **487** the controller is to take into account:

- the state of the art,
- the implementation costs,
- the nature, extent, circumstances and purposes of the processing as well as
- the varying likelihood and severity of the risk to the rights and freedoms of natural persons.

[136] Frenzel, in: Paal/Pauly, *GDPR*, 2nd ed. 2018, Art. 5 mn. 49.

[137] Cf. Karg, in: Wolff/Brink, *BeckOK DatenSR*, 25th ed., as at 1.8.2018, § 9 BDSG mn. 68.

[138] Martini, in: Paal/Pauly, *GDPR*, 2nd ed. 2018, Art. 24 mn. 21 et seq.

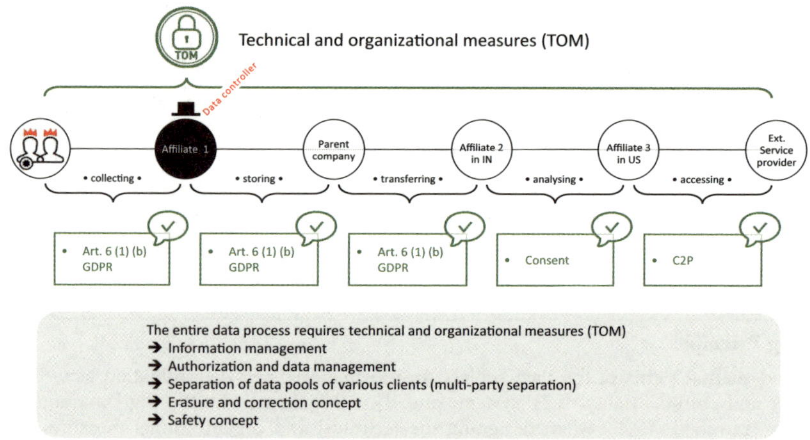

Figure 63: Technical and organizational measures in a sample chain

488 In general, it will therefore have to be assumed that particularly the scope and type of processing in Big Data analyses are considered to be particularly risky in view of the above explanations on their possible effects. Therefore, it is to be expected that for a compliant (from a legal sense) Big Data application, relatively high requirements will be to be put on the technical and organizational measures, even if neither the GDPR nor the BDSG a.F. contain specific or even requirements specifically aligned to Big Data applications to ensure compliance.

489 Against this background, possible technical and organizational measures that may become relevant in connection with the storage of personal data, especially in Big Data systems, are listed below. Due to the fundamental rights aspect, they focus on technical and organizational measures to maintain confidentiality and integrity. Finally, a further point to be considered is the storage limitation pursuant to Art. 5 (1) (f) GDPR. For this reason, this list naturally provides only reference guidelines regarding these measures.[139] The measures to be taken were already explained in detail above under mn. 445 *et seq.*

Confidentiality	– if necessary, even greater **access controls** to the data processing systems for Big Data applications – where appropriate, even greater **access controls** to prevent the use of data processing equipment for Big Data applications by unauthorized persons. – **encryption** of data (cf. Art. 32 (1) (a) GDPR) – separate storage of different data sets that are evaluated together without ever having been merged (through **secure multiparty computation**)[140]; logical separation; allocation of metatags in order to be able to separate data sets[141]

[139] Cf. to the whole Martini, in Paal/Pauly, *DS-GVO*, 2nd ed. 2018, Art. 24 mn. 35 et seq.
[140] Fundamentally Lindell/Pinkas, in: *The Journal of Privacy and Confidentiality*, 2009, p. 59 et seq.
[141] Hackenberg, in: Hoeren/Sieber/Holznagel, *Multimedia-Recht*, 46th update, January 2018, part 16.7 mn. 45.

Integrity	– **access and transfer controls** that only allow specifically authorized persons access to the data processing systems, especially for big data applications, ensure protection from unauthorized changes to the data and also guarantee protection from unauthorized transfer. – **input controls**, which make it easy to follow by whom the data were stored or changed – use of **electronic signatures**
Availability	– protection from **accidental destruction** and **accidental loss**, in particular, by a backup plan – ensuring the **undisturbed operation** of the data processing system, for example, through an uninterruptible power supply.
Resilience	**Establishment of resistance** (in particular against (D)DoS attacks)

Figure 64: Technical and organizational measures

It remains to be seen whether the rules of conduct approved for Big Data applications or an approved certification procedure will be available. Such procedures could facilitate proof that the controller has fulfilled the aforementioned obligations (Art. 24 (3) GDPR). **490**

II. System data protection for non-personal data only in a Big Data Application

If a Big Data application contains solely non-personal data (factual data or anonymous data), only the company's own requirements regarding the technical and organizational security of this Big Data application must be implemented, which the company itself sets with regard to the importance of such data. **491**

> **Guiding Principle:**
>
> Comprehensive system data protection is particularly important for Big Data applications. For personal data, the regulation in Art. 32 GDPR forms the standard, while for non-personal data the security requirements are defined by tConfidentialityConfidentialityhe company itself.

M. PROTECTION OF BIG DATA APPLICATIONS

Finally, the question must still be answered as to how a Big Data application can and is to be protected within the company. 492

I. Technical and organizational measures

On the one hand, this can include measures to protect data sets. The known server security measures will have to be applied here (cf. mn. 474 *et seq.*). In view of the sensitivity of the data, the requirements for such measures are generally to be classified as rather high, especially since this data is also susceptible to industrial espionage. As this information can represent company and trade secrets, e.g. within the meaning of § 2 No. 1 GeschGehG), there is also an increased interest in maintaining confidentiality. 493

It will usually be advisable to implement a process that regulates access to this data in the company. In many cases, affiliates and departments will be interested in accessing the data. In view of the aforementioned requirements, it must be assessed on a case-by-case basis whether it is permissible to grant access. In addition, the data protection requirements for processing this data must be made clear to those accessing the data. 494

It should also be (contractually) clarified which data – including non-personal data such as sensor data from industrial machines – may be used. At the same time, it may also be in the interest of the company, for example within the scope of a research cooperation, to grant other companies access to data sets. However, such use must also comply with the legal framework. 495

II. Protection of the algorithms underlying the Big Data application

On the other hand, it is also in the interest of the company to protect the algorithms used for evaluation and analysis in Big Data applications. However, it is questionable whether the mere algorithm can be granted legal protection at all. Firstly, the problem lies in the fact that there are various definitions of the term algorithm. One could focus on individual program loops, so that more extensive computer programs contain numerous different algorithms which are either protectable either individually or at least in their whole as computer programs. In computer science, in contrast, an algorithm is seen as a precisely formulated processing rule that solves a problem in a certain way in finite arithmetic steps. This is probably also how German courts understands the term algorithm in defining it as *"the rule of calculation considered in the computer program and relating to a given computer"*.[142] 496

In this latter interpretation, the algorithm thus has a certain degree of abstraction and must therefore be distinguished from the specific program code protected by copyright alone. As a general calculation rule or method, an algorithm is therefore not eligible for copyright protection. The way in which subroutines and work routines are linked to branch instructions is then only protected by copyright in the specific program code. 497

---

[142] BGH, *CR* 1985, 22/30 – Inkasso-Programm; OLG Frankfurt a.M., *GRUR* 1983, 753 (755); OLG Karlsruhe, *GRUR* 1983, 300 (305).

Algorithms are therefore generally not capable of being protected by copyright, but they can be the subject of trade and business secrets within the meaning of § 2 No. 1 GeschGehG, in which case, however, the company's particular need to maintain confidentiality should be expressed by corresponding access restrictions and controls as well as other mechanisms to secure secrecy of the algorithms.

498 Algorithms are not covered by patent legal protection because, e.g. according to Art. 1 (3) No. 1 Patent Act (PatG), discoveries as well as scientific theories and mathematical methods and, according to Art. 1 (3) No. 3 PatG, schemes, rules and methods for performing mental acts, as well as programs for data processing systems themselves cannot be patented by law.

Guiding Principle:

The algorithm on which a specific evaluation in a Big Data application is based is typically as such not included in copyright protection; only the specific program code in which the algorithm is reflected is eligible for copyright protection. Algorithms may at most be the subject of trade secrets within the meaning of § 2 No. 1 GeschGehG.

III. Compliance management system

499 Big Data activities should be part of a compliance management system. In practical terms, the data and its evaluation can entail a multitude of legal requirements. As shown here, this concerns data protection and the protection of intellectual property; in addition, competition law, for example, may also become relevant, which may be the case in particular if the respective operator has either itself attained a dominant position, e.g. within the meaning of §§ 19, 20 Competition Act (GWB) with its Big Data application, or if it has to grant third parties non-discriminatory access to evaluation results, or if it wishes to have access to raw data (which in turn can only be obtained by a holder with a dominant position within the meaning of §§ 19, 20 GWB). Pursuant to § 18 (1) GWB, an undertaking is dominant in the market where, as a supplier or purchaser of a certain type of goods or commercial services, it is active in the relevant product and geographic market in the following manner:

- has no competitors,
- is not exposed to substantial competition, or
- has a superior market position in relation to its competitors.

500 In assessing the market position of an undertaking in relation to its competitors, § 18 (3) GWB requires that:

- its market share,
- its financial strength,
- its access to procurement or sales markets,
- close links with other companies,
- legal or factual barriers to market entry by other undertakings,
- actual or potential competition from undertakings located within or outside the scope of the GWB,
- the ability to switch its supply or demand to other products or commercial services, and
- the possibility for the opposite market side to switch to other companies,

501 be taken into account. In the case of multi-sided markets and networks in particular, § 18 (3a) GWB stipulates that when assessing the market position of a company, the following must also be taken into account:

- direct and indirect network effects,
- the parallel use of several services and the effort required for users to switch between them,
- its economies of scale related to network effects,
- its access to data relevant to competition, and
- any innovation-driven competitive pressure.

Finally, pursuant to § 18 (4) GWB, it is presumed that a company is dominant if it has a market share of at least 40 %, whereby in the area of Big Data applications in particular the determination and delimitation of the relevant market may be difficult, but it is also of primary significance. **502**

Guiding Principle:

For its part, the operator of a Big Data application may be subject to competition restrictions if it has acquired a dominant position within the meaning of §§ 19, 20 GWB, so that it may have to grant third parties non-discriminatory access to raw data and evaluation results.

IV. Aspects of copyright contract law in the database management system

Due to the complexity and scope of Big Data applications, specially-developed database management systems are used to ensure data interconnectivity and satisfactory processing performance. The technical implementation of storage in such database systems must be within the limits of copyright law, i.e. the operator of the Big Data application must not only possess a legally acquired and valid right of use (= license) for the database management system used for the specific Big Data application but the license itself must also include the specific Big Data application its scope (objective, temporal and spatial). Contrary to opinions often encountered in practice, the license granted to (acquired by) a group company does not contain any right for all other companies in this group to use this license unless explicitly stated. **503**

Guiding Principles:

The database management system used to establish a Big Data application must be licensed in such a way that both the operator and all other users of the Big Data application possess a legally acquired and valid right of use.

Insofar as the data included in a Big Data application enjoy legal protection (cf. mn. 117–121), the handling of such data in the Big Data application must comply with the limits of the right of use granted thereto (cf. §§ 31 *et seq.* UrhG). **504**

If a database system is used which duplicates data (cf. § 16 UrhG), this process may result in a copyright infringement. This may be the case, for example, if data records are stored in distributed form for scaling purposes. It must therefore be ensured at all times that it is clear which data enjoy which protection and under which conditions they may be used. For example, the use of corresponding attributes in the database can prove to be useful here. **505**

Reproduction in this sense also occurs when legally protected data are extracted and transferred to a database for the purposes of a Big Data application.[143] **506**

[143] Cf. Spindler, *GRUR* 2016, 1112 (1113).

507 Overall, apart from agreements on rights of use, it also seems possible that copyright holders may consent to reproduction on the basis of implied conduct, for example by placing works online without restrictions[144] (the case is different for Open Data, which typically has special requirements and usage restrictions). From the perspective of data protection law, it should also be pointed out that, also against a background of the rights of data subjects, it must be clear where which data are located.[145]

508 The legal exception in § 44a UrhG also permits temporary acts of reproduction and exempts reproductions understood in this sense from the protection of § 16 UrhG. This is the case if the following conditions are cumulatively present:

- fleeting or concomitant duplication,
- which is an integral and essential part of a technical process,
- the sole purpose of which is to enable a transfer in a network between third parties through an intermediary or lawful use, and
- which has no independent economic significance.

509 However, there is often – also in the context of *sharding* – not just fleeting duplication, as the data is permanently stored in a *shard*. Something else could apply to in-memory database systems. Similarly, the duplication might often have be of separate economic relevance.[146]

Guiding Principles:

If only temporary acts of reproduction occur in Big Data applications, the legal exception to the reservation of the right of reproduction in § 16 UrhG regulated in § 44a UrhG may be relevant.

---

[144] Zieger/Smirra, *MMR* 2013, 418 (419).

[145] Hackenberg, in: Hoeren/Sieber/Holznagel, *Multimedia-Recht*, 46th update, January 2018, part 16.7 mn. 56.

[146] Doubtful overall, even if not specifically with regard to sharding – Spindler, *GRUR* 2016, 1112 (1114 et seq.); Zieger/Smirra, *MMR* 2013, 418 (419).

N. LEGAL CONSEQUENCES OF NON-COMPLIANCE WITH THE LEGAL REQUIREMENTS SET OUT IN THIS GUIDE

The legal consequences of the breach of data protection laws vary depending on which data and thus which laws are affected. These legal consequences may also occur cumulatively. 510

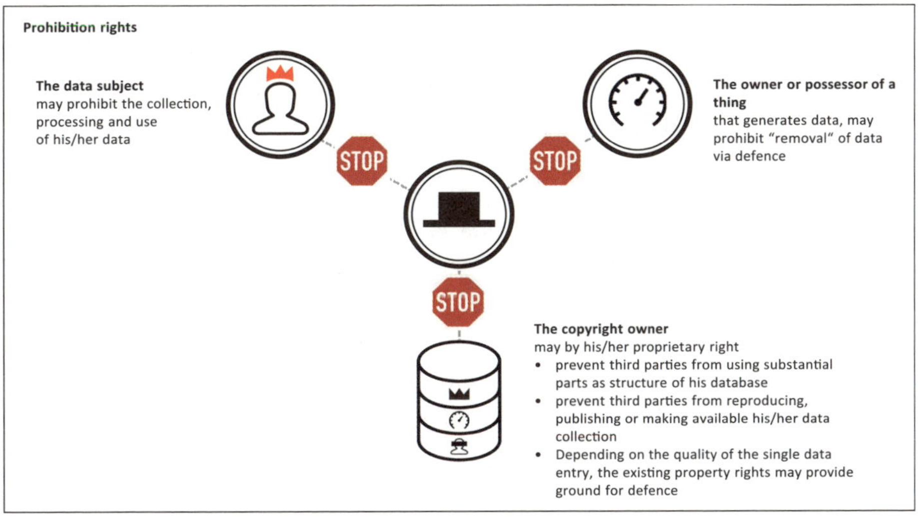

Figure 65: Prohibition rights

In detail, this means the following: 511

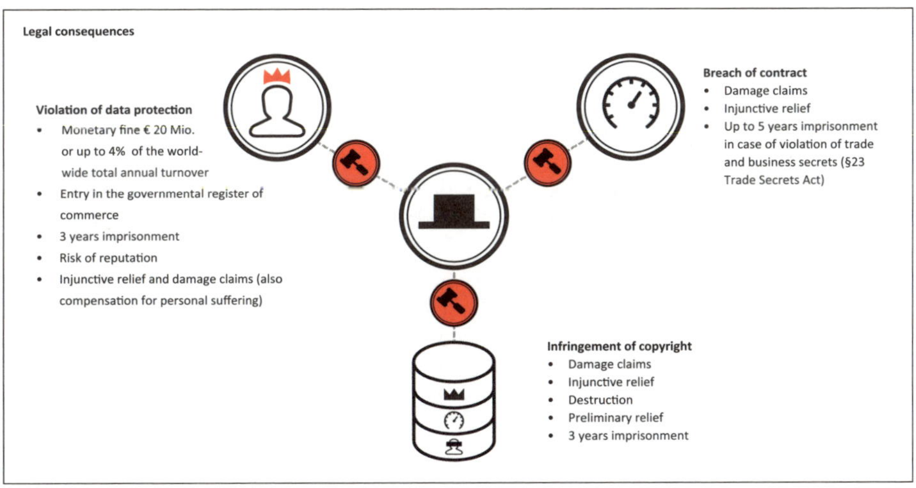

Figure 66: Legal consequences

I. Sanctions in case of violation of data protection regulations

512 The exploitation or use as well as the storage of personal data in a Big Data application beyond legal retention rights (generally Art. 6 (1) (f) GDPR) or retention obligations (Art. 6 (1) (c) GDPR) is only unlawful if the data concerned could not be materially evaluated in the Big Data application. Unlawfulness also exists in the case of other infringements of data protection obligations, in particular, in the case of not undertaking technical and organizational measures or where such measures were not sufficient to protect personal data from unauthorized access (Art. 32 GDPR), of information that has not been provided or is insufficient for the data subject (Art. 13 and 14 GDPR in conjunction with §§ 32, 33 BDSG), or of data protection impact assessments that have been wrongly omitted or are incorrect (Art. 35 GDPR).

1. Administrative fines

513 Art. 83 (4) GDPR provides for possible fines of up to EUR 10 million or 2 % of the worldwide group annual turnover in the preceding financial year for breaches stemming from unlawful evaluation and exploitation or unlawful storage as a result of a non-existent erasure concept. This includes the obligations of the controller and the contract processors in accordance with Art. 8, 11, 25–39, 42 and 43 GDPR:

- a violation of the conditions for the consent of a minor under 16 years of age in accordance with Art. 8 GDPR,
- [Art. 11 GDPR here probably not relevant],
- the obligation to ensure data protection through technical design and through data protection-friendly pre-settings in accordance with Art. 25 GDPR (cf. mn. 289 *et seq.*),
- the obligations to conclude a corresponding agreement with joint responsibility for a Big Data application (Art. 26 GDPR, cf. mn. 141 *et seq.*)
- the obligation to conclude a C2P agreement pursuant to Art. 28 GDPR (cf. mn. 127 *et seq.*),
- the obligation to establish and maintain processing inventories in accordance with Art. 30 GDPR (cf. mn. 441 *et seq.*)
- the obligation to implement technical and organizational measures to protect personal data from unauthorized access in accordance with Art. 32 GDPR (cf. mn. 445 *et seq.*),
- the obligations to report data protection breaches to the supervisory authority and to inform the data subjects in accordance with Art. 33 and 34 GDPR,
- the obligation to carry out a data protection impact assessment and to consult the competent supervisory authority in accordance with Art. 35 and 36 GDPR (cf. mn. 467 *et seq.*), and
- the obligation to appoint a data protection officer in accordance with Art. 37–39 GDPR (*cf.* mn. 164 *et seq.*), to provide the necessary material, technical and personnel resources and to integrate the data protection officer into the organization
- [the obligations from Art. 42 and 43 GDPR are not relevant here].

Pursuant to Art. 83 (5) and (6) GDPR, serious infringements can be punished with fines of up to EUR 20 million or 4 % of the worldwide consolidated annual turnover in the preceding financial year. In the area of Big Data applications, these are mainly breaches pursuant to Art. 83 (5) (a) GDPR of the following: 514

- the basic principles for processing, including the conditions for consent, in accordance with Art. 5 GDPR
- the collection, storage and processing of personal data or their transmission or making accessible to third parties as well as the evaluation of such data in Big Data applications, without one of the lawful grounds in Art. 6 (1) GDPR being present or the Big Data subject having consented to it in each case (cf. in this context mn. 184 *et seq.*),
- the conditions defined in Art. 7 GDPR for an effective consent (cf. mn. 197 *et seq.*), as well as
- the conditions defined in Art. 9 GDPR, under which the collection, storage and processing of special categories of personal data (cf. mn. 59 *et seq.*) or their transmission or making accessible to third parties as well as the evaluation of such data in Big Data applications.

The definition of a company under competition law pursuant to Art. 101 and 102 TFEU applies in assessing the amount of the fine.[147] This means that a decisive factor is the turnover of the entire group of companies to which the controller belongs. The turnover of the data protection authority alone is irrelevant for the assessment of the fine framework. The framework for fines can thus typically go well beyond the nominal amounts of EUR 10 or 20 million specified in Art. 83 (4) or (5) GDPR for companies within a group. 515

According to Art. 83 (2) sentence 2 GDPR, due regard is to be given to the following factors are decision on the particular fines in the individual case[148]: 516

- nature, gravity and duration of the infringement, taking into account the nature, scope or purpose of the processing concerned, the number of data subjects affected by the processing and the level of the damage suffered (Art. 83 (2) (a) GDPR);
- intentional or negligent character of the infringement (Art. 83 (2) (b) GDPR);
- any action taken by the controller or processor to mitigate the damage suffered by the data subjects (Art. 83 (2) (c) GDPR);
- the degree of responsibility of the controller or processor taking into account technical and organizational measures implemented by them pursuant to Art. 25 and 32 GDPR (Art. 83 (2) (d) GDPR);
- any relevant previous infringements by the controller or processor (Art. 83 (2) (e) GDPR);
- degree of cooperation with the supervisory authority in order to remedy the infringement and mitigate its possible adverse effects (Art. 83 (2) (f) GDPR);
- categories of personal data affected by the infringement (Art. 83 (2) (g) GDPR);
- the manner in which the infringement became known to the supervisory authority, in particular whether and, if so to what extent, the controller or the processor of the order notified the infringement (Art. 83 (2) (h) GDPR);
- where measures referred to in Art. 58 (2) GDPR have previously been ordered against the controller or processor concerned with regard to the same subject matter, compliance with all those measures (Art. 83 (2) (i) GDPR);

---

[147] Recital 150 GDPR.

[148] See also the recently published "Concept of the independent data protection supervisory authorities of the German Federal Government and the German Laender for the imposition of fines in proceedings against corporate entities", as of 14 October 2019.

- adherence to approved rules of conduct pursuant to Art. 40 GDPR or approved certification mechanisms pursuant to Art. 42 GDPR (Art. 83 (2) (j) GDPR); and
- any other aggravating or mitigating factor in the case, such as financial benefits gained, or losses avoided, directly or indirectly, from the infringement (Art. 83 (2) (k) GDPR).

2. Material and non-material damages supplemented by power to bring collective actions

517 Art. 82 (1) GDPR provides a basis for the data subject to claim compensation for material and, above all, non-material damages for data protection infringements; in this way, compensation for pain and suffering for data protection infringements will be possible in the future. Since this standard for damages for pain and suffering is new in data protection law, there is currently (May 2019) no experience as to the extent of the amount of damages to be awarded for pain and suffering; in general, however, a certain trend can be observed in case law whereby damages for pain and suffering awarded in the jurisdiction for breaches of the general right to personality, for example, due to an illegal press report, were higher in recent years. On this basis, the assessment of damages for pain and suffering is not unlikely to be in the lower five-figure range.

518 The debtor of such a claim for damages for pain and suffering is primarily the controller responsible for the unlawful data processing. In contrast to the BDSG a. F., this also results in a direct claim against the processor. The prerequisite under German law is an adequate and causal violation of a data protection law which leads to the cause of damage. However, this only applies to the processor's own statutory or contractual breach of duty with regard to breaches in duty in his function as processor.

519 Furthermore, there is a power for associations to institute collective actions, as defined in § 2 (1) No. 11 Act on Actions for Injunctive Relief for Breaches of Consumer law and Other Laws (UKlaG) and Art. 80 (1) GDPR.

3. Misdemeanours

520 § 130 Regulatory Offences Act (OWiG) sanctions the violation of supervisory duties by the owner of the company. If this is a legal entity, § 9 OWiG provides that the sanctions also apply to its authorized representatives. A violation of § 130 OWiG can either be attributed to the owner or, via §§ 130, 30 OWiG, to the company itself.

4. Entry in central trade register (loss of entitlement to participate in public tenders)

521 Finally, a fine imposed on a board member due to a company's breach of data protection law, is entered in the central trade register when the fine exceeds EUR 200. The Federal Office of Justice can request extracts from this register. These, in turn, can be passed on to authorities and public clients if there is a legitimate interest. This, in turn, can lead to the loss of entitlement to participate in any public invitation to tender.

5. Penalties according to the BDSG

522 Punishment of data protection violations results from § 42 BDSG: Thereafter, imprisonment of up to three years or a fine will be imposed on anyone who knowingly transmits or otherwise makes accessible to a third party personal data of a large number of persons that are not generally accessible without being entitled to do so, and who also acts for commercial interests. Furthermore, anyone who processes personal data that is

not generally accessible without being entitled to do so, or who obtains incorrect information by fraud, and in each case acts against payment or with the intention of enriching himself or another person or damaging another person, may be punished with a custodial sentence of up to two years or with a fine.

However, such acts will only be prosecuted upon request (§ 42 (3) BDSG). The data subject or the Federal Commissioner for Data Protection and Freedom of Information and the competent data protection supervisory authority are entitled to file an application. **523**

6. Supervisory intervention rights of the data protection supervisory authorities

In accordance with Art. 58 GDPR, each data protection supervisory authority has the following investigative powers relevant in the context of Big Data applications: **524**

- to order the controller, the processor and, where applicable, the controller's or processor's representative to provide any information necessary it requires for the performance of its tasks;
- carry out investigations in the form of data protection audits;
- to notify the controller responsible for a Big Data application or the processor of an alleged infringement of the GDPR;
- to obtain, from the controller of a Big Data application and/or its processor, access to all personal data and information necessary for the performance of its tasks,
- to obtain access, in accordance with Union or Member State procedural law, to the premises, including all data processing equipment and means, of the controller of a Big Data application and/or of the processor of that application.

In accordance with Art. 58 (2) GDPR, in the context of Big Data applications each data protection supervisory authority is authorized to: **525**

- issue warnings to a controller of a Big Data application or its commissioned data processor that intended processing operations are likely to infringe the GDPR;
- issue reprimands to a controller of a Big Data application or his commissioned data processor where processing operations have infringed the GDPR;
- order the controller of a Big Data application or his commissioned data processor to comply with the data subject's requests to exercise his rights pursuant to the GDPR,
- order the Big Data application manager or his contract processor to bring any processing operations into compliance with the GDPR, where appropriate, in a specific manner and within a specific period,
- order the controller of a Big Data application to communicate a personal data breach to the data subject,
- impose a temporary or permanent restriction on processing in the Big Data application, including a ban on the continued operation of the Big Data application,
- order the rectification or erasure of personal data or the limitation of processing in accordance with Art. 16, 17 and 18 GDPR (cf. mn. 365 *et seq.*) and the notification of such action to the recipients to whom such personal data have been disclosed pursuant to Art. 17 (2) and 19 GDPR;
- impose a fine in accordance with Art. 83 GDPR (cf. mn. 513 *et seq.* above) in addition to or instead of measures mentioned Art. 58 (2) GDPR, depending on the circumstances of the individual case,
- order the suspension of data flows from a Big Data application to a recipient in a third country or to an international organization, including, in particular, the results of analysis still targeted at specific Big Data users.

526 Finally, on the authority of Art. 58 (3) GDPR, each supervisory authority is authorized to advise the controller of a Big Data application according to the procedure of the prior consultation pursuant to Art. 36 GDPR. Subsequent approval and/or consulting powers, which are listed in the GDPR, are not directly relevant here.

II. Legal consequences of infringement of copyrights in collective works or database protection rights

1. Injunctive relief

527 The infringement of copyrights in collective works or database protection rights entitles the right holder to assert a claim for injunctive relief; under German law these are standardized for copyrights and database protection rights in § 97 (1) UrhG. A cease and desist claim can always be asserted if, either risk of further, repeated infringements can already be presumed due to an infringement of the law, or if, due to the circumstances of the individual case, there is a risk of a first infringement and the cease and desist claim can be asserted as a preventive measure. The claim is meant as a non-imminent infringement of a right or, if the infringement continues permanently, for the cessation of the permanent infringement. In contrast to the claim for damages explained in mn. 528 below, the injunctive relief does not depend on fault. The claim is also valid, therefore, if the controller does not even know the circumstances which justify the unlawfulness of these infringements and therefore does not even know that he infringes copyrights or database protection rights of third parties by using such data.

2. Damages claim

528 The infringement of copyrights to collective works or database protection rights also entitles the right holder to assert claims for damages. Under German law, the claim for damages also results from § 97 (2) UrhG. When calculating the amount of damages, the right holder can choose between three different methods of calculation. In addition to the calculation on the basis of the actual damage (e.g. the profit lost by the right holder), the absorption of profits, i.e. the claim to payment of the entire profit received by the infringer through the violation (*skimming-off*), results from § 97 (2) sentence 2 UrhG, and, as a third method, the license analogy listed in § 97 (2) sentence 3 UrhG, in which the damage is calculated according to the amount of the license fees which the infringer would otherwise have paid if it had concluded corresponding data use or license agreements. These claims for damages only compensate the past infringements of copyrights or database protection rights; if the infringer wishes to continue to use the data concerned in a manner that impairs the copyrights or database protection rights within the scope of his Big Data application, it must acquire the necessary rights of use for the future, despite payment of damages, and accordingly pay further usage fees/license fees.

3. Enforcement of copyright claims

529 In contrast to claims for damages, claims for injunctive relief can also be enforced in interim legal protection proceedings by means of an interim injunction. Decisions in interim relief can be obtained at short notice within a few days, in case of doubt even without the defendant having been heard. Such interim injunctions must be observed immediately after they have been served by a bailiff appointed by the applicant, i.e. the Big Data application in question may no longer be operated or used from this point in

time. Appeals concerning an interim injunction do not have a suspensive effect, i.e. they must continue to be considered during ongoing appeal proceedings until the interim injunction is revoked by a new court decision. for The defendant who has suffered damage as a result of an unjustified injunction, may have a claim for damages under § 945 ZPO against the claimant; however, as the benefit of a Big Data application lies in the evaluation and analysis of data available almost in real time and the business opportunities created as a result are possibly irretrievably lost, a claim for damages due to a Big Data application having been temporarily switched off due to the enforcement of a preliminary injunction will not fully compensate the detriments incurred by the defendant.

A decision on the merits of a case can only be given after appropriate preparation of an oral hearing by exchanging several written briefs, after the oral hearing thus prepared has been held (in one or more hearings before the court) and, if necessary, after further hearings regarding evidence collection. Thus, investigative procedures as part of the main proceedings may take several years. **530**

4. Destruction claim

Of the claims for destruction, recall and release made pursuant to § 98 UrhG, the claim for destruction pursuant to § 98 (1) sentence 1 UrhG is particularly relevant for data from collected works or databases unlawfully used in Big Data applications. The right holder may claim destruction of the unlawfully-made copies of data still in the possession of the infringer of copyright or database protection rights, i.e. ultimately the removal of this data from the Big Data application. **531**

5. Liability of the controller

Injunctive relief pursuant to § 97 (1) UrhG as well as destruction claims pursuant to § 98 (1) sentence 1 UrhG may also be asserted against the company owner, i.e. here the relevant responsible entity that uses data in or for Big Data applications in violation of copyright or database protection rights, regardless of negligence or fault. This claim against the responsible entity is independent of a claim against the acting employee of that entity. As this is a strict claim against the owner of the responsible entity, the latter also has no possibility of exculpating himself by referring to a careful selection and supervision of the acting employees pursuant to § 831 (1) sentence 2 BGB.[149] **532**

6. Right to information

In order to quantify the claim for damages and to secure evidence, the owner of copyright or database protection rights also has the right to information pursuant to § 101 UrhG as well as the right to presentation and inspection pursuant to § 101a UrhG. **533**

7. Criminal offences

The unauthorized use of copyrighted works is also punishable under criminal law: **534**

Anyone who reproduces or distributes a copyrightable work without the consent of the copyright holder may be punished with a fine or imprisonment for up to three years pursuant to § 106 (1) UrhG; any attempt is punishable by law (§ 106 (2) UrhG). **535**

---

[149] Reber, in: Ahlberg/Götting, *BeckOK Urheberrecht*, 21st ed., as at 20 April 2018, § 99 UrhG mn. 1.

536 The exploitation of databases contrary to § 87b (1) UrhG without the consent of the authorized party may also be punished with a fine or imprisonment for up to three years, (§ 108 (1) No. 8 UrhG); any attempt is punishable by law (§ 108 (2) UrhG).

537 However, these acts are always prosecuted only on application, whereby the copyright holder is entitled to apply in the case of criminal liability according to § 106 UrhG and the owner of the database protection rights in the case of criminal liability according to § 108 UrhG (§ 109 UrhG). The public prosecutor's office, as the prosecution authority, can only intervene *ex officio* and initiate prosecution where it establishes a special public interest in the prosecution.

III. Violation of virtual householder's rights

1. Injunctive relief

538 In analogy to § 1004 BGB, the owner of a virtual householder's right is also entitled to injunctive relief in the form of claims against the infringer that are independent of negligence and fault, i.e. against the infringer who deducts data from the relevant installation/IT system in violation of the virtual householder's right without the householder's consent. As with the right to an injunction under copyright law (cf. mn. 527 above), a risk of repetition is presumed in the case of a breach of virtual property rights that has already been committed. Otherwise, the specific circumstances of the individual case may give rise to the risk of an initial breach of the virtual householder's right, on the basis of which injunctive relief claims could be asserted.

2. Damage claims

539 Virtual property rights law, which is constitutionally based in particular on the fundamental right to the integrity of information technology systems (cf. mn. 481 *et seq*. above), can be qualified as miscellaneous law within the meaning of § 823 (1) BGB. The possessor of virtual property rights could therefore also be entitled to claims for damages in accordance with § 823 (1) BGB. Case law and legal literature have not yet come to a conclusion whether damage can also be calculated according to the three damage calculation methods already recognized for copyright infringements (cf. mn. 528 above). Due to the affinity of virtual property rights with copyrights, there are, however, good reasons for being able to calculate the amount of the claim for damages for infringement of virtual property rights according to these three alternative calculation methods.

540 With regard to the consequences under procedural law, cf. mn. 529–530 above.

3. Subordinate claims

541 The owner of a virtual householder's right is entitled to a claim for the provision of the information necessary to calculate the amount of damage against the infringer in accordance with §§ 242, 259 BGB.

4. Relevance under criminal law

542 The violation of a virtual property right is not expressly defined as a criminal offence in the German Criminal Code (StGB). However, depending on the circumstances of the individual case, criminal liability according to § 202a StGB for unauthorized access to data not intended for the perpetrator and particularly secured against unauthorized

access may be considered, which can be punished with a fine or imprisonment for up to three years. Depending on how the data is obtained under the circumstances of the individual case, criminal liability for unauthorized interception of data in accordance with § 202b StGB is also possible and punishable with a fine or imprisonment for up to two years.

IV. Sanctions for infringing business or trade secrets pursuant to the German Trade Secrets Act

1. Criminal offences

The protection of business or company secrets under the German Trade Secrets Act (GeschGehG) is a matter of both civil and criminal law. Any employee who discloses a trade or business secret entrusted or made available to him or her in the course of his employment during the term of the employment relationship without authorization to someone for the purpose of competition, for his own benefit, for the benefit of a third party or with the intention of causing damage to the owner of the enterprise shall be punished by a fine or imprisonment for up to three years (§ 23 (1) GeschGehG). **543**

Similarly, pursuant to § 23 (2) GeschGehG, a person may be punished who, for the purposes of competition, self-interest, for the benefit of a third party or for the purpose of causing damage to the owner of the undertaking, obtains or secures a trade or business secret without authorization by using technical means, producing a physical reproduction of the secret or taking away an object in which the secret is embodied or anyone who exploits or discloses without authorization a business or trade secret which he or she has obtained by means of one of the notifications referred to in § 23 (2) GeschGehG, may be punished if he or she, for the purpose of competition, for his own benefit, for the benefit of a third party or for the purpose of causing damage to the owner of the undertaking, obtains or secures a trade or business secret by using technical means, producing a physical reproduction of the secret or taking away an object in which the secret is embodied . **544**

In particularly serious cases, the custodial sentence may even amount to up to five years in both offence alternatives, whereby a particularly serious case exists if the offender acts commercially or if he or she knows at the time of notification in accordance with § 23 (1) GeschGehG that the trade secret in question is to be exploited abroad (§ 23 (4) GeschGehG). In all the cases mentioned, the attempt is already punishable by law (§ 23 (5) GeschGehG. Offences under § 23 GeschGehG will only be prosecuted at the request of the aggrieved owner of the business or trade secret concerned, unless the prosecution authority considers intervention *ex officio* necessary because of the special public interest in the prosecution (§ 23 (8) GeschGehG). **545**

2. Civil law Claims under the German Trade Secrets Act

Under § 10 (1) GeschGehG, the aggrieved owner of the business or trade secret concerned is entitled to a – fault-based – claim for damages against the infringer. **546**

Pursuant to § 6 GeschGehG, the aggrieved owner of the infringed business or trade secret is also entitled to injunctive relief in the scope of content, regardless of negligence or fault, as already described above under mn. 527 for copyright injunctive relief claims and under mn. 538 in the case of infringements of the virtual householder's right. For consequences under procedural law, cf. above under mn. 529–530. **547**

V. Contractual claims

548 If data is tapped and further processed in a Big Data application upon performance of a contract, such as a maintenance contract or a repair order for a technical system, without the knowledge and consent of the system operator, or if appropriate precautions are taken on one of these occasions so that the system permanently transmits such data to the operator of a Big Data application in the future without the knowledge and consent of the system operator, this can be qualified under civil law as a breach of contractual ancillary obligations within the meaning of § 280 BGB, which leads to a claim for damages by the system operator. Only the causal damage caused by this breach of ancillary obligations and which can be demonstrated and proven by the system operator, together with any lost profits, are eligible for compensation.

549 If and to the extent that such a maintenance or repair contract does not provide for the tapping of data or the establishment of corresponding transmission operations, the system operator shall also be entitled to contractually corresponding injunctive relief in analogy to §§ 249, 1004 BGB. For consequences under procedural law, cf. mn. 529 above.

550 Under criminal law, such tapping of plant data may be punishable under §§ 202a (unauthorized access to data), 202b (interception of data) or 303b (computer sabotage) StGB, which may result in fines or imprisonment for up to three years.

O. BIG DATA APPLICATIONS AS A SERVICE

The basics and individual aspects of Big Data have been discussed in detail in the preceding chapters. However, what does this mean for a controller who wants to operate Big Data professionally? 551

The controller must know his rights and obligations in handling the data and strategically use the legal scope for manoeuvre with regard to its business models. For example, a provider who wants to offer big data applications to third parties as a service from a public or private cloud platform must not only have the infrastructure to operate a cloud but must also guarantee the legal requirements. If the purpose of such a cloud provider is merely to offer storage capacity to its customers, the cloud provider requires authority for this (usually C2P agreement) and must ensure the following: client separation, appropriate technical and organizational measures, if necessary also for foreign customers adapting to the applicable law, erasure at the request of the customer, etc. The cloud provider must also ensure that its customers are able to access storage capacity for the duration of the contract. In addition, it must document the data processing operations and be transparent to his customers with regard to storage, forwarding and access from/to data. 552

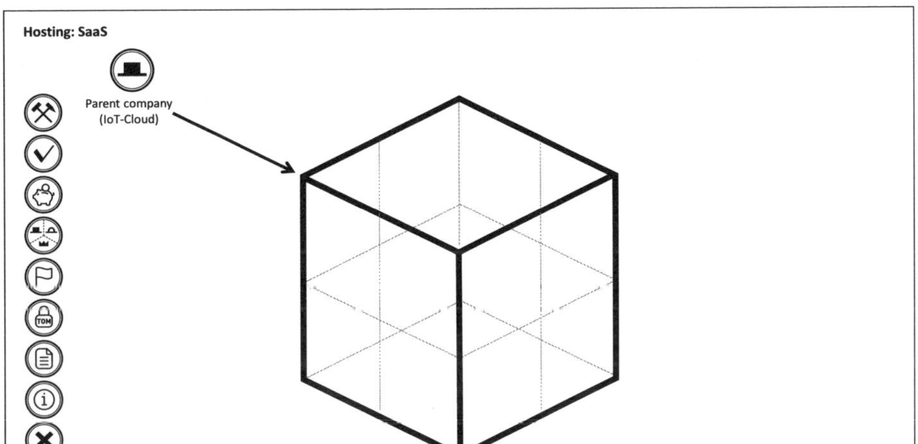

Figure 67: Responsibilities of a hosting provider

The customer of the cloud provider is the controller himself and has rights and obligations vis-à-vis his customers if it outsources customer data – including employee data, if applicable – to external storage space for various purposes/business models. These rights and obligations are not identical to those of the cloud provider, as the respective purposes, lawful grounds, customers, etc. are different. As described in the chapters above, a cloud user also requires a lawful ground for each purpose of his business models with regard to the various types of data, their combination and analysis, and must guarantee appropriate separation, provide organizational and tech- 553 nical measures, document its data processing (e.g. in the process directory) and inform his customers in a transparent manner about his actions and those of his contracted data processors.

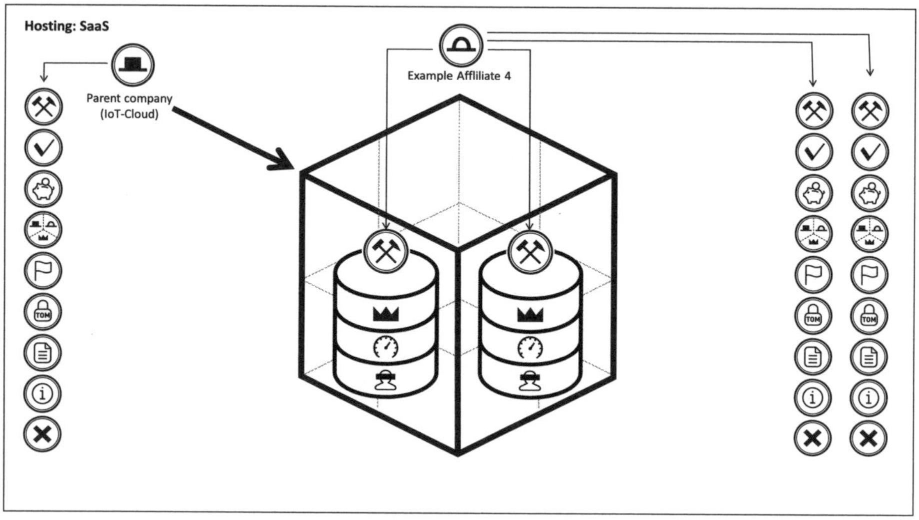

Figure 68: Responsibilities of a hosting user

554 The same applies if the provider of Big Data applications from a cloud has not only one customer but many different customers with different business models. Each of these customers is responsible for his own customer data and must observe rights and obligations when processing his customer data – including employee data, if applicable. Accordingly, the cloud provider must be in a position to consider and implement different customer requirements at the same time.

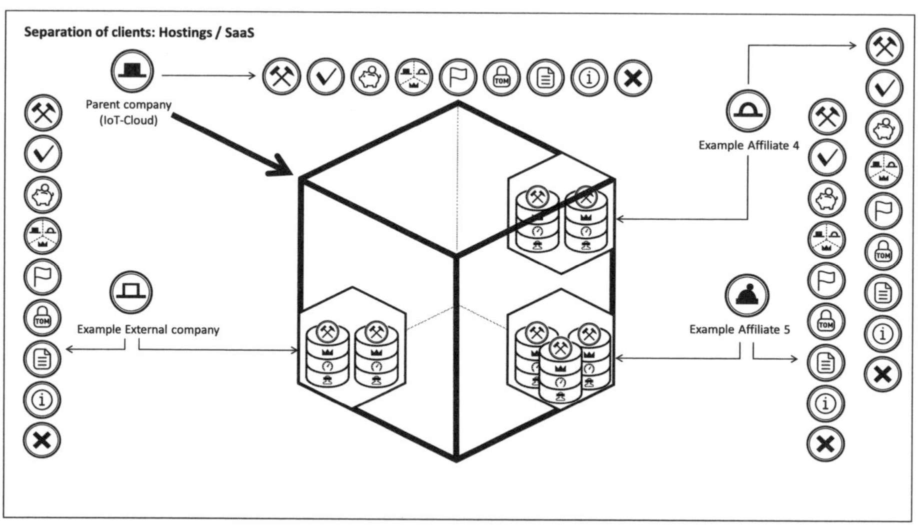

Figure 69: Separation of clients in a hosting/SaaS environment

The rights also result from the different roles and thus the purpose and lawful grounds of the controller. For example, a cloud provider may store the data of his customers and their customers, but may not view, analyse, change or otherwise do so on his own initiative and responsibility if it has no lawful ground. 555

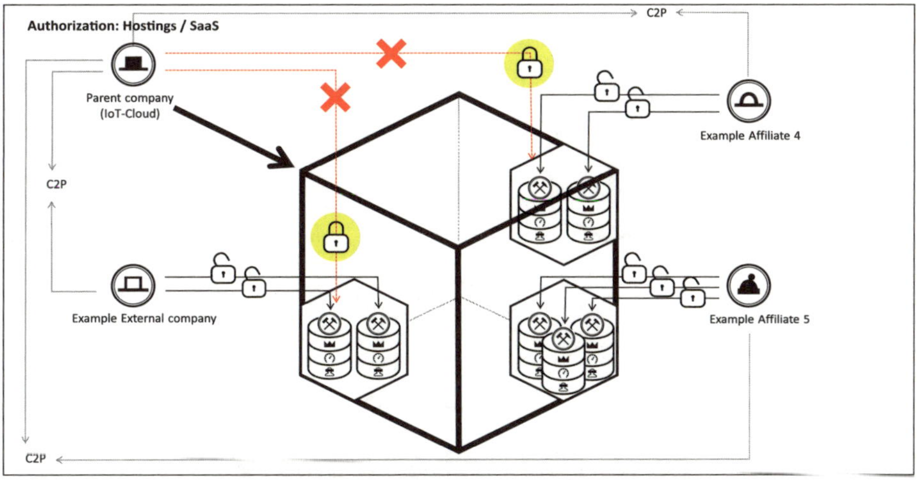

Figure 70: Authorization of a hosting/SaaS provider

The customers of a provider of Big Data applications from a cloud must grant the provider the right to inspect or analyse the data, i.e. there must be a purpose beyond the mere provision of data storage and it must be offered as a service so that the cloud provider has more extensive authorities. The customer of a cloud provider can only grant this authority to the cloud provider if the customer himself has the authority to do so from his customers. 556

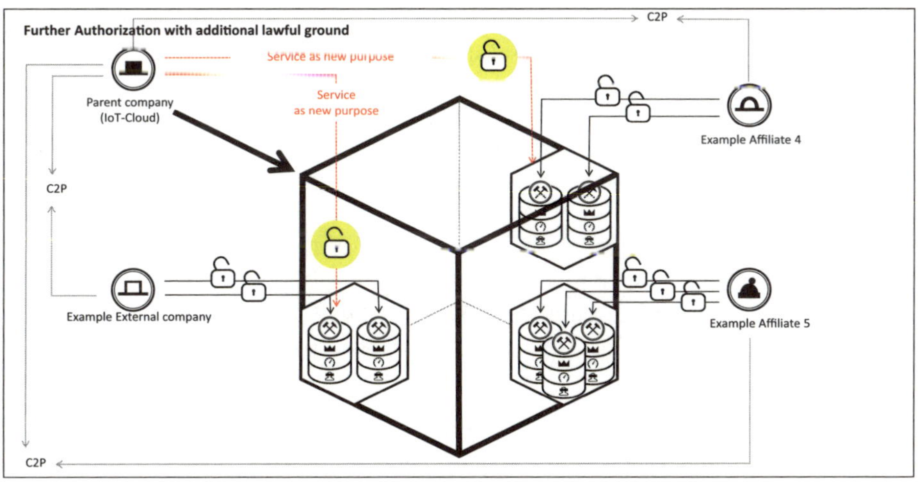

Figure 71: Further authorization with additional legitimization

If the provider of Big Data applications uses other cloud-subcontractors in Germany and abroad because his storage space is not sufficient or he wants to offer a 24/7 *follow* 557 *the sun* service for his international clientele, further controllers (*subcontractors*) are added, each of which also has his own rights and obligations as a cloud provider and in terms of data protection law as a contract processor. In addition to his own cloud, the provider must also consider and legitimize its rights and obligations – for example, the transfer and storage of data to/by his *subcontractors*.

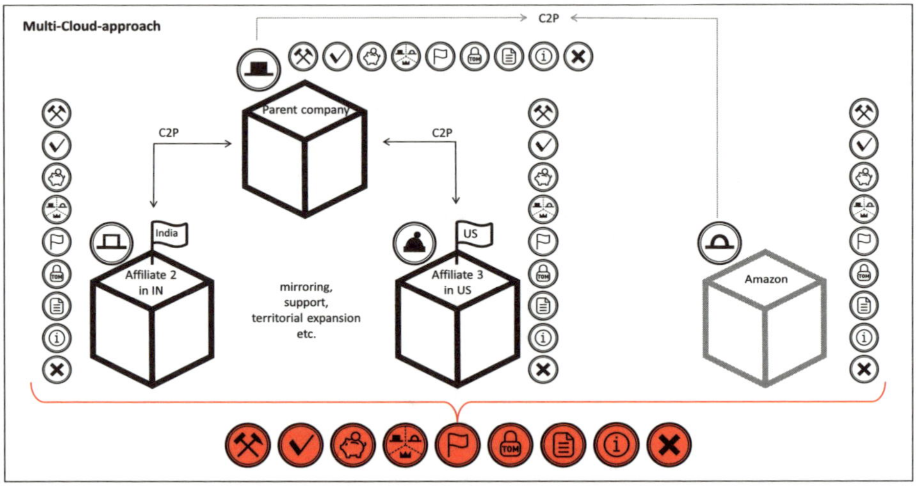

Figure 72: Multi-Cloud-approach

558 It can be seen from the various configurations that a controller has numerous tasks in his own company, both in terms of receiving and forwarding as well as processing. Particularly in the case of personal data, the data controller should ensure the lawfulness of the data and the data processing to be carried out before it is received, disclosed or processed, since, as explained in the previous chapters, there are either no or only limited subsequent remedies. Anyone who wants to participate in the Big Data business and become a serious player must therefore know and maintain his legal rights, obligations and scope in order to avoid fines and lawsuits.

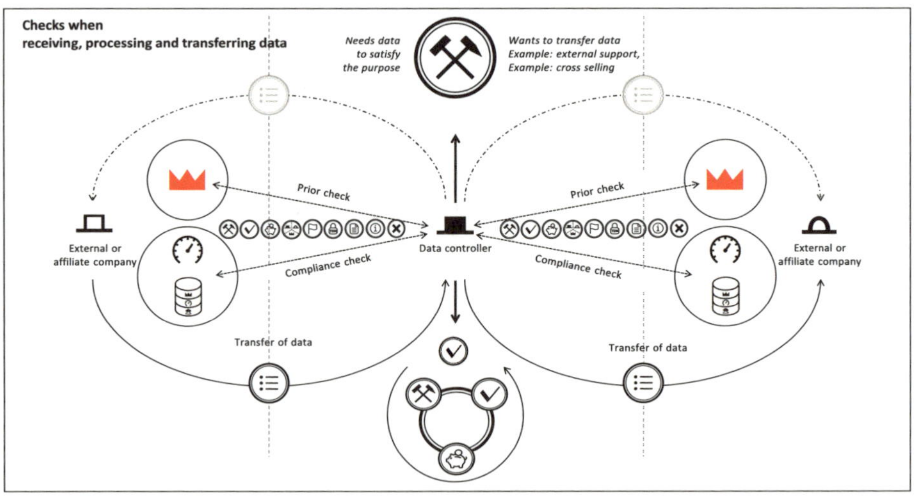

Figure 73: Checks when receiving, processing and transferring data

The rights and duties of the controller vary depending on the business model offered by the controller on the market. If the controller sells trend data that it has acquired from anonymous data or freely accessible data, the rights and obligations are different than if the controller acts as a provider with storage space in the market or even offers services with data (e.g. carrying out analyses, etc.). 559

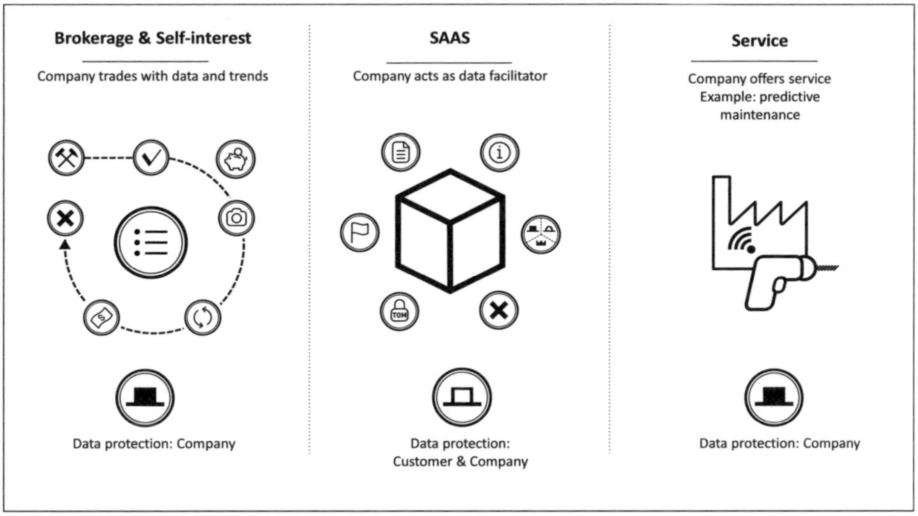

Figure 74: Data protection with different Big Data providers

Guiding Principle:

The provider of a Big Data platform operating on a cloud must be technically capable of maintaining client separation within his cloud application and of ensuring compliance with all data protection obligations incumbent on his customers as data protection clients, such as different retention and erasure periods, requirements for the involvement of subcontractors and, if necessary, the satisfaction of data subjects' rights.

P. RECOMMENDED ACTIONS

In summary, the following 10 actions can be recommended for your Big Data business: 560

1. Include data and rights management in the structure of your data set to allow the use and analysis of the data and avoid fines, claims for damages and injunctive relief.
2. Collect and process data lawfully only if you know and apply the legal basis precisely and examine this in advance by means of a prior review.
3. Choose suitable pseudonymization and anonymization tools in order to make use of additional analysis possibilities.
4. Plan the combination of data beforehand so that the data stock is not contaminated, and the analysis results remain lawful.
5. Implement an erasure policy to ensure data economy and remove data whose purpose has been fulfilled and which is thus no longer needed.
6. Select and implement a security concept through appropriate and necessary technical and organizational measures.
7. Plan an authorization concept for employees and administrators of your data stock to ensure client separation as well as admission, access and transfer authorization.
8. Document the processes in your data stock for your own monitoring and control and steering as well as observe the requirements for a procedure directory and a data protection impact assessment as well as information rights of data subjects.
9. Network across national borders by observing foreign legal systems on data protection.
10. Manage your Big Data business model by collecting data accurately, completely, consistently and with integrity as a *single point of reference* and on a *need to know basis*.

Index of keywords

The numbers refer to the margin numbers